The Ministry and Mental Health

THE MINISTRY

and

~ Edited by

MENTAL HEALTH

HANS HOFMANN

ASSOCIATION PRESS · NEW YORK

THE MINISTRY AND MENTAL HEALTH

———

Library of Congress catalog card number: 60-13142

72

To BETTY and JOHN MUSSER

Contents

Introduction

That there exists a relation between religion and mental health is self-evident. Religion prompts the believer to assume a specific attitude toward his environment which deeply influences his feelings and his actions. Since religion constitutes a profound and ultimate commitment, it provides either an orientation which channels the expressions and activities of the person positively or one which curtails the self-realization of the person when his religious tenets are contradicted.

Psychotherapy and especially psychoanalysis have challenged the role of religion in human development. The goal of psychotherapy is to unfold the innate potentials of the human personality as far as this is possible without endangering interpersonal relations and an appropriate co-operation with social demands. In this light, religion is to be blamed for creating undue dependence on an authority which at first was linked with the parental influence and later transcended the family structure and turned into reliance on an omnipotent father. Psychotherapy suspects that religion leads to an immature dependence and hampers the growth of personality into the freedom to take independent actions based on independent judgment and decision.

For the minister the relation between religion and mental health becomes an acute problem. Is he to go on to stress the sovereignty of God and absolute obedience on man's part to the will of God? Or is he to seek first the fullest possible unfolding of human potentials and concentrate on helping his parishioners to find self-realization as far as environmental demands will allow it? The minister is well aware that strict adherence to religious beliefs is widely undermined today by the influence of science and the economic progress which governs the social structure of our communities. He finds that his parishioners more and more are seeking the help of specialized experts even for their personal problems, which heretofore they had discussed mainly with their pastor.

On the other hand, a resurgence in popular interest in religion is apparent. It is hard to say what has caused it. Probably the mechanized and impersonal way of life and work which permeates the whole country has raised the question in the minds of people whether there is any innate and inalienable dignity left to the human personality. The question about the unique being and purpose of individual lives faces man today and deeply influences his feeling of emotional and even physical well-being. It is indeed thinkable that the present religious revival is in itself the expression of the individual's lack of confidence in himself which prods him to look for support from outside and beyond his own world. Quite possibly such a trend will further deflate the confident initiative of individuals within the pressure-constellation of modern life.

The first part of this book represents an attempt to cope with the problem which arises from the juxtaposition of religion and mental health. The role of religion and of the minister are scrutinized from the point of view of sociology and clinical and social psychology. The theme undergirding the first three papers is a respectful appreciation of the role of religion. This positive attitude toward religion leads the writers to investigate quite critically whether the traditional setup of the churches and the ministry is able to liberate and make available the most vital resources of religion. It is difficult for anyone to accept a critical evaluation of one's own professional role from the outside. But, it is to be hoped, the ministers will sense the sympathetic note in these writings. No authoritarian dictate or insensitive judgment is passed. The answer to the questions raised can come only from the ministers thus challenged.

The second part deals with the possibility of enhancing the personality growth of prospective ministers through their education in theological schools. A careful investigation of the motivations which lead a young man to seek training for the ministry is in this respect quite as essential as due attention to his personal development while he undergoes an intensive study program toward ordination into the ministry. The relevance of psychological findings for the minister's own understanding of himself and of his parishioners is expounded. Finally, one way of acquainting the theological student with the problems of mental health and how they are coped with in psychotherapy is explained in a discussion of the pastoral clinical training program.

The third part presents specific applications of the theories developed in the second. Teachers in different interdenominational schools report on the way their respective institutions have wrestled with the concrete problem of bringing adequate instruction in the area of mental health into the theological curriculum. Since this is a new endeavor with far-reaching possibilities but also delicate problems, it is good that other theological schools in the country may profit from positive and negative experiences which these schools have gathered. Although it is neither possible nor desirable to iron out all the denominational, geographical, and academic differences of the different schools, the stimulation which comes from such reports will help to focus on the opportunities and limitations which are given in the respective schools. Not all the schools have the same resources within the school, the same clinical opportunities or the co-operation of other departments within a large university. Nonetheless, once theological schools have recognized the importance of this area of teaching they are certain to find ways and means through which they can accomplish the goals on the basis of their own opportunities.

The end of the book takes up the problem which was mentioned first in this introduction. Through an exclusively descriptive survey of counseling activities of ministers in metropolitan areas of the East and of the West Coast the relation between the theological and religious orientation of the minister, his personality, and his job analysis on the one hand, and his effectiveness as counselor on the other, is established without forcing upon the reader premature or biased conclusions. For those ministers who are willing to read on and between the lines, the presentation of factual data is more convincing than many theories or biased suggestions. The editor wants to make it very clear that at least as far as he is concerned this volume is designed to sharpen the issues between religion and mental health as they bear on the ministry. Its purpose is to pass on suggestions born out of the experience of teachers in theological education without offering ready-made and therefore limited answers or an over-all and hence far too generalized solution to the problem. It goes without saying that the most effective form of a minister's co-operation in the area of religion and mental health is that which takes place in the privacy of his painstaking and sensitive work among his parishioners and confident collaboration with the psychiatrist and other private or public agencies within his community. Often the minister is so preoccupied with his own problems and duties that he fails to see beyond them. The editor would like to give him a broader acquaintance with the nation-wide approach and to offer the minister the added assurance that in his struggle to be relevant to the mental health of his parishioners he is in the good company of many who are searching with him and who would like to be of any possible help to him.

The National Institute of Mental Health established, through a grant, the Harvard University Project on Religion and Mental Health and thereby made this volume possible among other results of its work. The editor wants to express his gratitude to the Institute, the supervisory council of the Project at Harvard, the faculty of the University, and all those students who through their interests and co-operation have stimulated and made possible the launching of this book. Special thanks go to the contributors who, in spite of their heavy responsibilities in their respective research and teaching obligations, were eager to enrich this volume with their insights. The editor is grateful to the publisher who has been willing to undertake the publication of this book. It is heartening to see how many people in widely different paths of life and work have been eager to co-operate in clarifying the issue and making the outcome of this project as fruitful as possible.

HANS HOFMANN

PAUL TILLICH ৯৬

Paul Tillich, University Professor at Harvard University, occupies today the position of the dean among contemporary theologians. His eminence among religious thinkers is founded in his approach to life. Tillich is not merely a brilliant systematic scholar, and not merely a man who speaks from the background of European intellectual history and his own personal struggle with the German disaster of the past decades: his prominence rests most of all upon his ability to take our entire life situation seriously. His own approach to matters of faith is to listen conscientiously to the problems and questions which arise out of the predicament of our existence and to correlate with them those lasting religious answers which come from God's revelation of Himself in history.

Such an open-minded approach to the life and faith of Western Christianity permits Tillich to address himself with keen insight to all those human phenomena which make up our life situation as it actually exists. It is therefore not surprising that he should have fully appreciated both the social and the individual significance which psychotherapy since Freud has brought to cultural self-awareness, especially that of Americans. Tillich has given serious thought to the religious understanding of the human personality, which takes into account the discoveries of modern psychology and psychiatry. He is convinced that psychoanalysts in particular are able to lay bare the most deep-seated and powerful human dilemmas, but also that they can reveal resources which allow us to be far more realistic about human nature today than at any period of the past.

In the following chapter [1] Tillich offers a short but penetrating evaluation of the contribution which psychotherapy has made. He embeds his reflections about psychotherapy in an historical survey of those problems in the understanding of man which have furthered the theological doctrine of man. With prophetic vigor Tillich here demands that theology avoid withdrawal into the splendid isolation of irrelevant speculations. He states that the most profound resources of the Christian faith lie precisely in an honest realism, and that from this source true vitality can again emerge in our faith, and give a new vision and sense of direction to any who have grown disappointed either in themselves, in Western culture, or in a traditional way of life which has failed to provide sufficient incentive for a courageous struggle with the human predicament, its dangers, and its possibilities.

The Impact of Pastoral Psychology on Theological Thought

&§ PAUL TILLICH

The ten years in which the magazine *Pastoral Psychology* has done its important work are the ones that have seen the function of "pastoral psychology" establishing itself as a significant section of practical theology. In reading the discussions collected in *The Minister's Consultation Clinic*,[2] I realized the many problems raised and insights gained in these years, and would feel completely at a loss if I had to contribute any answers of a practical nature to the questions asked by the contributors of that book. The only thing I can do, as an early member of the Editorial Advisory Board of *Pastoral Psychology,* is to ask myself: What does all this activity going on in pastoral counseling and in its psychotherapeutic foundations mean for systematic theology? It is my conviction that its significance is great and should not be ignored by anyone who discusses problems of systematic theology. But if this can be shown, the other side also is obvious—that the theology which underlies pastoral counseling should be one which itself has been influenced by the insights of psychotherapy, not only in the questions it asks, but also in the formulation of the answers in correlation with the questions.

Naturally, the most direct influence of pastoral psychology on systematic theology concerns the doctrine of man, for psychology (in spite of the importance of animal psychology for certain dimensions of man's psychosomatic nature) is predominantly "doctrine of man." And pastoral psychology, even if using the insights of general psychology, deals with man both in his *essential* potentialities and his *existential* actualities. If we ask what are these insights of psychotherapy which systematic theology must introduce into its own constructive endeavor, then the first and most fundamental point is the rediscovery of the truth of the doctrine of man's predicament as professed by Augustine and the Reformers. Original Pelagianism, as well as semi-Pelagianism of Roman Catholic theology, emphasized the partial freedom of man in relation to God. The obedience or disobedience to the commandment of

13

love is a matter of man's conscious decision. They did not deny the distortions of man's created nature and the necessity of grace in co-operation with man's freedom. But their understanding of sin and grace weakened the valuation both of the hidden power of sin and the unconditional power of that grace which reconciles man with God, and consequently with himself and his world.

Present-day Protestantism has combined a basically Pelagian doctrine of man— if not in official theology, certainly in the popular understanding of its message— with a serious emphasis on morals, individual as well as social. The most conspicuous symbolic expression of this attitude is the idea of a progressive actualization of the kingdom of God on earth by the "men of good will" (with the secret and sometimes open claim that the men of good will are "we" and those who belong to us).

All these forms of open and hidden Pelagianism are undercut by contemporary psychology and the experience of everyone who does pastoral counseling. When a "pillar" of a suburban community, outstanding in moral and social activity, admits having suicidal tendencies, or if the mother of a happy family reveals, voluntarily and involuntarily, hatred against her children—then a Pelagian interpretation of these situations and any appeal to "free will" break down. The only thing the helper can do is to mobilize the healing powers, the forces of grace which are still working in the counselee and which may be strengthened by the way the counselor accepts him without moral demands. Such behavior in the pastoral situation follows the Augustinian-Reformation type of theology and is equally opposed to the Roman-legalistic and to the Protestant-moralistic attitudes. It is an astonishing fact that Protestant theology had to rediscover its own tradition about what man is, and about what healing powers are, through the impact of the psychology of the unconscious. To the degree in which the unconscious motivations were discovered, even in our fully conscious acts, the appeal to "free will" became impossible. The question now had to be: How can unconscious motivations be changed? And the answer was: By forces which enter the unconscious even if the entering door is consciousness. So the search for these forces started, producing a new climate in all theological disciplines, but especially in systematic theology.

A presupposition for any answer to the question of healing in the sense of salvation is a reformulation of the idea of God. If asked whether the experiences of pastoral counseling and its theoretical support, psychotherapy, had any influence on the idea of God, I would say, profoundly so; just as Augustine's awareness of the labyrinths of sin and guilt and his experience of saving forces in the community of the Church influenced his idea of God. In the same way, Luther's experience of the breakdown of the will to be good and the hearing of the message of forgiveness affected his idea of God; and likewise Kierkegaard's feeling of despair about the combination of finitude and infinity in his centered self, and of the necessity of the leap of faith, influenced his idea of God. In all these cases, basic insights into the human situation led to basic insights into the inexhaustible depths of the idea of God. Perhaps the contention will be made that it was not the insight into the human predicament which has produced new interpretations of the idea of God, but that it was a new experience of God which produced new insights into the nature of man. Yet such an objection is only verbal, because no statement about God can be made which is not rooted in the correlation between man's self-awareness and the experience of the divine Presence. Every change on one side of this correlation changes the whole correlation. With this understanding in mind, we can speak about a change in the idea of God which is at least partly dependent on the psychotherapeutic insights of our period and on the use made by them in pastoral counseling.

One can say that psychotherapy has replaced the emphasis on the demanding yet remote God by an emphasis on his self-giving nearness. It is the modification of the image of the threatening father—which was so important in Freud's attack on religion—by elements of the image of the embracing and supporting mother. If I were permitted to express a bold suggestion, I would say that psychotherapy and the experiences of pastoral counseling have helped to reintroduce the female element, so conspicuously lacking in most Protestantism, into the idea of God.

The impact of psychotherapy and the experiences of pastoral counseling on the ideas of man and of God necessarily have consequences for an understanding of the relation between God and man. This is manifest in two doctrines which seem to be in quite different fields but which actually belong together, the doctrine of divine acceptance and the doctrine of the religious symbol.

The doctrine of divine acceptance, traditionally called the doctrine of "justification by grace through faith," is the central doctrine of Protestantism. In fact, the Reformers called it the article by which the church stands or falls. But it has been almost completely lost in average Protestant preaching and teaching. Even when the doctrinal formulation was preserved, as in Lutheranism largely, the spirit of the doctrine—the good news that he who feels unworthy of being accepted by God can be certain that he is accepted—had been buried under doctrinal rigidity and aridity. In many denominations with Calvinistic and Evangelistic traditions, however, it is not the doctrinal but the moral legalism which has nullified the message of acceptance. For instance, the words of Jesus were not interpreted as expressing a new reality in which the law is conquered, but as a collection of moral prescriptions, called the "teachings of Jesus." In some cases, as in the fundamentalist groups of this country, the burden of the doctrinal law was added to the burden of the moral law. It is understandable that many people broke down under these burdens which are the opposite of the words of Jesus about the "light burden" and the "easy yoke" he imposes on his followers.

The tremendous growth of mental disturbances on Protestant soil is at least partly caused by the legalistic distortion of the Protestant message. In vain, biblical theologians emphasized the precedence of the "Covenant" between God and man over the law in the Old Testament, and the precedence of the "new eon" over moral commands in the New Testament, and of forgiveness of sins over the good works in the Reformation. They were not understood because these symbols did not fit the state of mind in the period of victorious industrial society. But when mental disturbances became a mass phenomenon, hampering both war effort and business progress, and when the disturbed theological students, together with many other disturbed active members of the congregations sought help, not from a minister, but from a psychoanalyst, the churches began to realize that something was wrong in their preaching and teaching.

This awareness expressed itself in theological attempts to understand in a new way the good news of the Christian message, the doctrine of acceptance. The psychoanalytic pattern of a nonjudging and nondirecting acceptance of the mentally disturbed became the model for Christian counseling; and through counseling, for teaching; and through teaching, for theological inquiry. Present theology can say again that acceptance by God of him who is not able to accept himself is the center of the Christian message and the theological foundation of preaching and pastoral counseling. However, since every effect is the result of many causes, it would be an exaggeration to say that all this is produced by the impact of psychotherapy alone. There is the existentialist movement in all its branches and there is the theology of crisis; and above all, there is the crisis itself—the world wars, the schizophrenic East-West split of mankind, and the threat of atomic self-destruction. But in spite of these contributing causes, the impact of the psychotherapeutic ideas and experiences on the theological interpretation of the Christian message is considerable. One can say that in spite of Freud's own antireligious assertions, the transformation of the intellectual climate by him was the greatest intellectual support for a rediscovery of the central Christian message, the good news of acceptance.

The other way in which theology reacted to the psychology of the unconscious was a new valuation of the religious symbol. Here also other causes were at work, especially epistemological and semantic considerations. But the decisive factor was the breakdown of the belief in the power of reasoning to determine the direction of the will. Intellectual and moral preaching fail to reach those levels of the personal life which can, however, be opened by authentic symbols—symbols which themselves have roots in the unconscious depths of individuals and groups. The impact of symbols on the totality of the personal life gives them revealing as well as healing power. Sectarian and radical political movements were conscious of this fact, and in the churches the traditional symbols never completely disappeared. But they were judged as imperfect and increasingly replaced by words and concepts. The Protestant emphasis on preaching, united with the humanist emphasis on teaching, emptied and reduced the realm of symbolic expressions. Liturgical and sacramental symbols lost their significance.

The situation is today different: Sacramental thinking has gained strength, the great liturgical traditions are being rediscovered and introduced into the life of the churches, artistic and religious symbols are seen in convergence. Important in all these movements is the spirit in which it is done. It is not done for "enrichment" or "enjoyment"—this may be a consequence, yet it is not the intention—but it is done as a "means of grace" in alliance with, not in subordination to, the word. The impact of the world of symbols on the unconscious is recognized.

It may be helpful to ask here the question of how artistic and religious symbols are related to the symbol-producing activity of the unconscious as it appears in dreams and free associations. The answer seems to be that "symbols of the unconscious" reveal something about the state of a personality in dimensions of which he is ordinarily not aware, but they do not reveal anything about reality as such; while historical, artistic, and religious symbols express, in a strict correlation, dimensions of the encountered world and of the encountering mind. Seen in this way the "symbols of the unconscious" are really more symptoms than genuine symbols. But it may well be that many of these symptoms are derived from what Jung has called "archetypes" and that they are symbols pointing to the situation of man in his world.

Theologically, this implies that an understanding of the term "Word of God" in the sense of "words inspired by God" misses a decisive element in the relation of God and man, the impact of the divine Presence on the unconscious—not magically by excluding consciousness, but totally, grasping all sides of the personal life. The theologian who speaks without qualification of the "teachings of Jesus" shows that he has learned nothing from psychotherapy and the rediscovery of the unconscious in the twentieth century.

The decisive test of the influence of psychotherapy on theological thought is the theological interpretation of salvation. Salvation of men—groups and individuals— is the ultimate aim of all divine activities in time and space. According to the Christian faith, it is the work of the Christ and through him the divine creation of a New Being. Though the early church understood salvation as a cosmic event in which man and his world are involved, the concept of salvation was increasingly restricted to the individual and his eternal destiny. Salvation was identical with being accepted in heaven, and condemnation was identical with being thrown into hell.

In this image of salvation the root of the word, *salvus* (being "healed and whole") is completely neglected. One consequence of this was that theology and medicine lost the intimate connection they originally had, and always should have—for saving the person is healing him. The tremendous importance which the healing stories have in the New Testament records is understandable only if one knows that the kingdom of God was supposed to come as the healing power on earth. But the church, although reading one of these stories in almost every Sunday service, did not emphasize their healing side, but their miraculous aspect, and this in such a supranaturalistic way that the conscience of innumerable preachers was thrown into conflict between their duty to interpret prescribed texts and their honest doubt about the miraculous element in them. The *rapprochement* between theology and medicine in our time has brought a great liberation to such men by opening a new way for preaching about the healing stories in the New Testament: The healing power of the New Being in the Christ, and not a miraculous interference of God into the processes of nature, is the religious significance of the stories.

The task of the theologian who is influenced by psychotherapeutic insights is a thorough re-examination of the doctrines which were called "order of salvation" and "the Christian life," and which tried to describe first the way of the Christian from "conversion" to "sanctification," and then his experiences and actions as a mature Christian. The general trend of doctrinal theology was directed toward an understanding of the objective factors that determine the Christian life: the divine Spirit, the Word, the sacraments, the church as the communion of faith and love, and the attack of the demonic forces in the Christian and in his world, the images of Christian perfection, and so on. All this was seen, so to speak, from the side of God and not from the side of man. An exception are the penitentials, the books advising priest-confessor about the endless variety of human predicaments, aberrations, and virtues. Under the religious dimension, they anticipate much of what has been found in psychotherapeutic practice and theory. But most of it was lost by abuse, mechanization, stagnation, and, above all, by the Protestant and humanist disregard of the unconscious and subconscious elements in the dynamics of the personality. Psychotherapy is one of the factors which have forced practice and theory to take the subjective side of Christian existence as seriously as the objective side.

Today no theologian should speak about the healing powers of faith without pointing to the ambiguities of religion and the ways present in religion for escape from healing for those who do not want to be healed. Neurotic withdrawal from reality can express itself as fanatical defense of a not-completely-affirmed position, or as compulsory legalism in fulfilling the assumed commands of God, or as a bundle of misplaced guilt-anxieties. This, of course, is not a plea for a so-called healthy religion which, for instance, enables a corporation executive to adjust himself to the demands of the business community. But the theological question of Christian growth and maturity and a state of "being healed" cannot be answered without consideration of the human predicament in its ambiguous mixture of saving and distorting forces.

Another problem within this context is the question of the relation of the divine Spirit to the human spirit. Psychotherapy makes two answers impossible: the neo-orthodox one and the humanistic one. According to the first answer, the divine Spirit never enters (a questionable spatial metaphor) the human spirit. No real union takes place: "I believe that I believe," but I am not grasped by the spiritual Presence in moments of faith and love. It is incomprehensible how such a relation of God and man can have healing power; and a religion without healing or saving power is irrelevant. The humanist answer is equally inadequate, however. According to it, the divine Spirit is nothing but the religious function of the human spirit. If this were so, healing would be self-healing. But only something healthy can heal what is sick. The sick cannot overcome itself by itself. It can only receive healing powers from beyond itself. The very existence of psychotherapy witnesses to this fact.

But if we now say that the divine Spirit grasps the human spirit, raising it beyond itself and healing it through the creation of faith and love, the psychotherapist rightly asks: How is this event related to the facts I know about the psychosomatic disturbances of my patients? Answering this, the theologian must show how the creation of a centered self by the experience of ultimate concern spreads healing forces over a personality in all dimensions of his being. He must show this in the dimensions of the spirit, of psychological self-awareness, of bodily functions, of social relations, and of historical self-realization. The general and rather empty notion of the divine Spirit must be filled with concrete material taken from man's existence under many dimensions and in many realms of life. In this way it may happen that the image of the mature Christian, which has been lost along with the image of the mature man generally, will reappear and provide an answer to the question of mature humanity as such.

A third problem implied in the question of the relation between the divine Spirit and the human spirit is the question of healing in the different dimensions in which man lives and through which he participates in all life. Psychotherapy presupposes that the relation of all elements of the personal life to each other has not the character of levels lying one above the other, and consequently open to mutual interference, but that these elements represent different dimensions of a unity. One can speak of the multidimensional unity of life as it appears in man. On this basis all functions of healing belong together. The helper must heal the whole person. There is no partial salvation. But there is fragmentary salvation under each dimension.

The divine Spirit, wherever it works, is related to the functions of the spirit as well as to those of self-awareness and bodily self-realization. It has effects on the expressions of the face, on the memory of the past and the anticipation of the future, on the moral act and cultural productivity, and, above all, on religious self-transcendence. In all these dimensions, it is healing—but fragmentarily, because we live in time and space, and under the conditions of finitude. Therefore, in a particular case, tuberculosis may be healed, but not a neurotic condition of the patient. Or compulsive withdrawal may be healed, but perhaps not an arteriosclerotic condition of the heart. Or this also may be healed, but not despair about the commanding character of the moral law and the feeling of meaninglessness about the cultural contents. This also may be healed, but perhaps not the doubt about the validity of the religious symbols and the feeling of profound guilt about these doubts. Or this also may be healed, but not the total despair about the meaning of history and one's own historical existence. All healing is fragmentary and preliminary. Therefore, specialized helpers and healers are necessary. But there is one question which transcends all others, the question of the participation of the whole being in unambiguous or eternal life. Psychotherapy has not abolished this question, but it has related it to all other questions of the human predicament. This is one of its gifts to theology.

It seems to me that a theology which is influenced in all these directions by psychotherapy is a better one than a theology without such influence; thus, the theologian would do well to remain in contact with the psychotherapeutic movement. The counselor and minister should be aware of the fact that through his work he not only serves individual human beings, but also theology and, in this way, many human beings whom he cannot reach, but who may be healed by a preaching which is based on a theology in which the results of psychotherapeutic experience and thought are effective.

REFERENCES

1. This chapter first appeared as an article by Paul Tillich in *Pastoral Psychology*, Vol. 11, No. 101 (Feb., 1960), 17-23. Permission granted by Simon Doniger, Editor of *Pastoral Psychology*, and by Dr. Tillich.
2. *The Minister's Consultation Clinic*, Simon Doniger, ed. (Great Neck, N.Y.: Channel Press, 1955). This is a collection of published and some unpublished inquiries sent in by readers of *Pastoral Psychology*, accompanied by answers and discussions of problems facing the minister in his work.

TALCOTT PARSONS ᢒᴖ

Talcott Parsons, Professor of Sociology in the Department of Social Relations at Harvard University, has rendered American sociology and especially the other disciplines which are interested in sociology an immense service. In the footsteps of his European forerunners, Durkheim and Weber, he has been able to bring together the empirically gained evidences of social structure and change into a system of thought, into an organized wealth of research material which heretofore had not become available to the field of sociology as a science. Sensitive as he is to all the forces which influence the social structure in our country, Parsons has investigated and effectively interpreted the phenomenon of religion. He is aware of the immense influence which psychotherapy wields not only on individuals but on our whole society.

Parsons fully recognizes that psychiatry as a medical discipline starts out with psychopathology, concentrates on individual patients, and draws all its conclusions from the point of view of its understanding of sickness and the sick personality. Nevertheless, psychotherapy cannot avoid dealing with problems which are caused by a general lack of orientation. He points out how the decay of clear social structure robs the individual of a sense of direction which heretofore religion was able to provide. On this ground Parsons relates mental illness to the general "spiritual malaise." It is obvious that psychotherapy is tempted to move into the vacuum and offer its own spiritual outlook. Although no psychiatrist confesses this intention, nor does psychiatry as a whole deal with the issue of ethical guidance, the therapeutic situation is bound to bring up this problem and, implicitly at least, suggest a solution. On the other hand, the representative of religion too easily slips into doing the job of the psychotherapist if he concerns himself exclusively with the care of the individual parishioners. Thereby he neglects the social component of religion and unduly narrows its significance.

Parsons makes a special contribution in pointing out the ambiguity which exists today between the social structure of the family and the social role of the church. He rightly centers his concluding observations around the problem of value, which ties together the area of psychiatry, the church, and the social impetus governing the family as well as contemporary society. Parsons' contribution promises to provide a broad and adequately solid basis for discussion of value orientation among psychiatrists, ministers, and other communal agents. The distinctive uniqueness of the different fields will become clear and their co-operation thus more fruitful.

Psychiatrists and ministers alike are apt to overlook the significance of the social aspect in the lives of their people and in the nature of their own professional work. It is helpful that a well-qualified sociologist should point out how much psychiatry and the ministry are really governed by social forces and in turn produce attitudes of great significance for society.

Mental Illness and "Spiritual Malaise": The Role of the Psychiatrist and of the Minister of Religion

*8 TALCOTT PARSONS

The recent period in the development of Western society generally, and of the United States in particular, has posed with increasing urgency the problem of this paper. Whatever the situation with respect to whether or not mental illness has increased notably in our time, there is no question that *concern* with the problem of mental illness has become very much more salient than it was, for instance, in the nineteenth century. Furthermore, a growing intellectual tradition of psychology and psychoanalysis which is concerned with the diagnosis of mental illness, and with the definition of appropriate therapeutic measures, has become an increasingly prominent feature of the cultural scene. The relation of this development to the traditional religious basis of concern for the individual is undoubtedly close, so close indeed that assertions that the psychiatrist has taken over the functions of the minister of religion have been common. It has also been asserted that movements in the mental health field, notably psychoanalysis, are themselves new "religions."

From the religious side there has also been much concern with the situation of the times, with what seems to be a relatively widespread state of "spiritual malaise." There is the same order of doubt as to how far, if at all, this is a new or more serious problem now than in previous periods. There is, furthermore, a marked concentration of concern in this area, as in that of mental illness, on the problems of the individual. How is he to achieve a sense of meaning, to be capable of faith in an uncertain, skeptical, and, many say, a "materialistic" age?

In such a situation it seems to be highly important that attempts should be made to sort out some of the different factors which bear on the "plight" of the individual in our time, in a context which is concerned with the question of whether and on what basis a meaningful line of differentiation between these two problem areas

23

can be drawn, how they are related to each other and what areas of overlap or at least joint concern may exist.

A good starting point is the well-known fact that treatment of problems of health with religious (including magical) techniques is, for practical purposes, a universal feature of "primitive" societies and cultures. Essentially this is to say that the health problem is "fused in with" the area of religion; the two are not differentiated. There are, however, very important variations in the extent to which primitive religions are oriented to problems of health. To take a well-known example, in the American Southwest the Navajos have a very strong religious emphasis on health whereas the immediately neighboring Zuñi are much less concerned in this direction.

Within a broader context—that is, in relation to Judaism—it can be maintained that the most distinctive feature of early Christianity was its religious "individualism," its concern with the fate of the individual soul. Since the problem of health is also—however much it is socially conditioned—a problem of the state of the individual, it is not surprising that early Christianity was permeated with concern with health, and that religious healing was one of its central bases of validation. The impact of the Gospels would certainly have been greatly diminished had this element been removed.

Perhaps the main starting point of a differentiation between the "cure of souls" in the religious sense and what we think of as the problem of health came from the juxtaposition of the Christian and the Greek traditions. Whatever may have been, in Greek terms, the religious elements in the "cult of Aesculapius," Hippocratic medicine was a genuinely scientific tradition and, if it remained alive at all, could never be completely reabsorbed into a tradition of purely religious healing. The basic fact that Christianity grew out of a synthesis of Hebraic and Greek cultural traditions, with a very distinctive contribution of its own of course, meant that the scientific strain was an essential one which could not be eliminated.

With all the qualifications which must be made in terms of a sociology of knowledge, I should interpret the emergence of modern psychopathology as, in its *main* trend and meaning, a development of modern science. It represents the gradual, difficult, and socio-culturally speaking, often painful extension of scientific knowledge and the scientific point of view into areas of concern from which it has tended in other cultures and in our own past to be excluded. It is, in this perspective, by no means to be wondered at that scientific medicine was first introduced in the somatic field and has only gradually spread to the "mental."

In this connection it should not be forgotten how very recent a development genuinely scientific medicine over a wide front is. I have suggested that the Hippocratic tradition is genuinely scientific. But, given its presence in classical Greece, perhaps the salient fact about its history is the extreme slowness of progress from its brilliant beginnings until quite recent times; it is indeed only since the middle of the nineteenth century that it can be said that a broadly scientific medicine was coming to be established. And even the beginnings of a scientific psychopathology belong to the present century. Clearly the field is still in a very elementary stage of its development.

The fundamentals of the religious aspect of the picture of course go much further back. They are found, in various forms and combinations, in many different religions, and the specifically Christian patterns go back to the earliest phases of its history. However, the whole process of development and differentiation which has occurred in societies with a predominantly Christian religious tradition, and which in its recent phases underlies the emergence of scientific medicine, has involved important changes in the religious definition of the situation as well as that of other phases of social life, and so a review of some highlights of the American situation in this respect will be called for. Before introducing that, however, a general analytical approach to the relation of the two main foci of reference in our problem will need to be worked out.

Religion, Society, and the Personality of the Individual

Let us start at the religious end. As I conceive it, religion roots in the most general cultural orientations of human action—orientations which underlie the structuring both of social systems and of the personalities of individuals. These orientations, following Max Weber, I should think of as orientations in terms of the ultimate "problems of meaning" which are involved in the human situation as such.

Not only must such orientations be grounded at the level of what Tillich calls "ultimate concern," but they must somehow define meaningful orientations *to* all the main areas of inevitable involvement of human beings. These may conveniently be classified as the physical world as such (one meaning of "material") including the human organism; the world of personality, of the individual human being (and in some degree nonhuman living things) as an acting, evaluating sensitive (including suffering) entity, of the social world in which numbers of persons are involved in relations of mutual solidarity and/or obstructiveness, and in which they share a common fate; and, finally, the world of cultural orientations and meanings themselves, including not only the religious aspects but the fields of secular cognitive culture, of art and other forms of expressive symbolization, and of values. All these areas of human concern and of the structuring of human action and relationships are closely interdependent and in many areas interpenetrating.

Any adequate analytical treatment must, however, start with their *conceptual* discrimination from one another. Our concern is with two principal contexts of relationship in which religious orientations are involved. On the one hand, there is the relation to the social system which I conceive above all as centering on the problem of values in their relation to the normative aspects of the structure of societies. On the other hand, there is the problem of the relation to the individual personality, which concerns the cultural level of values also, but this time in relation to the definition of the goals of the life of the individual by their relations to what

Weber called his "religious interests," and the bearing of his inevitable involvements in social relationships, and with the organic basis of his own life, on these.

I conceive religious orientation as inherently independent of any of these other contexts of action. But it is the kind of independence which also implies interdependence; it is not "lack of relationship to. . . ." However, this independence implies an inherent possibility of *tension* as between a religious orientation and the exigencies imposed by involvement in nonreligious aspects of the culture, in society, in other aspects of the personality, and in the physical world. But by the same token, since human life is inherently involved in all these sets of exigencies, no religious system can cut loose from them too drastically if it is long to survive as a mode of shaping actual life, and there are certainly inherent tendencies to try to establish bases of working integration between them so that the tension, though not necessarily eliminated, is still kept within moderate bounds. Finally, the conception of interdependence implies that the adjustments which are involved in integration may in principle be mutual; there is no a priori reason why they must come in any particular degree from one side or the other. Furthermore, we must allow for ranges of difference in intensity of influence from either side.

In the social direction the most fundamental relationship is the religious grounding of the institutionalized values of a society. What I call the societal value system is in turn the apex of the structure of its "normative culture," which in turn is the primary constitutive element of its structure as a system. But a societal value system is never a simple function of religious orientations. It is rather a result of the specification of the implications of these orientations through several steps in relation to a variety of exigencies and factors having at most only secondarily a religious reference.

Among the most important of these is first the involvement of the social system with the cognitive culture—above all, in the fields of science and philosophy. The two areas of cognitive culture most directly independent of religion are, first, science, dealing all the way from the physical world, through the aspects of medical science which closely involve the personality of the individual, to that dealing with the society itself as an object. Second, merging into science is what we call ideology. This is the empirically oriented but evaluative set of conceptions of a system of social action, notably a society itself or its parts, in which the holders of the beliefs in question are themselves involved. It is the area in which their values are integrated, more or less successfully, with their cognitive conceptions of the objects evaluated. The same considerations apply to the personality as a system.

A next category of factors and exigencies involved in social systems which are independent of religion are of course those concerned with the structural differentiation and conditions of functioning of a society itself as a system. Here, above all, political organization and its relation to phenomena of authority, power, coercion, and at some point the use of force come in. Another primary focus is the institutionalization of economic production and the attendant relationships: the existence of monetary systems, markets, productive organization, and, underlying it all, the necessity for the average human being to make his living by the "sweat of his brow." Still another focus is in the phenomena of social stratification. Most sociologists would argue the inevitability, particularly in complex societies, of substantial ranges of inequality, though of course the bases on which they are structured vary greatly.

Last, but in the present context perhaps not least among these specifically social exigencies, is that of religious organization itself. A church, sect, denomination, or religious movement is, among other things, a social organization. If it has special functions, they must be staffed; there must be problems of how to structure internal authority; and indeed the activities of the organization must be financed. Successful meeting of the exigencies of running churches as organizations is *never* a simple function of the religious orientations which govern them, alone.

Finally, the human personality is certainly subject to exigencies which are both independent of the religious and other components of the cultural tradition and of those of the society in which the individual has been brought up and lives. I shall return to certain of these later.

There is a crucial sense in which the structure of the society stands between the cultural system including its religious components on the one hand, the personality system on the other. And the focus of the set of interconnections is the set of values institutionalized in the society and internalized in the personality. Crucial as social values are in the dynamics of the social system, in the nature of the case they cannot be the sole determinants of processes in the society. These also are a function of the resources which are available for the implementing of values and goals, including the organizational resources. They are a function of many processes of internal adjustment within the society by which various strains and tensions can be handled. And, it goes without saying, every society is subject to varying exigencies outside itself.

Furthermore, let us remember that what I have called societal values do not themselves stand at the religious level of human values. The former can be reached only by a process of specification from the latter, in the course of which the *relative* valuational significance of interests in effective implementation of the values of his society and of the subsystems of it in which he may be involved (which is never quite the same thing), of the interests of personalities including both his own and others, of organic welfare, again both his own and others, and of course the preservation of his conception of the imperatives of religious ultimate concern itself.

It follows from these considerations that as Max Weber was so acutely aware, the bearing of religious orientations on the values institutionalized in a society is *always* and in the nature of the case problematical; there can never be an assumption that religious imperatives require either acceptance or rejection of particular values institutionalized in the society, or at what level. Furthermore, actual situations in the society are never fully in conformity with institutionalized values and always vary independently of them. Thus, we may say that leaving out the problems of personality as such, the relation between religious orientation and imperatives of action in society is inherently complex, and that this complexity tends to come to a focus on moral problems. The fundamental form the question takes is that of whether my obligation as a responsible member of my society is compatible with my religious commitment, and on occasion the conflict may be very acute indeed. Putting the question in this broad way, however, clearly does not get very far, since it provides only the most general framework. Anything like the resolution of tension which might bring something like a feeling of "good conscience" requires a very much more detailed working through of the almost endlessly ramifying particularities of the problem.

Naturally also the problem is the more complex, on the one hand the more complex the society is in which the individual is placed; and, on the other hand, the more it has been and is involved in a process of change so that traditional formulae prove to be inadequate.

In the discussion above I have stressed the factors by virtue of which a clear and simple relation, either of conformity or of opposition between the values institutionalized in a society and the imperatives of religious obligation, cannot be assumed. This position should not be allowed to obscure the fact, for which I believe there is overwhelming evidence, that in the very long run religious orientations and the values associated with them constitute crucially important factors in determination of the major patterns worked out in the organization of societies. This fact should be enough to caution those who tend to assume that there is always an inherently unbridgeable gap, that the "world" in its social aspect is always in the most fundamental sense in radical conflict with religious values. Such positions appear from time to time in religion, but certainly cannot be ascribed to religion in general. At the same time the process of religious influence is slow and halting, and is cross-cut by many factors independent of it. Hence, however much the positive side may be stressed, at any given time the moral complexity of the relation I have been outlining is always a very real problem.

From the point of view of the relation of religion to the social system this problem comes to a head in the question of the nature of religious collectivities and their relation to the rest of the structure of the society. Two major types may be distinguished, though they may on occasion be combined. One is the collectivity organized around the conception of a specifically "religious life," participation in which is dependent on conditions incompatible with the ordinary lives of people embedded in any type of secular society and, not least important, those who are obligated to important responsibilities in the operation of the secular society, such as political responsibilities, those of economic production, and not least the socialization of children through the family and the educational system.

The second type is an organization primarily of the "laity," of persons who are basically anchored in the life of a society and whose secular obligations, if not taking precedence over their religious commitments, must in some sense be treated as compatible with them to the extent that remaining in a secular status and performing the obligations attached to it is not declared to be radically unacceptable from the religious point of view.

The first type is of course above all illustrated by the religious order, organized about a segregated monastic life. The Protestant denomination of contemporary society is an almost pure case of the second type. The Catholic church of course combines the two. Subsequent discussion in this paper will be confined to the second, and the prototype of the role of the clergy will be the Protestant minister whose primary responsibility is the leadership of a congregation, the membership of which consists overwhelmingly of people who are not devoted to the religious life in the sense of withdrawing from worldly participations. Clearly the problem of moral complexity as just outlined is most acute for this group.

Personality and the Social Structure

Let us now turn to the side of the personality of the individual. This of course is rooted in the physical organism with its genetic constitution and its metabolic needs for food, respiration, elimination, and so forth. But more importantly for our purposes, the main structure of the personality is built up through the processes of social interaction. It develops through the internalization of social objects and of the normative patterns governing the child's interaction in social situations.

Of course the primary agency of early socialization is the family in which the child is brought up—very centrally in our society, and with some important qualifications over the whole of humanity. The process in general starts with the development of a deep, in some senses an indelible, attachment to the mother. This in due course is used as a basis of leverage to motivate and reward the autonomous behavior, within the framework of a basic security of acceptance. Erotic components, as we know since Freud, play a central role in these early relationships, particularly as a bridge between the needs of the organism and the generalization of motivation to the level of socially organized patterns of behavior.

With the oedipal transition the child emerges from a life primarily contained within the family. His sex role has become emotionally consolidated to a considerable degree; and he enters upon a new and rapid process of instrumental learning especially concerned, in our society, with the school and with informal relations to his age peers. Then, as he enters adolescence, he becomes capable of a much more differentiated set of commitments, not only to the continuance of formal education, but to responsible participation in associational activity, to a re-emerging basis of concern with his relations to the opposite sex, leading eventually up to marriage, and, on a new level, with the problem of his personal moral commitments and their backing with reference to an orientation to the problems of meaning.

Any individual person is inescapably bound within the framework not only of the genetic constitution of the organism and the condition of its healthy functioning, but of his personal life history, which is never exactly like that of any other, and its bearing on his interests, goals, and capacities for dealing with the problems of adult life. And these involve all his roots in the biological, social, and cultural soil of his experience. He is what and who he is by virtue of the time and status of his birth, his sex, his parentage, his many associations. In this sense every human life starts from an ascriptive origin and can depart from the fixities of this origin only by the paths of structured "opportunity" provided by the structure of the culture and society in which he is embedded and by the exigency of his own personality.

Whatever its origins and constraints along the way, however, this personality always comes to be a system with its own distinctive constitution, its own goals and imperatives of internal integration, its own characteristic ways of dealing with life situations. These were developed in the closest involvement with *one* part of the society and the culture, through a widening series of circles from his relation to his own particular mother, through the family of orientation, to the school system and local community of his latency and adolescent periods. But he is never socialized into "the" society so that he becomes just a standardized cog in the machinery. Mothers, families, schools, and communities are all widely and subtly variant, as are the initial constitutions of individuals. It is a striking case of interdependence and interpenetration, but most emphatically not of the sort which implies the extinction of independent distinctiveness.

I have made the relation to the values of the social system the main axis of the present discussion of religious orientation on the one hand, personality structure on the other. This is indeed a crucial common factor, but it should now be clear that it enters in a very different way and on very different levels in the two cases. In the religious case, as noted above, the religious anchorage of societal values stands at a higher level of cultural generality than do the societal values themselves. At the valuational level they involve the basis of relative valuation of societal obligations, personal obligations and those independent of either, for example, to scientific "truth" or to religious salvation. On religious levels these very highest valuational choices are "grounded" in the highest-order orientations of meaning.

Nothing could be more important than the proposition that the personality of the individual is organized about internalized values. But these are not, in any simple sense, "religious values." The initial reference point of personal values is at the opposite extreme of a scale of generality to specificity of values from the religious level. It is the value system which can come to be shared in common in social interaction by a helpless, unformed small child and *one* adult, his mother, in a two-person relationship system. This value-pattern must be very specifically tailored to the capacities and exigencies of a very small child acting only with a very specific, limited and controlled environment. It is highly dependent on the idiosyncratic characteristics of the mother as a person and her relation to her child. Only on this foundation are successive layers of value-internalization painfully built up step by step in the socialization of the child.

Looked at from the point of view of a societal, to say nothing of a religious, value-system, this relationship seems to be a slender reed indeed on which to build the main foundations of a personal character. The essential point, however, is that the crucial problem of personality development in its earliest stages is not how to get commitment to the "right" values, but how to get commitment to *any* values. It is the persistent fallacy of "emanationist" theories of human behavior to hold explicitly, or to imply, that if you have the "right" orientations, their implementation in action follows automatically. This could not be farther from the truth. From its very nature the process of building up a personality structure is one in which preparation of the "soil" for the growth of value-commitments must take precedence over concern with the content of those commitments. The basis of this view is the conviction of how very precarious a truly human level of personality development in any sense is. And the safeguarding of minimum conditions of this development concerns factors which are at the furthest range of independence from religious orientations, the ineluctable needs of organisms, and the exigencies of successful development of any sort of personality. The role of erotic factors in personality development constitutes a particularly important focus of this problem.

The erotic-need system of the individual, which has caused so much concern and conflict in religious connections, is only in a relative sense the focus of "bodily" needs. It is, for instance, not at all on the same level as the need for nutrition. It is rather, in the genetic development of the individual, the most important *bridge* between the biological and the social levels. It is an essential component in the first genuine *attachment* to another human being and hence in the building up of capacities for higher levels of attachment, of love, including eventually the religious levels of love and devotion. It is of the first importance that the erotic attachments of childhood must be transcended if these higher levels are to be attained. But it now seems entirely clear that they must be genuinely transcended, not bypassed altogether or, once developed, merely repressed again.

In the normal process of "socialization," as sociologists call it, this transcending occurs in two most important stages. The first of these takes place within the family in which the child grows up, his family of orientation. Freud made the famous statement that the infant is "polymorph perverse." This is to say that the form his erotic motivational structure will take is not determined in advance by genetic factors (in the hereditary sense), either with reference to the object choice, that is, whether he is heterosexual or homosexual, or with reference to zonal primacies, that is, whether he is oral, anal, or genital in primary focus of erotic need. A process of developing learned organization takes place in the early years, which can be profoundly disturbed if the relationship structure of his family situation is abnormal.

At the end of this period, in the oedipal transition, childhood erotic interests are normally more or less fully abandoned (in a certain sense repressed) and during the next few years the child is in what Freud called a state of "latency." This is a period of tremendous advance in instrumental learning, and in the development of emotional capacities in nonerotic connections. His relations to his parents are greatly altered in the direction of affection and respect rather than erotic attachment. He must also develop a respectful attachment to teachers and loyalty to peers of his own age. Then, in adolescence, the erotic component begins to emerge again, but this time with two crucial differences. In the first place, the normal object is a person of opposite sex outside his family and belonging to his own generation. And second, this component no longer dominates his whole personality in the old sense, but is built into and controlled by a structure of values and interests which far transcend the scope of this component. In his adult life only one of his principal role complexes, that of his family and his devotion to cultural commitments, including those of religion, will have other primary bases of anchorage in his personality system. In a *genetic* sense, however, the system in which the erotic component is central remains at the "root" of his whole personality system. It is this circumstance which underlies the element of truth in Freud's conception of the "sexual"—I prefer to say erotic—basis of all the neuroses.

From one point of view the process of transcending childhood erotic needs may be regarded as, at the same time, the process of internalizing higher levels of value. The first major step here is the internalization of what Freud called the *superego,* which essentially is the level of internalized control that makes the renunciations of childhood eroticism in the latency period possible. This, however, is far from being the end of the road. Every major step in achieving greater maturity involves the internalization of still higher levels of value-commitment, up to the level of full adulthood.

If, as was noted above, religious collectivities constitute the primary social context in which the religious commitments of the individual are directly expressed and in certain respects regulated, for his personality as a system the corresponding area of social involvement is clearly the family. Here, however, a very special duality of structural relation of the individual to kinship collectivities becomes of central importance. This is to say that the normal individual is, in his lifetime, a member not of one family, but of two, that into which he is born and grows up as a child and that formed by his marriage in which he functions in the role of spouse and parent.

There is a very fundamental dynamic relation between the two in which the personality of the individual constitutes the primary link. For the adult his family of procreation is clearly the most important focus of his personal "security" as an individual person. It is the motivational foundation on which the stability of his capacities for participation in what—from the point of view of the society—are the "higher level" functions of adult life, is built. These include of course contribution through occupational performance, through community responsibility in various associational forms, and through cultural concerns.

For the living individual the stability of this foundation is not to be taken for granted. It may be suggested that the most important set of mechanisms of its regulation consists in the fact that the basic motivational themes and components of childhood are directly involved in the life of the family for the adult. It is well known that in the process of socialization the reciprocal role relation of interacting partners is internalized. From this point of view performance of the parental role is, for the individual, the acting out of the obverse role pattern to that which he in fact played as a child. Functioning as a parent, then, constitutes a long succession of recapitulations in reverse roles of the individual's own childhood experience, reaching from early infancy to the final emancipation from the family of orientation. Then, in a subtler and in some ways deeper sense, the relation of marriage partners is not only a living out of the relationships of their own parents to each other, but in its erotic phase, involves deep symbolic references to the direct eroticism of early childhood. Very broadly it may be said that the act of heterosexual intercourse is a symbolic recapitulation of the erotic tie between mother and pre-oedipal child.

The crucial point here is that these symbolic recapitulations are carried out within the context of socially responsible adult life situations. The primary tests and rewards come, particularly for the adult male, in these situations. But the motivational commitments which make socially acceptable achievements, and those acceptable to the higher-level consciences of individuals, possible are deeply regulated by the subtle emotional interchanges of family life.

Family and Church as "Boundary" Structures

It has been suggested that however fragmented in particular cases, a religious tradition is inherently part of a culture and that this in turn is in the first instance integrated with a society rather than the personality of an individual. With reference to the theme of values, it is closest to the level of value-commitment which is institutionalized in the society—it is the highest level in the general scale of "ultimacy."

Given this very fundamental difference between the involvement of values in the personality of the individual in the genetic sequence on the one hand, in the culture and from it the society on the other, can there be said to be any analogy between the duality of involvement in the individual in two families, and his involvement in religious organization? I should like to suggest that there is, but that the sense in which this is the case must be very carefully formulated.

There is a critical sense in which the preoedipal child is not yet "in the society"; he is in his family. The family is the borderline structure between the roots of the personality of the individual and his beginning participation in the society. As an adult he is a full participant in the society, but through his family of procreation he still participates in this "presocietal soil" of his being as a human personality. There is an analogous sense in which, in all the higher religions, but notably Christianity, the religious collectivity is not fully "in the society." It is in an important sense "set apart," a field of participation which, to use the old phrase, is "in the world but not of it." The ways in which this is the case may of course vary immensely, but I should like to postulate an essential element of constancy in this respect.

In the case of a church or denomination in the modern sense, however, its typical member is, in his other roles, very much a member of society. But the church is a partially segregated area where the concerns of secular life can, within limits, be held in abeyance. This would seem to be an important aspect of the more general phenomenon of the "set-apartness" of the realm of the sacred.

Churches, in their symbolic and ritualistic traditions, utilize a set of references of meaning which are particularly "set apart" even from intelligibility in the context of secular life. My general hypothesis here is that these references are to what may be called metaphorically the "childhood of the culture." They do not refer primarily to stages in the life history of the individual, but to the "foundations" on which the present stage of religious commitment, particularly with reference to "the world," have been built up. In the Christian case, this reference is to the basic constitution of the early Christian church. There are four basic references, involved in all Christian ritual from this point of view, to God the Father as the transcendental reference of the ultimate ground of meaning; to the Christ figure as the mediator between Divinity and humanity and hence as the symbolic head of the church; to the church itself as the brotherhood of Christians imbued with the Holy Spirit, and to the individual Christian as participant in the church and, through it, in Divine grace.

From the point of view of adequate adjustment to and involvement in a society of the modern type, the early church was clearly "archaic." It was quite literally not "of" this world, particularly a modern world. Modern churches are the product of a complex process of evolution from the early church, but they of course still perpetuate this same fundamental complex of belief and symbolism and make it the focus not only of their ritualistic practices but in some sense of their organization as collectivities. In the "middle" period of this evolution the church became a very elaborate organization, which in a sense commanded jurisdiction over something approaching a half of life in society. Since the Reformation there has been a process of social differentiation in the course of which the church has become a more specialized agency to the point where, in the modern Protestant denomination, it has become predominantly a private association which has "lost" many of the functions of the earlier, particularly the mediaeval, church, notably with respect to jurisdiction over secular culture, education, and family life, whereas the political and economic spheres had earlier been predominantly institutionalized in secular terms. The pattern of the denomination has, particularly in the United States, profoundly influenced the religious organization of Judaism, and even considerably that of the Catholic church in that through its minority position and the separation of church and state the religious collectivity is deprived of many of the prerogatives it had traditionally enjoyed and still does where it is the established church.

The most important point for present purposes is that churches as social organizations constitute only a small fraction of the framework of organization of a complex modern society while the rest of the society is specifically categorized as secular. There is a certain parallelism to the fact that the family has, in the course of recent social evolution, also become a more differentiated, specialized agency, less diffusely embedded in larger social structures, such as the nexuses of extended kinship and local community.

This differentiation does not, as it is often contended, imply that either or both have lost most of their "importance" in modern society. It means that the influence they do exert is not through organizational jurisdiction over certain spheres of life now structurally differentiated from them, but through the value-commitments and motivational commitments of individuals. In spheres outside their families and their churches, then, individuals have come to be by and large free of organizational control and in this sense to act *autonomously,* on their own responsibility. But this is by no means to say that their behavior in these "external" spheres is uninfluenced by their participation in the family and the church respectively.

In modern society, then, the family and the church are "boundary-structures" vis-à-vis, respectively, the motivational and the value components of the individual personality. Let us try to sum up how these are related to each other. The axis on which I have tried to relate them is that defined on the one hand by the series of steps in the specification of orientation of value, from the highest religiously grounded level, down through the value system institutionalized in the society, to the levels which can become meaningful in the orientation of the particular individual, faced with a particular life situation within the society. The other series is grounded in the most general exigencies of the organization of the motivational system of the personality, starting in the earliest attachment to the mother, going up through the oedipal stage, through latency and adolescence to adulthood.

The latter series may, from one point of view, be regarded as a series of internalizations of value-patterns, of their "combination" with motivational components. But it starts with highly specific values, and only gradually works up to more and more generalized levels. Conversely the "religious" series is in the first instance one of the specification of values. It, however, starts at the *most* general level and must work "down" from there. Moreover, this process also, to be effective in conduct, must include the *institutionalization* of the values, and one major component of this process of institutionalization is the motivational commitment of individual personalities to them.[1] The church or churches have been the primary social agencies of this process of *institutionalization.*

For the given individual there must of course be a process by which the religious values are internalized in his personality; various aspects of religious education are involved here, but we cannot take space to go into them. Once internalized, however, their reinforcement and maintenance operate through mechanisms which are analogous to those operating in the family of procreation. This is universally the processes of religious observance and teaching, perhaps notably observance, on the ritualistic level. The most important point is that in both cases the stabilization functions operate mainly through institutionalized mechanisms which do not require any elaborately specific attention to the problems of the particular individual. It is rather that he normally participates in a nexus of social relationships and the attendant activities, and this participation normally regulates his pattern of commitments.

Now we may raise the question of where and how these two series meet in the structure of the society and the life-pattern of the individual. Looking at the problem from the life-cycle point of view the evidence seems to be that a specially crucial point is adolescence. There are certainly normally what we would call religious components in the orientations internalized throughout the life cycle, and certainly in the preoedipal and latency periods. But it is in adolescence that the child first comes to play a more highly differentiated set of roles in a variety of different contexts of participation. Furthermore it is here that he first, in a sense implying real commitment, faces the formation of the basic pattern of his adult life, notably with respect to choice of occupation and of marriage partner. Late adolescence brings both these commitments and also the first formal admission to participation in community responsibility, in modern societies especially symbolized by the right to vote. Finally, most modern religious groups institutionalize full religious participation through ceremonies such as confirmation sometime during this period.[2]

We may thus say that it is typically in adolescence that the individual enters into full participation in his society; that he becomes a contributor through occupational performance to its functioning, and thereby economically self-supporting; that he assumes his share of collective responsibility; and that he begins to participate in the socialization function through marriage. Here for the first time he is really confronted with the problem of the nature and extent of his value-commitments as an adult member of the society.[3]

We have emphasized that this extent and nature of societal commitment is in the nature of the case problematical on cultural—that is, eventually religious—levels. Somehow societal interests must be balanced against others, notably those of the individual's own personality itself, and the balance grounded in some orientation defining the meaning of *his* life.

Our very broad conclusion is that the problems of the groundwork of the motivational structure of the personality come to a head in relation to the oedipal stage of personality development, and to the relation between the individual's participation in his family of procreation, as spouse and parent, as an adult. The problems of value-commitment and its grounding in the individual's relation to the deeper layers of the cultural tradition of his society come to a head in his life history in adolescence, and in principle in terms of the current social structure, in his relation to the organized religion in which he was brought up or toward which he may be drawn.

Social Differentiation as Affecting the Statuses of Family and Church

Let us now attempt to look at the problem from the point of view of the social structure. Here the salient fact about modern society is the high development of structural differentiation, and the rapidity with which processes of structural change at the requisite levels have gone on. It has already been noted how the family has become a substantially more specialized agency, more fully differentiated from other agencies. By virtue of this fact its members are placed in a position of far greater autonomy in their relations outside the family, and these spheres constitute an increasingly large share of their life-interests. For the child of course this increasing autonomy centers in his schooling, and the relations to his age peers which are closely associated with the school, but are also in important respects independent of it.

At the other end of our scale, the church in the denominational pattern has also become a more specialized agency and by virtue of this fact has lost many of its former functions. Its organizational involvement in the "things of this world" has in one important sense steadily receded. It has certainly lost notably in political power, relative to the situation in which established churches existed. It takes far less of a role in the control of economic production, and most notably perhaps it has renounced much of its formal jurisdiction over secular culture and education, and over family relations. By the same token as the family, it has tended to come to exert influence increasingly through its "moral" hold on individuals rather than through the more "massive" societal means of exerting influence.

Like marriage for the adult, church affiliation has become a voluntary matter. This is closely associated with the system of religious toleration, separation of church and state, and denominational pluralism. Religious adherence has become "privatized."

The fact that both institutional complexes have been so involved in the process of differentiation means that a gap has been created between them, which did not previously exist to the same extent. The "wedge" which symbolizes and has in part created this gap is, above all, secular education—in the United States, the public school system. But it is also clearly signalized by the tendency to deny to *organized* religion even directly moral, to say nothing of legal jurisdiction over marriage and divorce and many of the problems of private morality, particularly those associated with the family.

It is in our opinion this process of structural differentiation in the society which underlies the emerging salience of the problem with which the discussion of this paper started. Our general thesis here is that the problems of mental health and illness root in the motivational organization of the personality of the individual. This in turn genetically is primarily concerned with the process of socialization down through the oedipal period, and in terms of the problem of adjustment of the individual, in the first instance with his roles in marriage and cognate relations and his role as a parent. Since mental illness ramifies into the personality as a whole, it affects all the behavioral contexts in which he is involved, but its structural core rests in the areas designated.

What has been referred to above as "spiritual malaise" is empirically often associated with psychopathology, but must be considered to be analytically independent of it. It concerns above all the individual's commitments to the values of his society and the various subsectors of it with which he is or potentially might be associated, and, from this point of departure, his involvements in problems of meaning. This is in turn genetically associated with his experience in the religious groups with which he and his parents and associates have been affiliated, an experience the personal significance of which has very generally come to a head in adolescence. It leads over into acute problems of the meaning of his life commitments.

Both sets of problems are closely related to strains which are inherent in the structure of a rapidly developing and differentiating society. The family itself has been rapidly changing its character. It is furthermore an important "residual legatee" of strains generated in other parts of the society and hence may often become disorganized under the impact of these strains. On the other side of the picture the religious organization is necessarily deeply involved in the structure of the society as a whole. Hence any major changes of the latter have a strong impact on organized religion. For these reasons, attitudes toward organized religion and its symbol-systems understandably play a major part in the impact on personalities of all the strains which are operative in a changing society.

Perhaps the most generalized formulation of the common factor in these two problem areas which is current in sociological thinking is the concept of *anomie*. This may be said to be the disturbance of the state of internalized expectations of persons occasioned by the processes of change in the normative components of the institutionalized culture, and hence in the definition of what can legitimately be expected of individuals and classes of them. The most essential point is that in the process of such change, what is expected often over wide areas becomes seriously indeterminate. Anomic components of the situation may, we feel, be propagated in both directions. On the one hand, they may raise questions on the more religiously based level of meaning. Where the normative structure involves serious anomic elements in particular, the balances between performance and sanction, between what is felt to be earned and the actual available rewards in fact forthcoming, will be upset. (The upset, it may be noted, may result from excessive as well as from inadequate reward.) In the other direction, looking to the motivation of the personality, life simply becomes more complex and there are problems of how far individuals are capable of "taking it" from the point of view of their own characters, particularly with respect to their "tolerance of ambiguity" and their capacity to handle risks.

This discussion has stressed the differentiation between the personality and religious contexts, between family and church. Before closing this structural analysis something should be said about one very important context of connection between them. Both the problem of mental health and that of religious commitment involve matters of intimate personal significance to individuals, what in a certain sense are highly "private" affairs. It is not fortuitous, therefore, that both center in the life of the local residential community and that by and large it is as family members that people are associated in churches. Both are hence somewhat withdrawn from the larger economic and political affairs of the society, and are associated together in this withdrawal. This situation has much to do with the sense in which the church has tended to maintain, and even develop further, a set of functions as a diffuse center of association at the first level beyond the household. It is a kind of substitute for the undifferentiated neighborhood, a place where "like-minded" people can get to know each other and be made to "feel at home" in contexts not specifically connected with religion.

It is not uncommon to suggest that this set of functions has in fact become primary, that modern churchgoers are "not really" religious at all, but are only interested in sociability. In my opinion this is a misinterpretation. This associational aspect of the modern denominational parish is a predictable feature of the general pattern of the development of modern society when the fact is taken into account that family and church have such intimate intrinsic relations to each other. The sociability pattern is the primary mechanism by which family and church are brought together with each other. Each, in its own specialized way, involves the "whole person." Unless they are to be, not merely differentiated, but *dissociated,* there must be some adequate mechanism of linkage. My hypothesis is that the church as a "social center" provides this mechanism, and that, as a result of the structural differentiation of modern society, this has become more rather than less important.

Family Structure and the Profession of Psychiatry

We may now return to our problem of the relation between mental illness and spiritual malaise and the structure of the social agencies oriented to them. It has been pointed out that in earlier societies the problems of illness and of the religious states of the individual have tended to be fused, and that a process of differentiation has occurred from there.

Very broadly it may be said that the first major complex to become differentiated (from the fusion, in earlier societies, of the problems of illness and of the religious states of the individual) was that having to do with somatic illness. The long history of the problem cannot be gone into here. Suffice it to say that a crucial stage was reached with the great scientific developments of the late nineteenth century and the full institutionalization of "scientific medicine" in this period. Generally this development posed few problems for religion since it was almost a dogma that only "the body" was involved in such illness. This relative insulation of the problems of the state of the body from those of "the mind" proved to be unstable and shortlived, however. Our own century has seen, particularly in this country, a progressively increasing salience of the conception of illness precisely in the area of the personality (mental illness) and its complex interrelations with the organism (the so-called "psychosomatic" field).

This development was certain to have a major impact on religion since it is a matter of the mechanisms by which human behavior is controlled. On one level mental illness could be defined as a Divine punishment; on another as a way in which the individual could evade his moral responsibilities. But whatever the difficulties, it is, as noted, clear that the main trend in the definition of mental as of somatic illness, and of the possible therapeutic measures for coping with it, has been in terms of the development of *science,* of its extension into spheres where its possibility and significance have in previous cultures been questionable. Certainly the scientific underpinning of the diagnoses and treatment of mental illness is still in a very early stage of development, but a relatively firm institutional pattern of this definition has become established, and it is one which specifically differentiates a problem of applied science from anything legitimately falling within the jurisdiction of religion. However indeterminate the boundaries between the two jurisdictions, and they are certainly far from having been settled, this is a firmly established fact of modern society which is extremely unlikely to be reversed by a return to an across-the-board conception of the primacy of "religious healing."

The function of dealing with mental illness has become, at least tentatively, institutionalized in the profession of psychiatry as a branch of the medical profession. There are many unresolved problems about the exact status of psychiatry, the ingredients which should go into psychiatric competence, and its relation to other possible therapeutic agencies. But, however these questions may stand, the broad location of this function in the social structure is certainly "appropriate." In its recent development medicine has centered in the bodily welfare of the individual, and the main residual locus of care for this welfare has of course been the family household. Hence there is an ancient and honorable tradition of the central importance of the "family physician" as the guardian of this welfare in the sense of "backing up" the more routine and common-sense operations of the family. Medicine has, seen in this light, been a "second line of defense" of the somatic welfare of the individual, tending to step in where the difficulties exceeded the capacities of the family to cope with them. As the conception of incapacitation through illness has broadened into the "mental" areas this same basic reference point has continued to be the central one, namely that of a professional agent who could treat the individual for the problems particular to him, in close collaboration with his family.

This is of course far from telling more than a fraction of the story, since the development of the hospital and various complex patterns of medical, including psychiatric, care, have greatly modified this simple pattern of an individual professional practitioner serving as a backstop to the family.

Nevertheless, I do not think that the significance of this pattern can be ignored. It certainly fits with the view put forward above that the personality of the individual is rooted in his experience in his family of orientation and is most intimately regulated, in his adult life, in his relationships within the family of procreation. It is an expectable development that there should be mechanisms in the society which backstop the family in this set of functions as well, and do so by and large in the tradition of "classical" medical practice.

However far hospitalization, group therapy, and various other arrangements have gone, for the present context it is important to note that in the field of mental health the main pattern has been that there should be, at the disposal of the individual in intimate relation to this family, an *individual* person, qualified by scientifically based competence, to deal with his individual problems. This person is, in his therapeutic role, to be sure, anchored both in the scientific culture of the society and in its moral standards, which define health and hence the respects in which a "sick" person deviates from those standards. The medical profession as a social entity is of course the primary institutionalized guardian of this definition of the role of psychiatrist. But the medical profession is not a collectivity which as a collectivity undertakes responsibility for the health of the community as a whole. It is rather an *association* of practitioners whose institutionalized roles as individuals are organized about their responsibilities—assuming the requisite competence, of course—for caring for the needs of particular patients. This, after all, is the primary basis of the difference between the medical and the public health professions in modern society.

The Churches and the Problem of Spiritual Counseling

I bring out this last point because it presents a notable asymmetry between the therapeutic function in the medical-psychiatric function and that of the trusteeship of the religious interests of the individual. The organ of this latter trusteeship has, historically, been the church. However much the character of the church has been modified in the course of its evolution, particularly in the recent denominational phase, the church has always been defined as primarily a *collectivity* which *combined* the trusteeship of the great religious tradition—in relation to the society of its primary values—with a concern for the spiritual welfare of individual persons. Thus, as has been suggested, the church is far more closely analogous to the family than to the psychiatric profession. The family and the church have both served as *collective* trustees, responsible to be sure for their individual members' welfare and development, but depending in this respect mainly on mechanisms which operated "nonrationally" in that the persons implementing them were not in a scientific sense aware of "what they were doing." As noted, the basic religious mechanism in this respect has been the ritualistic function.

Seen from this point of view the minister of religion is not parallel to the psychiatrist in his relation to individuals.[4] If we look at the problem in terms of structural parallels he is in a certain sense parallel to the "father" of the family. What I mean here is that he is, in certain respects which need careful defining, the responsible leader of a collectivity, a collectivity to which the welfare of individuals in very crucial respects has been entrusted, but where his primary function is responsible leadership *of* the collectivity, not individualized attention to individuals. In religious terms these functions have centered on the administration of the ritualistic cult, and on the teaching function with reference to maintenance of the cultural tradition itself. These are both contexts in which the maintenance of uniformity takes clear precedence over individuation.

The problem of the "cure of souls" has of course by no means been absent from Christian tradition. Its most massive institutionalization has perhaps been in the Catholic confessional, and of course very generally in the "pastoral" function of the clergy. In a few variant, if not deviant, cases like Christian Science, it has been elevated to a primary level, but, in this case, in terms directly competing with the medical treatment of illness—a role which most religious groups have understandably avoided.

Our general line of argument is that this pastoral component of the role of the minister of religion is, structurally speaking, far more closely analogous to the sense in which good parents take an individualized interest in and responsibility for the psychological welfare of their children than it is to the role of psychiatrist. In both cases, however, this must in the nature of the case be an "auxiliary" function since their primary responsibilities in both cases are inherently focused on the collectivities in question.

I take it that the important feature of the development of psychiatry for present purposes is the emergence of a professional role which is structurally differentiated and hence in a sense segregated from that of parent or spouse in the family, but which is adapted to the task of dealing with problems of the personality of the individual which root in the family, but which, precisely because of the nature of the family as a collectivity, cannot be effectively dealt with simply as a function ascribed to familial roles. This structural segregation can be shown to provide an essential condition of the permissiveness which is central to the psychotherapeutic process, and for exercising the leverage necessary for getting out of vicious circles of involvement with familial problems which are often both symptoms and determinants of psychopathological conditions.

Hence it seems logical to suggest that a corresponding problem exists in the religious context. The minister is in the first instance the responsible leader and administrator of a congregation and a parish. He is the guardian of the cult tradition and of the church's responsibility for the morality of its members. In this connection he is subject to the same order of handicaps in dealing with his parishioners' intimately personal problems of religious orientation, as are family members in dealing with each other's psychological problems; in both cases of course the problems become acute when they get beyond a certain level of complication, above all when they involve irrational mechanisms of defense which are not accessible to the ordinary appeals at the "rational" level of belief and teaching which is taken for granted in most Christian and Jewish denominations.

I have argued that perhaps the most important keynote of the process of social change in modern society is structural differentiation. This has been very much involved in the changing status of religion and the pattern of its social organization. The present American system of denominational pluralism is a product of such a process of differentiation. But there is no reason to believe that the process has reached a limit.

Clearly Christian ministers and their Jewish counterparts have come into a difficult and in some respects anomalous position with respect to their functions as "spiritual advisers" to individuals. On the one hand, there is the tendency to encroach on the functions of psychiatry as a branch of science-based medicine and thus not to differentiate the problems of the individual's commitments to values, and to solutions of the problems of meaning, from the problems of the underlying organization of his personality as a motivational system. On the other hand, there is the set of problems concerned with the conflict between the minister's primary responsibilities as leader of a congregation and the kinds of permissiveness and support which are indicated in a role that is trying to deal with the complex inter-weaving of religious problems with the personality structure of the individual.

My suggestion is that it is in the logic of the present situation that there should soon emerge a distinct, differentiated professional role which might be called that of "spiritual counselor," differentiated, that is, both from the role of psychiatrist on the one hand, and from that of minister in his capacity of leader of a congregation, on the other.

The essential bases of the differentiation vis-à-vis the psychiatrist should be clear from the discussion above. It is probably a fact that psychiatry has tended to take over certain of the functions which properly belong in this area, and that it is likely it will tend to retreat in certain respects to a more restricted area. As I see it, the primary focus of the psychiatric role should be on the problem of the *capacity* of the individual to *implement* the values and other commitments which he may come to regard as legitimized for his life.[5] The complexity of borderline relations is such that such capacity can seldom if ever be improved without attempted clarification of *what* it is that the patient most fundamentally wants. But however important this interpenetration, it is not the psychiatric function to consider the bases of the legitimation of this "what," above all to confront the individual with the underlying problem of choice-and-meaning terms. This is not to say that psychiatric clarification does not or should not extend to consideration of the consequences of the individual's value-commitments to himself and to others; this it necessarily does, but this is not the same problem as that of legitimation.

In drawing the line vis-à-vis the traditional ministerial role, the distinction out-lined above between familial and psychiatric roles can, if properly qualified, provide a model. Just as the family is the primary locus of the regulation and stabilization of the motivational structures of the individual, so it may be argued that the church is the primary locus of the regulation and stabilization of his spiritual commitments. Seen in terms of its relation to the institutionalized value-system of the society this is indeed the primary function of the church. But, just as in the case of the family certain problems of the personality come to be beyond its capacity to cope with, so for the church, certain of the value- and meaning-problems of its members become too acute to be coped with within the traditional framework of church organization. If not adequately handled, in both cases there is a tendency to the establishment of vicious circles, involving "alienation" of different types.

The conditions necessary for coping with such vicious-circle tendencies are known in a broad way. These include a sphere of institutionalized "permissiveness" within which the individual may freely express his attitudes and sentiments without being exposed to the normal negative sanctions in case they deviate from those accepted in the relevant collectivities. They include a "floor" of supportiveness so that a generally accepting attitude is not jeopardized by these deviant expressions. At the same time, however, they include only selective rewarding of specific over-tures toward new "definitions of the situation," the standards being their conformity with a higher-level conception of the relevant values and beliefs. Finally, they include the availability of a consistently reinforcing pattern of sanctions which will consolidate a renewed orientation in terms of the values and beliefs to which the agent of this "therapy" is himself committed.

A slightly different way of putting it is to say that any therapeutic agency in this sense must be capable of operating at two levels in relation to the internalization and institutionalization of the relevant cultural components. On the one hand, it must be firmly anchored in the higher institutionalized level—in the psychiatric case, in that considered normal to the "mature" personality. The therapist must not let himself be drawn into the "pathological" expectations of his patient in such a way as to reciprocate them. He must firmly "stand for" the values of health. At the same time, however, he msut also be able to "empathize" with his patients "deviant" preoccupations, which in the psychiatric case are psychologically regressive. He must give a properly controlled opportunity for their expression, and not let this expression undermine the generally supportive attitude indicated.

Turning back to the case of the minister, I should suggest that the leader of the congregation is handicapped in performing this role in a sense directly parallel to that in which a family member is handicapped in performing a psychiatric role. In the nature of the case he is the primary focus of the sanction system on which the functioning of the collectivity he leads is dependent. He is responsible for exhorting to proper participation in ritual, proper affirmation of belief and proper moral conduct. At the very least he must show disapproval of acts and attitudes which are deviant from these standards. Furthermore, by and large his implementation of these sanctions is public within the collectivity, though some modification of this is possible.

The exigencies of this collective leadership role constitute a formidable barrier to effective implementation of the permissive and supportive components of the "therapeutic" role, and indeed of the element of tentativeness which is necessarily involved in what I have called "selective rewarding." Experience in the psychological field has shown clearly that these functions are greatly facilitated if the agency responsible for them is clearly differentiated from that of the "normal" implementation of sanctions, and if these two agencies are mutually insulated from each other by a pattern like the privileged communication which is so deeply rooted in the traditions of the medical profession. It is precisely crucial that the patient's deviant phantasies should *not* be communicated to the members of his family. My suggestion is here that the minister is a "parental" figure in his psychological significance, and that it is important for the individual in religious quandaries to have a forum of expression of religious attitudes, which will be guaranteed against communication to his minister since the latter is inevitably put, by such knowledge, in the dilemma of how far to exert pressure to "correct" the deviance.

That a profession of spiritual counselors in this sense should be a specialized group clearly separated from the parish ministry, and that the function should not be treated as an auxiliary function of the minister himself, seems to me to be strongly indicated. I would even suggest the possibility of going a step beyond this, namely to the point where such a group should be independent of at least formal denominational affiliation. It is of course a very serious question how far different denominational groups could tolerate entrusting their members to intimate religious counselors who were not committed to the particular denominational position. But it seems to me that the existence of the substratum of religious and moral consensus which is to me the necessary condition for the functioning of a system of denominational pluralism indicates the feasibility of such a separation. It would certainly greatly facilitate the impression of the genuineness of the "disinterestedness" of the counselor, namely, by removing the suspicion that he was simply an agent of the denominational authorities, not sincerely concerned with his client's personal religious problems, not only commissioned to bring him back into the fold by whatever pressures were necessary. Just as the conception of mental health in our society permits of leading a healthy life within a wide range of social statuses, occupations, and indeed family situations, so it would seem to be logical that a life of approved spiritual commitment could be lived within any one of a range of denominational affiliations, or indeed independently of any, and that a profession of spiritual counselors might well hold themselves formally free of commitment to any of them within an institutionalized range.

This of course is not to say that the members of such a group should be empirically independent of closer ties to some denominational groups than to others. The same set of forces which make our particular denominations in fact more closely connected with some parts of the social structure than others would operate in this direction. It is not considered deviant for some psychiatrists to have mainly a Jewish clientele, or mainly an academic one. But this is a very different thing from the profession being broken up into sectors which are formally committed to the service of particular social groups and these only.

The main tenor of this paper has been to emphasize the importance of the *differentiation* between the focus on the motivational foundations of the personality as these root in the process of socialization and in the family and, on the other hand, the involvement of the individual in religious and value-commitments at the more mature levels, as these are institutionalized in churches and in the value-patterns of the society at the more generalized levels. But this emphasis should not distract attention too much from the fact that these two levels are in fact intimately connected as well. Were this not so, the early fusion of the problems of health and of religious "purity" which is of such great historic significance would not be understandable. Both spheres involve the "deeper" and often unconscious layers of the personality of the individual. They are, moreover, deeply and subtly intertwined so that at many points they are only analytically distinguishable. This circumstance does not cancel out the importance of the process of differentiation which has been analyzed here, but it does make clear that it is a differentiation of deeply interconnected elements and that, since it is not a dissociation, their relations to each other remain of the first importance. Nothing said in this paper should be construed to minimize the importance of these interconnections.[6]

Conclusion

There is, by something like common consent, much spiritual malaise in our time. Diagnoses of the situation differ widely. My own inclination is to put considerably more emphasis on the processes of social and cultural change, including growth, which have gone on in recent times and which certainly have not ceased to go on, rather than, as is so commonly done, on factors of spiritual decline or moral collapse.[7] In my opinion the severity of the adjustments that have to be made in the processes of change which we know to occur are quite sufficient to account for the order of magnitude of the phenomenon.

In the nature of the case a major part of these adjustments must take place at levels entirely out of reach of the suggestions put forward in this paper. They must involve the major symbol-systems and ritualistic practices of churches, their organization as social collectivities and their place in the societies of which they are parts. No individualized measures can take the place of such readjustments. By exactly the same kind of reasoning much of the psychopathology of our time is a function of these same processes of social and cultural change, and certainly the psychiatric treatment of individuals cannot by itself control these processes or prevent them from having all deleterious impact on individuals.

At the same time, when due account is taken of these considerations, certainly the therapy of individuals at the psychiatric level can save many of the casualties of the social maladjustments and malintegrations with which we are so familiar and can mitigate their impact. In so doing it can greatly lessen the spread of personality breakdowns which make the stabilization of social situations and the assimilation of structural changes more difficult. By the same token, though individualized handling of spiritual malaise cannot hope to eliminate it, it can in principle have the same order of effect in raising the levels of commitment of large numbers of individuals, and in softening the severity of the phenomena of religious and to some extent moral crises on a societal level. It can, that is to say, mitigate the cost of religious changes, and certainly in individual instances, if not on some collective levels, it can avert some acute crises and possible shipwrecks.

It should be clear from the preceding argument that the prospects of success of any such institution as a profession of spiritual counseling rest on the existence of a sufficiently institutionalized consensus, above all with respect to what constitutes "moral integrity" in our society. This is parallel to the sense in which psychiatry rests on a consensus with respect to what constitutes mental health. This consensus need not be explicit in detail nor very tangible, but it must exist. It is my own view that it does in fact exist, that without it the degree of stability which our type of society has shown could not be understood. This is perhaps the main point at which issue must be joined with the prophets of spiritual doom who are so prominent in our time.

REFERENCES

1. On the general nature of this process see "Christianity and Modern Industrial Society," by Talcott Parsons, in *Festschrift for Pitirim A. Sorokin,* Edward A. Tiryakian, ed. (to be published by The Free Press, Glencoe, Ill.).

2. Particularly illuminating observations on the significance of adolescence for the religious orientations of the individual are presented in Robert N. Bellah, "The Place of Religion in Human Action," *Review of Religion,* March, 1958.

3. An important, relatively new factor seems to have entered into this situation, the implications of which are far from clear. This is the increasing participation of the population in higher education even beyond the college level through advanced professional training. Just what are the limits of adolescence is a moot question, but certainly the middle twenties are beyond them. Anyway the effect is to postpone the full assumption of occupational roles and the attendant responsibilities and rewards to a much later point than has been typical of most of the population for most periods. It may well be that this is an important factor in the ferment about problems of meaning in our own time, since there is a certain conflict between the general emphasis on early independence and responsibility on the one hand, and the kind of tutelage in which persons in the system of formal education generally, and of professional training in particular, tend to be kept. One possible tendency may be to treat the higher commitments of meaning as even more tentative than before, since only the fully "mature" person should enter into them. But if this is the tendency, one would expect much conflict in the process of the working out of the new pattern, and that certain groups should feel a particularly urgent need to have firm "answers" almost immediately.

4. On this difference cf. Kaspar D. Naegele, "Clergymen, Teachers, and Psychiatrists," *Canadian Journal of Economics and Political Science,* February, 1956.

5. Cf. my paper "The Definitions of Health and Illness in the Light of American Values and Social Structure," in E. Gartly Jaco, ed., *Patients, Physicians and Illness* (Glencoe, Ill.: The Free Press, 1958).

6. An exceptionally fine and perceptive analysis of these relations has recently been made by Erik H. Erikson in *Young Man Luther* (New York: W. W. Norton & Co., Inc., 1958). Contrary to the tendency of many psychoanalytically inclined writers to attempt to "reduce" the religious components of the problem to what we have here called "motivational" terms, Erikson consistently keeps the distinction clear, yet noting the highly intimate nature of their interdependence.

7. I have stated the main case for the growth- rather than the decline-hypothesis in "Christianity and Modern Industrial Society," in Tiryakian, ed., *op. cit.,* and cannot take space to repeat it here.

DAVID C. McCLELLAND ❧

His training in experimental psychology has enabled David McClelland, Professor of Clinical Psychology in the Department of Social Relations at Harvard University and Director of the Center for Research in Personality, to bring to his work in clinical psychology the precision and practicality of the natural sciences. That his development as a scientist should have moved in the direction of clinical psychology shows that his real concern is with people and the unity of the human personality. His concern includes at least a tangential awareness of problems which heretofore were dealt with by philosophy, theology, literature, and the arts. McClelland is well aware of the relevance of these fields and does not shy away from taking them into consideration.

He does not carelessly mingle properly religious or philosophical concepts with those which belong to psychology as a social science. On the contrary, McClelland desires to bring clarity into the distinction between the social sciences and the humanities. When one of his colleagues tried to demonstrate how much Freud in his approach was really influenced by religious forces in his own tradition rather than being as scientific and clinical as he professes to be, McClelland was bound to be much affected by such a suggestive hypothesis.

In this chapter of our book he uses the hypothesis of Bakan—perhaps too confidently—in order to demonstrate the religious overtones in psychoanalysis. Under his treatment Freudian analysis becomes a secular cult with mystic overtones. McClelland feels that this allows him to explain certain utterances and attitudes of Freud himself but especially the turn which Freudian analysis has taken today. The popular response to Freudian analysis thus arises out of a widespread need for a mystic religion and its absence in traditional American Protestantism.

Even if the term mystic religion is not so understandable or palatable to many readers as it is to the Quaker McClelland, the impact of his argument should not be ignored. Traditional Christianity in this country has in many instances sold out the genuine inward vitality of faith to the frenzy of outward activities. To build a church or to have many different programs and a gymnasium or swimming pool in the basement of the church building has often become far more important than the issue of personal faith and conviction in the life of the individual church member. The psychologist McClelland points out that this neglect is not accidental. The outward appearance of a church may be impressive while the individual members have little or no awareness of the relevance of the Christian faith in their daily life. This shallowness of church experience explains why so many devout Christians lose their ability to deal constructively with their personal problems and seek the help of a psychiatrist rather than the advice of their socially busy pastor.

McClelland seems to be convinced that if the Christian faith does not come back to the strength of its inward reality, it will be swept aside by the secular movement of psychoanalysis, which lives inwardly on the vestiges of Jewish mysticism. Even if the direct connection between psychoanalysis and Jewish mysticism is not so tenable as McClelland believes, the problem for the Christian Church, as he points out, is a real issue and ought to be faced by ministers and theologians.

Religious Overtones in Psychoanalysis

§ DAVID C. McCLELLAND

Speaking publicly about religious matters presents many difficulties for a behavioral scientist today. To admit to a religious point of view, to some personal commitment, is to violate the most fundamental rule governing the behavior of a scientist—namely, to be objective. Personal bias serves only to distort the search for truth. So it is part of the professional role of the scientist, particularly if he is interested in human affairs, to keep himself free from entangling commitments, to remain in a state of suspended judgment so far as many of life's most serious issues are concerned.

And most of my colleagues live up to their professional role with great strictness so far as religion, and in particular Christianity, is concerned. I can hardly think of a psychologist, sociologist, or anthropologist of my generation who would admit publicly or privately to a religious commitment of any kind. Furthermore, it is my impression that the taboo on religion holds for more than those who should remain professionally objective. Very few intellectuals in my circle of any kind take Christianity seriously except as an historical or social phenomenon. The only exceptions are those whose professional role more or less requires them to take a religious stand—those who teach religion and those who are in a position of public responsibility. I have known men whose interest in religion appears to have begun the moment they assume public office. It is apparently just as inconceivable for a President of the United States to be irreligious as it is for a professor of psychology to be religious. The requirements of their roles are just different, and are normally followed without much deviation. With the two exceptions noted, objectivity or suspended judgment on religion is the rule, at least in the intellectual circles in which I move. A psychological colleague of mine has told me that the same condition exists among undergraduates. He has found in his intensive study of a number of them that they talk readily enough about their sex lives, but unwillingly and with great hesitation about their religious convictions. He has concluded that it is not sex which is a delicate subject in our generation but religion.

49

So I am faced with great difficulty. I do not teach religion nor am I a public figure. What is more, I am a psychologist who should remain objective. Yet I must "break role," transgress the taboo against religion and reveal at least to a certain extent my personal religious convictions. I have had to overcome considerable internal resistance to do so, and you may well wonder why it was necessary. Why could I not deal with a subject like psychoanalysis and religion objectively without revealing my own personal convictions? The answer lies in part in what I shall have to say and in part in my own personality. It will be necessary for me to talk at length about the unconscious religious assumptions of psychoanalysis and I thought it only fair to reveal my own so that whatever bias I bring to the task may be discounted and corrected by others. Furthermore, in religious matters I am a nonconformist from a long line of Dissenters, and I suspect that my desire to speak out is motivated by a culturally nurtured spirit of opposition which in this case has turned itself against the conspiracy of silence on religion. Be that as it may, let me confess at the outset that my remote ancestors were Huguenots and strict Presbyterians from Scotland and northern Ireland, that my mother was reared a Covenanter—one of the most radical forms of Presbyterianism, that my father is a Methodist minister and that I am a convinced Quaker whose approach to religion is primarily mystical. It would be hard to find a background of more "radical" Christianity. Its relevance to my theme will become clearer as I proceed.

Psychoanalysis stands in striking contrast to Christianity in intellectual circles. It is enthusiastically accepted, or at least taken very seriously, by the very same men who ignore or despise Christianity. Unfortunately I have no precise figures, but it is my strong impression that an influential minority among both faculty and students in our great urban universities have either been psychoanalyzed or would like to be. It has been seriously proposed in one university department known to me, that a psychoanalyst be added to the permanent staff of the department whose function would be largely to analyze his fellow staff members. In Cambridge where I live it is as difficult to spend an evening with friends without discussing some aspect of psychoanalysis as it was perhaps a hundred years ago to spend the same kind of evening without discussing Christianity. But is it fair to compare the two phenomena in this way? After all, psychoanalysis is not overtly a religious movement. It is a technique for helping the mentally ill and for discovering some of the ways in which the mind works as a contribution to scientific psychology. But whatever its conscious intention, as a *social movement* its functions are much broader than these. Its leading practitioners have charisma: they are looked up to, admired and treated as beyond the ordinary run of humanity in much the same way as ministers and priests have been at various times in the past. Psychoanalysis has managed to give meaning to life to many troubled intellectuals who could find no meaning elsewhere. Its metaphysics—Freudian and neo-Freudian conceptions of the nature of man and existence—are seriously discussed by leading intellectuals of the day in much the same way as theological questions were discussed in an earlier day. Above all, it *heals,* and we should not forget that one of the basic and most fundamental appeals of Christianity as described in the New Testament was its healing power. At least on the surface then—and the idea is by no means original with me—psychoanalysis has many of the characteristics of a religious movement. Nowhere that I know of is this more simply and movingly expressed than in Thomas Mann's treatment of psychoanalysis in *The Magic Mountain*. Mann came into contact early with analysis around the time of the First World War and, with what appears now to be an unusual flash of poetic insight, understood its basic religious character. At the tuberculosis sanitarium where the scene of *The Magic Mountain* is laid, there is a resident psychoanalyst, Dr. Krokowski, who concludes his first lecture to the assembled patients on psychoanalysis by stating that "symptoms of disease are nothing but a disguised manifestation of the power of love; and all disease is only love transformed." The reference here is of course to the Freudian theory that all neurosis has at its root some sexual difficulty, some deformation in the normal development of the libido, but Mann purposely phrases Dr. Krokowski's conclusion in religious terms. He then continues:

> Dr. Krokowski had raised his voice and so drawn attention once more upon himself. He was standing there behind his table with his arms outstretched and his head on one side—almost, despite the frock coat, he looked like Christ on the Cross!
>
> It seemed at the end of the lecture Dr. Krokowski was making propaganda for psychoanalysis; with open arms he summoned all and sundry to come unto him. "Come unto me," he was saying, though not in those words, "Come unto me, all ye who are weary and heavy laden." And he left no doubt of his conviction that all those present *were* weary and heavy laden. He spoke of secret suffering, of shame and sorrow, of the redeeming power of the analytic.[1]

Perhaps Dr. Krokowski is pictured as proselytizing a little too openly for the Psychoanalytic Institutes of today, but I can personally vouch for the fact that his missionary zeal is not altogether dead among contemporary psychoanalysts. They are committed people. They *believe* in the "redeeming power of the analytic" in a way which many Christian ministers might envy.

Is the resemblance of psychoanalysis to a religious movement superficial, a mere compelling metaphor, based on a few functional similarities in meeting people's needs? I think not. The resemblance is far more deeply rooted than that. It is based on the fact that psychoanalysis did not spring full-blown from Freud's mind, like Minerva from the head of Jove. Rather, as a remarkable little book by Bakan has recently demonstrated,[2] it drew heavily on the traditions of Jewish mysticism, particularly as they flowered in Hasidism in Central Europe late in the nineteenth century. Freud was himself of course violently antireligious, although he always considered himself culturally a Jew. Nearly all the early leaders in psychoanalysis were likewise Jews in varying degrees of rebellion against orthodoxy. Bakan argues that although they consciously rejected religion, they nevertheless borrowed heavily from mystical traditions which were widely influential in the milieu in which they grew up.

The goal of Hasidism was self-actualization, self-fulfillment by direct contact with the Divine. It therefore had much in common with various forms of radical Christianity like Methodist "enthusiasm" or Baptist "revivalism" which also became widely influential in the nineteenth century. Like them it was a mass movement which gained much of its strength by being opposed to traditional orthodox religion. From the seventeenth century onward rabbinical Judaism was on the defensive throughout Central Europe. It had taught that only by living up to the minutiae of the Law could the Jews as a people expect to be favored by God, that in return for their obedience and fulfillment of his commands, God had entered into a cove-nant to reward them and to treat them as his Chosen People. However, the Jews suffered from continuous persecution culminating in pogroms from the seventeenth century on. How could the average Jew believe that by living up to the Law, he was going to be favored by God? He had apparently tried it without success. The orthodox answer, then as in the time of Job, was of course that he must have failed in some respect to live up to the Law or he would not have been so punished by God.

So the more the Jews suffered, the greater was the traditionalist religious pressure to live up more exactly than ever to the many requirements of Jewish Law. Mysticism represented a revolt against such rabbinical "legalism." It argued that salvation for the Jews as a people was not likely to come about by increasing conformity to the Law. Rather individuals could be fulfilled and the group "saved" by direct contact with the Divine here and now. Such contact was characterized by joy and release rather than by the more traditional suffering and repentance. A few great rabbis— the Baal Shem—became noted for their miraculous healing powers, their ability to release individuals from the burden of suffering, rather than for their detailed knowledge of the Talmud as in orthodox Judaism. Mass enthusiasm swept religious meetings. Emotional release replaced the hard, cold, rational legalism of orthodoxy. False messiahs appeared—Sabbatai Zevi and Jacob Frank—who promised to lead the Jews immediately into a better life, and who even went so far as to argue that sinning was a good thing since it would help bring about the millennium sooner.

The goal of psychoanalysis is practically identical with that of Jewish mysticism— to release and fulfill the individual by contact with emotional, irrational forces. Freud's image of man is of one hemmed in by conflicts and anxieties arising pri-marily out of the thwarting of natural impulses by society. The central problem of neurosis is the need for freedom, for release from guilt, from an oppressive superego representing the demands that society makes on the individual. For ex-ample, a common cause of mental disturbance is the Oedipus complex, according to psychoanalysis. What, in its simplest terms is the Oedipus complex? It is an *inevitable* tragedy which arises in the development of the impulse life of man from being born into society, or more particularly into a family. Every little boy is fated to fall in love with his mother, to hate his father, to feel guilty, to suffer—because he is a human individual born into a matrix of other individuals. He must obtain release from the tragedy of social existence, and psychoanalysis is the instrument for obtaining release from the oppressive social responsibilities of Jewish orthodoxy. In other words, Freud and the Jewish leaders of psychoanalysis saw man's central problem in terms of his need for self-fulfillment as over against the oppressive forces of social obligation because this was the central issue in the cultural milieu in which they grew up. For them the crippling pressures of the group, of traditional Jewish orthodoxy, were very real and obvious. Probably only in Calvinistic Puritan circles have they ever been so great elsewhere.

Two often-noted peculiarities of traditional psychoanalytic practice appear to have arisen at least in part from the way man's central problem was conceived. The first is the obvious fact that psychoanalysis has never had much success among psychopaths or among working-class people.[3] The neurotic problems of psychopathy and of many lower-class people often arise from the *absence of well-defined moral standards*. So a therapeutic movement which sees the central problem of neurosis as oppression by excessive moral demands is not apt to be of much help to such people. Psychoanalysis has just never been comfortable with the problem of providing people with a consistent set of values, even when "moral education" is what is obviously needed. It still works best for those who factually do need release from an oppressively moral upbringing.

A second "peculiarity" of psychoanalytic practice is that it has traditionally refused to have anything to do with the welfare of anyone else in the patient's milieu. That is, the therapist's relationship to his patient is much like the defense lawyer's relationship to his client. He does not try to represent the interests of his patient and society at one and the same time. In fact he gains much of his power to help the individual by openly allying himself with the patient, as over against the demands of society. Since many psychoanalysts are also physicians, this idea fits in well with medical ethics which state that the doctor should do everything for the welfare of his patient. But there is an important difference between physical and mental illness, which psychoanalysts have been slow to recognize. In curing physical disease a physician ordinarily does not have to worry whether his remedy will harm anyone else. Medicine may cost money but giving it to one person does not make another person sick. Yet such problems do arise in mental illness since it is such an interpersonal affair.

For instance, in the course of psychoanalysis a man may come to realize that what he needs is release from his wife, a divorce. The wife may be upset by this, in fact she now may become "ill," and may even want to talk to her husband's analyst about the problem. He may well refuse to see her on the grounds that getting involved in her problems may make it more difficult for him to help her husband. If she needs help she should get her own analyst. The patient's family is not the analyst's responsibility, and if he is a doctor, he may feel that medical ethics justify his point of view: he must do everything he can for his patient's welfare, even if it may by some mischance harm someone else. I am not now of course accusing the whole psychiatric profession of being socially irresponsible. I know as individuals that they do often consider their social obligations. I know too that modern analysts like Spiegel argue that the whole family may need treatment to help any member of it really successfully. What I am saying is that the major emphasis of the psychoanalytic tradition in psychiatry is on the welfare of the individual and that it has real difficulties in the area of moral education and of social responsibilities. The reason lies at least partly in the fact that psychoanalysis originated as an individualistic revolt against the oppressive orthodoxy of legalistic Judaism.

But it is not only the aims of psychoanalysis and Jewish mysticism which are parallel, as Bakan has pointed out.[4] The techniques they employ are also very similar. Jewish religious scholarship has always been noted for its exegesis on the text. Rabbis were trained in complex interpretations and reinterpretations of the details of Jewish Law. What Jewish mysticism did was to adopt the same detailed textual approach but in a less rational, less logical, looser or metaphorical manner. Abraham Abulafia had recommended a technique which he called "skipping and jumping" in dealing with the text as early as the thirteenth century. Cabalistic writings over the succeeding centuries provided a body of magical, emotional lore which served as a constant contrast to the "cold" legalism of Jewish orthodoxy.

Jewish mysticism drew on such sources and on the direct inspiration of its chief writers to produce the *Zohar,* a book of allegorical reinterpretations of religious traditions which was for the Jewish mystic what the *Talmud* was for the orthodox Jew. The *Zohar* is a work of imagination not of reason. Its key technique is allusion and metaphor as opposed to logic and close reasoning. The psychoanalysts employed the same technique and called it "free association." Furthermore, they had a traditional basis for using free association to understand man, since according to Bakan, the *Zohar* suggests that man may be conceived as a text (or Torah) requiring exegesis and more particularly in Hasidism, the holiness of the Zadik (or religious leader) was to be understood as a kind of living Torah. In other words, in psychoanalysis as in Jewish mysticism it was the technique of employing the imagination, of interpreting free association, dreams, and metaphors which was going to serve to release man from the bonds of traditionalism, of oppressively rational, moral obligations.

And what exactly was it that was revealed by the technique of free association that proved so therapeutic to man? It is here that one of the most striking parallels with the tradition of Jewish mysticism appears. Freud was openly a rationalist. He felt that knowledge of the unconscious irrational forces in human nature ultimately gives man control over them. But it is knowledge of a very special sort that heals. It is *sexual* knowledge. It is precisely at this point that Freud stands at the very center of the Jewish mystical tradition. In Hebrew the word for "knowing" (*jaddah*) can have a sexual connotation as is illustrated by the English translation of the verse "and Adam knew Eve his wife"; that is to say, he "knew" her sexually. As the story of Adam and Eve further illustrates, in biblical tradition, "knowledge" (eating of the fruit of the tree) is intimately associated with sexual knowledge: "And the eyes of them both were opened, and they knew that they were naked."

The ceremony of Bar Mitzvah, observed for Jewish boys at puberty, apparently celebrates the fact that only when he has achieved full sexuality (that is, genital maturity) can he overcome the ignorance and the impulsiveness of childhood. Though sexual associations to knowledge had been present in all Jewish traditions, they were most highly developed in the *Zohar*. In fact the *Zohar* recasts much of Jewish religious tradition in sexual terms. For example, Israel is conceived as the female part of God, the Holy Shekinah, which is cast aside and then redeemed by God in a mystical union described in sexual terms.

In short, the sexual image is all-pervasive. Real knowledge, real understanding of the world must *ultimately* be sexual. Freud and the orthodox analysts adopted this viewpoint rigidly. They insisted that all attempts to understand man and his conflicts in other terms, such as Jung's religious archetypes, Adler's drive for power, or Rank's birth trauma, were necessarily superficial and misleading. At its most fundamental level life must be interpreted in sexual terms just as the *Zohar* had demonstrated.

There is more, much more, to Bakan's analysis of the connections between psychoanalysis and Jewish mysticism.[5] Freud saw the sexual instincts in a sense as the root of all evil. The young infant was born with powerful drives which, if he were only strong enough, would lead him to commit every crime in the calendar—incest, rape, murder, and so on. In the mystical tradition the source of all evil is the Devil and by entering into a pact with him one can gain control over the occult forces which are his to command. To the non-Jewish world, this idea is best represented in Goethe's *Faust,* a work much influenced by Jewish cabalistic writings. There is evidence that Freud felt in his psychoanalytic work that he was entering into a pact with the Devil, that by exploring the underworld of the mind he could gain control over the evil forces within it. There is also considerable evidence that he suffered from a "Messiah complex," that he feared to enter Rome where the Jewish Messiah was traditionally supposed to be proclaimed, that he at least unconsciously thought of himself as founding a new religious movement which would replace the outworn traditions of orthodoxy. But enough of Bakan's case has been presented to make the main point. Psychoanalysis was religious in its origin, a secular outgrowth of the Jewish mystical tradition in its continuing struggle with Mosaic orthodoxy.

It should by now be much easier to understand why psychoanalysis has had such a great appeal for American intellectuals. It fitted in readily with their spirit of revolt against Christian orthodoxy, with the nineteenth-century spirit of romantic individualism which was concerned with fulfillment rather than one's duty to social institutions, to the state, or to the church. Its insistence on the evil in man's nature, and in particular on the sexual root of that evil, suited the New England temperament well which had been shaped by a similar Puritan emphasis. In fact to hear Anna Freud speak of the criminal tendencies of the one- and two-year-old is to be reminded inevitably of Calvinistic sermons on infant damnation. Echoes of Calvinism can also be found in Freud's thoroughgoing determinism, and his insistence on the inevitability of certain emotional conflicts like the Oedipus complex. After all, for people schooled to believe in predestination or even more, in the complete absence of chance in the universe because God controls everything, it takes no great stretch of the imagination to accept scientific determinism. In science, Nature simply replaces God in making everything inevitable.

But above all psychoanalysis could succeed among intellectuals where traditional religion failed because it was presented as science, not religion, in an increasingly secular age. That is, it provided many of the values which religion had traditionally provided, but did so without consciously posing as religion. If the intellectuals who so enthusiastically espouse psychoanalysis knew that they were supporting an honorable offshoot of religious mysticism, they might be considerably less enthusiastic about it. It is because it is not religious but scientific that they can let themselves believe in it.

Is it then my purpose in calling attention to the religious roots of psychoanalysis to discredit it in their eyes, to destroy their faith? Certainly not, although there is no doubt that we have laid open an issue which was a matter of grave concern to the founders of psychoanalysis. Freud reports how disturbed he was that psychoanalysis seemed to be largely a Jewish movement in its early days, and how his eagerness to include Gentiles led him to support Jung for the presidency of the International Psychoanalytical Association even when it was already becoming clear that Jung differed with him on a number of basic issues. Despite Freud's efforts, the leading psychoanalysts in both Europe and the United States were for a long time nearly all Jews. The fact is not at all surprising if Bakan's thesis is correct that psychoanalysis drew many of its key traditions from Jewish mystical religion. But why then did they not admit it? Why did Freud not explicitly acknowledge his indebtedness to earlier traditions? There are several possible explanations.

To begin with, it should not be overlooked that many psychoanalysts may not have realized they were drawing on Jewish religious traditions in exactly the same sense that many secularized Protestants may not realize their view of life is strongly colored by their religious background. They were secularized Jews and had every reason to reject consciously anything that had to do with religion. But even if they had realized their indebtedness (and Bakan feels that Freud might well have recognized it), there was every reason for them to conceal the Jewish origins of psychoanalysis. Freud was convinced that he was practicing a scientific technique which produced objective knowledge about human behavior. To admit that there was anything Jewish or religious about it would be to undermine its scientific status, to admit the possibility of bias. Worst of all, to admit to Jewish origins would be to open psychoanalysis to the tide of vicious anti-Semitism which was sweeping Central Europe in Freud's day. After all, neither then *nor even now* was it as harmless to speak of a Jewish school of psychoanalysis as it was to speak, for example, of Scotch realists or American functionalists. Finally for many Jews the emotional excesses of the mystical tradition, particularly since they had a distinctly sexual flavor at times, were a very discreditable part of Jewish history and if anything only served to provide some factual basis for the anti-Semitic tales circulating in Europe at the time. It would certainly not help a new "science" to be associated with mysticism, with occultism, with cabala, and every form of obscurantism. So psychoanalysis had every reason not to want to talk about its Jewish origins even if it had understood them. To speak of them even today is to run some risk of bringing a "taint" on psychoanalysis by association.

But my intent has been quite different. It is to show that psychoanalysis was successful in part because of its religious roots, because it has continued to serve man's needs in the way that religions have always served them. To demonstrate this thesis requires much more than an historical analysis. After all, one can admit that a movement was religious in origin, just as natural science developed out of radical Protestantism, without implying that it *continues* to be religious in any way. Suppose psychoanalysis did draw some of its ideas and practices from Jewish mysticism. So what? Has it not become increasingly scientific and perhaps even abandoned many of these ideas? Psychoanalytic practice has certainly been modified in America despite the resistance of the more orthodox Freudians. In fact, the psychoanalytic viewpoint has gradually pervaded the entire psychiatric profession, but in the process it is gradually undergoing some changes. Many new ideas are afloat, at least in the most advanced medical centers, but they highlight even more sharply how psychoanalysis functioned as a religious movement by showing how the same religious needs can be met in slightly different ways. Let me illustrate.

As we have seen, psychoanalysis, because of its individualistic, mystical origins, tended to see man's main problem as centering in his need for release and fulfillment as over against oppressive moral obligations. The psychoanalyst was tacitly the patient's ally in his struggle for fulfillment. At least one modern variant of psychoanalysis no longer regards this problem as central by any means for all neurotics. Instead, the patient's key problem is not the need for release but the need for love. He must learn that somebody cares for him, somebody respects him as an individual whatever he may do or whatever he may have done. The therapist is still his ally but not necessarily in his struggle for release from crippling moral demands. Therapeutic skill lies in the ability to convince a neurotic or psychotic that the therapist really does care for him. Neurosis, according to this view, in large part developed because the person feels he can no longer trust people, because he suspects everybody. Needless to say in such an atmosphere of distrust and suspicion, the therapist cannot get away with *pretending* he cares. He must genuinely be able to respect his patient if his efforts at cure are to be successful. It takes very little reflection to see that stripped of its accidental historical opposition to orthodoxy, the concern of psychoanalysis for the individual has developed into the traditional mystic's concern for "that of God in every man," as Quakers would phrase it.

The orthodox analytic emphasis on the central importance of sex has also undergone changes. There are probably fewer and fewer analysts who act in their daily practice on the assumption that only the sexual image has genuine healing power, although many of them still continue to write up their cases in terms of Freudian metaphysics. I know of one individual whose analysis significantly turned on images from James Joyce, another whose cure centered in a verse from the thirteenth chapter of I Corinthians ("For now we see through a glass, darkly; but then face to face: Now I know in part; but then shall I know even as also I am known"). But again Freud's instinct seems to have been correct when he refused to yield to those who insisted that sexuality was not of central importance but a *mere* metaphor for something else. For him the sexual nature of man was far more than a mere metaphor in the ordinary sense of the term. It represented *power*—above all the power to heal.

Modern psychoanalysts though they may reject the sexual image as necessary, all accept the idea that whatever imagery the patient uses, it must have power, the same kind of power for him that the sexual image had for Freud. It is here that psychoanalysis, both orthodox and modern, reveals most clearly its mystical character. What the religious mystic has testified to throughout the ages and in all forms of religion is his direct emotional experience of something, above all a power, *beyond himself.* This "something" he has usually called God and has sought to describe his experience in terms of whatever religious imagery is readily available to him in terms of his time and culture. But always he protests at having to find words to describe his experience. Words, images always seem to distort it for him, though he must find some way of expressing the inexpressible.

For Freud and others in contact with the Jewish mystical tradition, the sexual image succeeded in conveying the power of the inexpressible. For others the image may be different. But that does not mean that the image is trivial or unimportant, a *mere* intellectualization. No, it must carry the emotional impact of contact with a power beyond the self—a power called by some the life principle or libido, by others a positive growth force, by religious mystics, God. Every neurotic suffers from a feeling of inadequacy: something has happened to him which is beyond his control. He cannot cope with it. In the course of his analysis he may suffer a long time in confusion, despair, and helplessness, but at some point if he is to get well, something begins to happen to him which he experiences emotionally as "outside self." He can do things now that he could not do before. He does not know exactly what has happened and may attribute his new-found powers to the influence of the analyst or some new discovery about himself, but the central inescapable fact of his *experience* is that he did not do it himself—that some power outside himself moved him. To speak of a "power not ourselves that heals" is at least in mystical religious terms to speak of God. The fact that the power was described in sexual terms by early psychoanalysis appears more and more to have been an accident of its Jewish mystical origins.

Other modern developments in psychiatry point in the same direction. They have tended to separate what was peculiar to the problems of Jewish mysticism in Freud's time from what is universally characteristic of religious mysticism as it attempts to respond to the human condition in all times and places. For example, there are psychiatrists now like Spiegel who have overcome the limitations of working with an individual quite apart from the effect of his "cure" on others. They do not see society or the family as so oppressive as those breaking away from Jewish or Christian orthodoxy did. They do not think that it is possible to consider the health of an individual apart from the health of those around him. They even argue that the family should be treated along with the individual. In all these developments the traditional religious concern for group as well as individual welfare has begun to creep back into psychiatric practice.

Or to consider just one more example, orthodox Freudians were pessimistic about human nature. They believed in a form of "infant damnation" and like the Puritans at times appeared to feel that the best that man could hope for in this "vale of tears" was stoic indifference. When Freudianism came to America, it tended to get more optimistic, to be influenced by the American pragmatic belief in the possibility of a much better world—so much so in fact that many European analysts have been very much disturbed by the easy optimism of some American analysts. Cultural relativity has been particularly suspect because it seems to argue that people are neurotic simply because they are brought up incorrectly. After all, other cultures rear their children differently and in such a way as to avoid many of the problems that beset our children when they grow up. All that is needed is proper child care. Similarly what the therapist has to do is to "retrain" the patient who has been brought up incorrectly.

Psychoanalysts originally took a much more serious view of the "existential" difficulties in which every man found himself and which no amount of proper child rearing could wish away. It can be argued, as Tillich has maintained,[6] that in a certain sense they were more religious in this respect than their American colleagues, many of whom succumbed to the typical American notion that man can do anything for himself if he only has the proper knowledge. But the real point I want to make is that modern psychology appears to be moving away both from Freud's easy pessimism or the relativist's easy optimism about the nature of man. Rather it regards man as neither basically good nor basically evil, but as having great *potentialities* for both good and evil. Existential difficulties are neither minimized nor exaggerated. They are accepted as part of life in exactly the same sense that man's capacity to transcend them (*not* remove them) is accepted. This development too appears to be more characteristic of the general mystical point of view than of the peculiar Freudian one. Of the Quaker mystic at least it has always been characteristic that he has recognized the seriousness of man's existential limitations —his all too human failings—at the same time as he has struggled for and occasionally found the Divine spark in every man, even himself.

But perhaps I am overdoing it, overstraining myself to find analogies between mystical religion and psychoanalysis. So far, psychoanalysis has been shown to have been religious both in its origins and further developments. But the skeptic may still ask, so what? After all, just because a movement functions in some respects like a religion, does that mean that it is really religious?[7] By this kind of reasoning couldn't almost anything be made to appear religious? To answer such questions requires a definition of what religion "really" is. But there are many definitions of religion. Which is the best one? Unfortunately I am not a theologian and therefore not even in a position to know what the best alternatives are. So I shall have to content myself with a general definition recognizing fully that in so doing I may simply be revealing my own religious background.

In its most general sense religion has to do with the transcendental, with a power beyond man and this world which is usually called God. Religion commonly functions in three spheres of life—intellectual, social, and personal. It gives intellectual meaning to existence through theology which attempts to provide answers to such ultimate questions as why people are born, where they go when they die, how the world got started, and so on. In the social sphere, religion has to do with ethics, with the moral principles governing the right conduct of men toward each other and with the sanctions (rewards or punishments in this life or hereafter) which follow when men do the right or wrong things. Finally in the personal sphere, religion or God has been invoked to explain unusual experiences which seem beyond the normal. In particular it has been associated with healing. All great religions have dealt with all three of these areas of life to a greater or lesser degree. For example, the New Testament deals extensively with intellectual matters, with the meaning of existence, as in the Gospel of John, with ethical questions as in the Sermon on the Mount and Paul's letters, and with the miraculous healing powers of Jesus.

Throughout its history Christianity has sometimes emphasized one or another aspect of religion. In the last hundred years, for instance, I think a case could be made for the fact that there has been a progressive shift in emphasis within Protestantism. A hundred years or more ago it was the theological aspect of religion that excited Christians the most. In fact they got so worked up over theological issues that Protestant Christianity split up into a number of different sects representing apparently irreconcilable theological doctrines. Today it is difficult for Christians of different denominations to work up much enthusiasm over theological disputes. The point of central interest has shifted.

Around the turn of the twentieth century ethical questions assumed paramount importance. Christians became primarily interested in the social gospel—in proper working conditions, prohibition, international peace or, in more recent times, racial discriminaton. In fact I recall a common definition of God as being "a Power not ourselves that makes for righteousness." Christianity both supported and was supported by the hope of a better world here on earth in the near future. But two World Wars, a depression, the tyranny of fascism and communism, the relative failure of the United Nations, the invention of atomic techniques for destroying mankind have all tended to discourage somewhat the search for God in the social order, in man's relationship to man. If He is really making for righteousness, He appears to be pretty slow about it. As a result the ethical emphasis in Christianity is losing some of the enormous appeal it had once, although it is still strong among many church leaders brought up in an earlier day. Some Christian leaders like Tillich and Niebuhr have revived interest in basic theological questions—in new analyses of the meaning of existence in Christian terms.

There is an alternative: to find God in the "healing power of the analytic." It is for this reason above all that I would classify psychoanalysis as a religious movement. To some extent it provides man with a theology, with a view of the nature of existence. Freud had quite a lot to say about the ultimate nature of things, although many contemporary analysts would regard them more as his personal philosophy than as anything essential to psychoanalysis as a therapeutic technique. Psychoanalysis also has had something to say about ethics, about man's relationship to man, particularly in the hands of such neo-Freudians as Erich Fromm who has specifically tried to work out what the implications for ethics are of Freudian assumptions about the nature of man. For many people the appeal of neo-Freudian ethics lay precisely in the fact that it seemed to be based on solid scientific facts rather than on religious assumptions about the nature of man. However, what has often been stated as fact turns out on closer examination to be simply value-assumptions more or less unconsciously carried over from the particular religious background of the author. It is more nearly the dominant view among modern psychoanalysts that their therapeutic technique is ethically "neutral" in the sense that it is valuable for a person whatever his ethical standards may be. In this sense it is nearer the mystical tradition in that it does not concern itself with particular ethical problems but rather with the basic attitudes that lie behind man's relationship to man, with the "changed heart."

But whatever its theological or ethical implications may be, psychoanalysis is above all a continuing testimony to a "power not ourselves that heals." As such it has particular though usually unconscious religious appeal for intellectuals offended by the "antique" theology of the Christian church and increasingly disillusioned about the ethical potentialities of Christianity. Viewed in this light, psychoanalysis, as a secular religious movement, fulfilled an historic religious function which the church was not fulfilling, and probably was able to do it better because it was openly antireligious.

So much for my argument. Let us suppose for the moment that there is some truth in it, at least in its essentials. What does it mean so far as the Christian church is concerned? What challenge does it present? It should stimulate some new thinking on at least two major points—one, the conception of the minister's role and the other, church doctrine.

There is little doubt that Protestant ministers are less important in the community today than they have been at various times in the past. It is not that they are not busy, extremely useful members of the community who are highly regarded. It is just that they are less important. The reason appears in socio-psychological terms to be that they have less of the charisma that goes with power. In the genuinely religious community of the past, the minister was God's representative who above all knew something about or even exerted some control over what was going to happen to a man after he died. He fulfilled at least to a limited extent the role of a gatekeeper—in this instance to the after-life. But as theology declined in importance and was replaced by ethics as the focus of interest, the after-life became less and less important. It was *this* life that counted, and so far as this life was concerned the minister became just one of a number of people who had ideas about how it ought to be lived. At the same time the power he used to have as a gatekeeper over life and death shifted to a considerable extent to a new profession—that of the physician who controlled the knowledge and skill which could at least keep a person alive. In a generation when the next world was of primary importance, the man who could keep you in this one (the doctor) was not so important, but he became much more so as man's interest shifted to this life.

But if our analysis has been correct, the doctor-psychiatrist should have even more of the charisma of power that formerly belonged to the minister. For he not only inherits some of the control over life and death of the physician (after all, neurosis can lead to psychosomatic disorder and death), he is also closely connected with the one manifestation of God's power that many men appear most willing to accept today—*namely, the power to heal* rather than to transform the social order or to give certainty about the meaning of life. The traditional healing functions of religion have never been much practiced by the Protestant ministry, although of course whole sects like Christian Science have developed around the attempt to exercise them. It is also true that there has been a growing interest in pastoral counseling in the Protestant church, though I doubt if much of it has been conceived at the level which I am discussing here. Instead it has been introduced as a social service like the many others the modern church provides (from sewing circles to basketball courts).

Am I therefore suggesting that ministers should get training in the religious significance of therapy, rather than just in its techniques? Lest the answer appear too simply to be "yes," since any attempt to recapture lost charisma may seem like a good thing, let me push the question further. Are ministers willing to undergo the three to seven years required for a psychoanalysis? It is my firm conviction supported not only by the experience of psychoanalysts but by the whole tradition of religious mysticism, that only by such prolonged self-examination can a man begin to understand and work easily with the healing powers he must be prepared to represent. Mystics—Jesus himself in the wilderness—have spent years in preparation, years in which they have searched sensitively for the leadings of the divine Spirit. Are Protestant ministers willing to "go and do likewise"? Are they for that matter willing to become mystics, to seek within themselves that which is behind and beyond the particular creeds and formulas of their church? Or would it be the better part of wisdom for the church to attempt to help psychiatrists understand a little better what they are doing in religious terms? Certainly few psychiatrists would now regard their mission in life as in any sense religious or would regard the healing power they deal with as in any sense a testimony to the power of God. Or would it be better to leave them alone, to let them go on representing religion unconsciously? Fortunately my task is only to raise such questions, not to answer them.

It has also been my contention that psychoanalysis has fulfilled a religious function for many intellectuals in a way which the Christian church has conspicuously failed to do. Why? The superficial answer already given is that psychoanalysis succeeded where religion failed because it was a secular scientific movement which could avoid the stigma of organized religion. But this only pushes the question further back. Why was there a stigma attached to organized religion? Here I must openly admit that my answer appears to be dictated by my own religious background, but to me it is a compelling one. The church lost out because it became insensitive to the revelations of God and stuck stubbornly to former revelations, ideas, and images which have lost much of their meaning for thinking people. To the mystic the church is a human institution, like a museum, full of artifacts which were infinitely meaningful and valuable to the people who made them. They may even be esthetically pleasing now, but still no longer fulfill their original function. Creeds, doctrines, rituals must be created anew in each generation and in each individual's heart. God reveals himself progressively, but the church as an institution is necessarily conservative tending to preserve earlier revelations long after they have outlived their usefulness.

To the mystic then it is no shock at all to read Freud's analysis of the Christian communion service, to discover that eating the body of Christ manages to symbolize both love and hate for a father-figure. Nor is he in the least disturbed by psychoanalytic interpretations of religion as projections of family conflicts or infantile frustration. He believes that religious images are always attempts to express the inexpressible and it is only natural that man should draw on his most profound psychological experiences in order to clothe the inexpressible with the meaning it deserves. As Tillich puts it, "every being chooses the symbols for the Divine according to what he himself is. . . . If we use the father-image in order to symbolize our ultimate concern, then the ultimate concern is not the father-image." [8]

Let me push the argument one step further. Whiting and Child have discovered [9] that those cultures around the world which discipline young children severely for sexual activity also tend to explain disease in sexual terms. Jews and Puritans were strict about sexuality in children. They should therefore be more likely to invent and approve of the sexual theories of disease which characterize psychoanalysis. Would it have shocked Freud to discover that his theory of neurosis was very likely determined by his own upbringing? It very well might have done so because he thought of his libido theory as a scientific fact rather than as a projection of his own childhood experience. He would have been shocked for the very same reason that many Christians were shocked when he pointed out the childhood basis of many of their religious beliefs and institutions. For he believed in the reality—in the ultimate truth of his image just as they did in theirs. And in a sense he and they were both right. The sexual image was and is "true" and compelling for many people—in fact, the *only* way in which the inexpressible can be meaningfully expressed for them. The same is true of the traditional images of the Christian church for many people.

The only mistake, according to the mystic, is to worship the image, to regard any revelation as final. Like the scientist he knows that what is true today will be untrue or at least very differently true tomorrow. The Protestant church on the whole has been opposed to iconography—to the worship of visual symbols of religious ideas—but it has been less opposed to worship of the ideas themselves, of *verbal* attempts to represent ultimate reality. Could it give up some of its reverence for formulas and seek more and more sensitively for new ones that speak for God to the condition of our times? Can it institutionalize progressive revelation without weakening its very foundations? I am not enough of a church historian—perhaps not even enough of a Christian—to know.

But the success of psychoanalysis as a lay religious movement squarely confronts the church with just such an issue. Growing out of a religious mystical tradition, psychoanalysis has managed to find new ways of interpreting existence, of interpreting man's relationship to man, and above all of testifying to the healing powers of what would have been called God in any other generation. These new insights have been profoundly meaningful to many thinking people. Can the church learn a lesson from this development? Can it go and do likewise? Can it absorb enough of the mystical approach to religion to respond more sensitively and flexibly to the revelations of God in our time?

It would be unfair to conclude without recognizing that the Christian church has, of course, already reacted to the challenge of psychoanalysis. Though it is certainly presumptuous for me even to try to give an account of its response, which by now is quite extensive,[10] I think one can easily distinguish the development of two main currents of thought, once the shock and anger at Freud's open attacks on religion were overcome. The first has been dominated by the liberal Christian's primary concern with ethics, with moral and social perfection.[11] It has seemed to argue as follows, if I may oversimplify to the point of caricature, just to make the position clear: Psychoanalysis is obviously a "good thing" because it helps man to overcome his neuroses and move toward perfection, both in terms of inner adjustment and outer relations to others. Freud's antireligious sentiments are "unfortunate"; but his basic assumptions, if properly stated, are not antireligious at all—in fact, they turn out to be very similar to liberal Christianity (see Hiltner).[12] Christianity also is a "good thing" because it helps people. So Christianity and psychoanalysis should get together and help one another to bring about a better world (see Outler).[13] Easily recognizable in all this is the typically American optimistic emphasis on the possibility of progress and on the nonessential character of theoretical differences so long as they lead to the same practical consequences.

The second current of thought centers around Paul Tillich,[14] who argues that psychoanalysis makes a far more fundamental contribution to Christianity than a mere therapeutic "bag of tricks" which is useful to the Protestant minister in his work. Tillich believes, correctly in my opinion, that psychoanalysis has helped man to realize the "existential" predicament—the meaninglessness, the loneliness of existence with which man is confronted when he awakes from the state of "dreaming innocence" of childhood to realize his own finitude, his own limitations. Freud certainly belonged with many of his European philosophical contemporaries in the emphasis he put on the "existential question." He explained with obvious pleasure how man's pride had received three great shocks; first, from the Copernican discovery that the earth was not the center of the universe; second, from the Darwinian discovery that man was not especially created without antecedents; and, third, from the psychoanalytic discovery that man was not even master in his own household but was controlled by forces beyond his knowledge. To Tillich, recognition of man's existential limitations is the root of Christianity because implicit in the notion of imperfection is *some* idea of perfection (essence) from which man has fallen away or is "estranged." Christianity represents the faith that the estrangement can be healed, that some "solution" (that is, salvation) beyond essence and existence is possible. Obviously Freud did not go beyond the first step of stressing man's existential limitations, but in so doing he has contributed greatly to helping man see the *necessity* for a religious—even a Christian—solution to the problem of existence. Recognizable in Tillich is an emphasis both on the healing and "meaning-giving" functions of religion as opposed to the ethical function stressed in the other Christian reaction to psychoanalysis.

Neither of these currents of thought has understood psychoanalysis as a *religious* movement, although Tillich has come much closer to doing so than American liberal Protestantism. For Tillich has sensed that American optimism about the infinite plasticity of human nature tended to destroy an essential point in Freud's understanding of man. American psychoanalysis, like American liberal Christianity, tended to regard all man's troubles (sins or neuroses) as being due to ignorance— to improper upbringing. Both groups could then unite in supporting a mental health movement which would remove trouble in the world by instructing parents and teachers how to treat children and by providing better counseling services for those who needed help. Both groups could agree that Freud's insistence on dark innate forces in human nature, in the inevitability of emotional conflict in human life (witness the universality of the Oedipus complexes), on the tragedy of existence, was not an essential part of psychoanalysis but simply a product of his personal pessimism. After all, nothing is inevitable: it all depends on how a person is brought up!

The odd thing about such a "cultural" reinterpretation of Freud is that it denies what is most religious (and probably most "healing") about psychoanalysis and not only for the reason that Tillich gives. Freud saw man's problems as arising far more from the conditions of existence than from improper upbringing, as Tillich correctly points out, but he also felt that the answer to man's problems lay in a very special kind of emotional experience of a sexual nature. Earlier I have argued that this experience which is felt as arising from beyond the self is really a testimony to a healing power which is called God by Christians and which was put in terms of sexual symbolism by Freud because he drew on the tradition of the *Zohar* which so described God and religious experiences. Cultural relativists and liberal Christians alike have joined in insisting that the specifically sexual nature of Freud's insight was a "mere" culturally determined metaphor, not recognizing that as Tillich puts it, "the symbol participates in the reality that is symbolized," [15] that the metaphor is and was a living testimony to the reality of the power behind it. So both liberal Christians and the cultural school of psychoanalysts fail to recognize two key religious elements in Freudian psychoanalysis—its insistence on the existential predicament, on the inevitability of anxiety *and* its testimony to the healing power of something which is beyond man. Tillich understands the first element, but not the second, perhaps because he is more of a rational theologian than an "experiencing" mystic.

He certainly understands religious mysticism and states, just as a psychoanalyst would, that the experience "cannot be forced" by the desire for self-salvation. "It must be given." [16] Almost any patient can testify to the truth of this statement so far as recovery in psychoanalysis is concerned. He feels that something has "happened" to him and that if he and the analyst have brought it about, they have done so only indirectly and were not able to force the issue. Renewal, rebirth, salvation, whatever it is called, is *directly experienced* but certainly cannot be produced by an act of will.

Tillich may have missed the religious significance of the mystical healing experience in psychoanalysis because mysticism tends to blur the severity of "the estrangement of ordinary existence" [17] which is for him the starting point of Christian theology. It also tends to shade over into naturalistic mysticism (pantheism and the like) which does not sufficiently recognize the enormous gap between the infinite and the finite, between essence and existence.[18] But is it necessary in terms of either Christian theology or ordinary experience to understand the gap in *negative* terms, in terms of deprivation, loneliness, meaninglessness? The true mystic, it seems to me, experiences the gap in *positive* terms, in terms of affirmation, joy, wonder, belonging, supra-existential *meaningfulness*. Certainly these experiences have been reported very commonly by religious mystics and by patients recovering in psychoanalysis.

In other words, they experience the gap in terms of "accentuation of the positive" rather than in terms of "elimination of the negative" as Tillich and the existentialists do. Is this an important difference? I think it is, but here I am really venturing into theology where others are much better equipped to speak than I am. All I wish really to emphasize is that psychoanalysis is more profoundly religious in its implications certainly than liberal Christians have realized when they have tried to explain away as due to culture its religious essentials—namely Freud's existentialism and his insistence on the healing power of a primarily sexual experience. It is even more religious than Tillich has realized because he failed to appreciate the testimony it gives to a direct, mystical experience of a "Power beyond ourselves that heals."

One final comment. Christianity was itself initially a response of mystical, individualistic elements within Judaism to the Pharisaic orthodoxy of the times. If Goodenough's evidence is to be believed, it was spread all over the Mediterranean world by Hellenized Jews; by Jews like Paul who were in contact with Greek mysticism and rationality. Are we witnessing a similar development today? Has the Christian church become so petrified, so insensitive to the needs of our times, that a new religious movement has again arisen out of Judaism, opposed to orthodoxy and spread by secularized Jews? Certainly psychoanalysis has all these characteristics. It is essentially individualistic, mystical, and opposed to religious orthodoxy. It originated in Judaism and it has been spread by Jews who had lost their faith by contact once again with the spirit of Greek rationalism as represented in modern science. Would it not be the supreme irony of history if God had again chosen his people to produce a new religious revolt against orthodoxy, only this time of Christian making? It is an interesting question, but time and the response of the Christian church alone can give the answer.

REFERENCES

1. Thomas Mann, *The Magic Mountain,* trsl. by H. T. Lowe-Porter (New York: Alfred A. Knopf, Inc., 1927). Used by permission of the publisher.
2. David Bakan, *Sigmund Freud and the Tradition of Jewish Mysticism* (Princeton, N.J.: D. Van Nostrand Co., Inc., 1958).
3. A. B. Hollingshead and F. C. Redlich, *Social Class and Mental Illness* (New York: John Wiley & Sons, Inc., 1958).
4. David Bakan, *op. cit.*
5. David Bakan, *op. cit.*
6. Paul Tillich, "Psychoanalysis, Existentialism and Theology," *Christian Register,* March, 1956, 135, No. 3, pp. 16-17, 34-36.
7. Seward Hiltner, "Psychoanalysis and Religion—the Search for Completeness," *Christian Register,* March, 1956, 135, No. 3, pp. 14-15, 32-34. Hiltner states explicitly that "psychoanalysis and religion are not of the same order" largely because psychoanalysis is not a "conscious" church openly believing in God. Though he is certainly correct, he is in danger of defining away one of the most important religious movements of our time, at least among intellectuals. It was Freud himself, as Tillich points out, who sparked the revolt against consciousness in philosophy. What more fitting though ironic climax to Freud's career could there be than the creation of an *unconscious* religion, a "church" functioning like one in most respects except in the recognition that it is one?
8. Paul Tillich, "Psychoanalysis, Existentialism and Theology," *Christian Register,* March, 1956, 135, No. 3, p. 36.
9. J. W. M. Whiting and I. Child, *Child Training and Personality: a Cross-Cultural Study* (New Haven: Yale University Press, 1953).
10. Seward Hiltner, "Psychoanalysis and Religion—the Search for Completeness," *Christian Register,* March, 1956, 135, No. 3, pp. 14-15, 32-34.
    Albert C. Outler, *Psychotherapy and the Christian Message* (New York: Harper & Brothers, 1954).
    Paul Tillich, "Psychoanalysis, Existentialism and Theology," *Christian Register,* March, 1956, 135, No. 3, pp. 16-17, 34-36.

11. Seward Hiltner, "Psychoanalysis and Religion—the Search for Completeness," *Christian Register,* March, 1956, 135, No. 3, pp. 14-15, 32-34.
    Albert C. Outler, *Psychotherapy and the Christian Message (op. cit.).*
12. Seward Hiltner, "Psychoanalysis and Religion—the Search for Completeness," *Christian Register,* March, 1956, 135, No. 3, pp. 14-15, 32-34.
13. Albert C. Outler, *Psychotherapy and the Christian Message (op. cit.).*
14. Paul Tillich, "Psychoanalysis, Existentialism and Theology," *Christian Register,* March, 1956, 135, No. 3, pp. 16-17, 34-36.
15. Paul Tillich, *Systematic Theology: Existence and the Christ* (Chicago: University of Chicago Press, 1957), Vol. II, p. 9.
16. *Ibid.,* p. 83.
17. *Ibid.,* p. 83.
18. *Ibid.,* p. 7.

FREDERICK C. KUETHER ଥ∾

The former executive secretary of the Council for Clinical Training, Frederick Kuether, B.D., who is now director of training for the American Foundation of Religion and Psychiatry in New York, represents a minister who is training others after he has carefully completed his own preparation. For Kuether the pastoral counselor is not a person who does something but one who is primarily a man with a certain attitude of openness, with a willingness to wrestle with the problems counselees bring to him. Too often in theological education the personality of the prospective minister is grossly neglected. All that matters is that he learn his lessons and know the intellectual and practical facets of the Christian tradition. Kuether has learned them too, but has grown beyond this and become a man who can afford to be spontaneously involved with the problems which come before him without getting lost emotionally in their intricacies. Only through this freedom do problems appear in their deep significance but appropriate proportions. In response to them the Christian faith can become alive as it perhaps never did before in the life of the counselee.

In this chapter Kuether tackles one of the most essential problems in the field of religion and mental health. Under the influence of European existentialist therapy, which now seems to have become a fad in the United States too, he has learned to look at the phenomenon of religion in the person's life differently. The Freudian approach, which considers religion merely negatively as an authoritarian power to repress instinctual drives, is replaced by scrutinizing the actual significance of religious symbols for the believer. Kuether goes one step further and investigates the religious aspect of the different images which a person has of himself or the world around him. He succeeds in achieving a positive evaluation of religion and demonstrates the religious but not intellectual expressions of people's everyday attitudes.

In his counseling with parishioners as well as in his preaching and teaching it is important for the minister to become aware of the many ways in which the person expresses his religious leanings even in the most secular terms and actions. The minister must be equally sensitive to the secular substitutes into which religious energy streams off if it is not captivated by properly religious practices and not stimulated by the religious appeal of the church. Protestantism has become casual in concentrating exclusively on traditional religious practices and neglecting the wide range of other human expressions. Such neglect depletes the vitality of individual faith as well as the relevance of the church and its ministry. The editor wishes to commend Kuether highly to the reader for having grappled with this tricky issue.

The Images of Man and Their Religious Significance

ঌ FREDERICK C. KUETHER

Until relatively recently man has been so involved in coming to terms with his external environment that he has had little time or energy to devote to an exploration of his inner world. Now that his mastery of the microscope, the telescope, and the cyclotron has given him control over at least a portion of his environment, he is confronted with a vastly more confusing task: that of understanding and coming to terms with himself. He has found that he does not know what to do with his knowledge of the world around him because he does not really know who he is. He finds himself constantly in the position of Paul when he spoke of doing what he would not, and failing to do what he would.

Coming to man's rescue, slowly but more surely every day, are the findings of the scientific study of man—depth psychology, sociology, anthropology, and the like. Today at least a portion of the terrain of man's inner world has been sketched in broad outline. Certain basic facts regarding his development and his orientation of himself to the world around him seem to apply generally to all men, regardless of the time or the specific culture into which they are born. For the purpose of this chapter only four of these findings will be discussed, and then only briefly.

First, man has the largest fore-brain of any animal. It has been discovered that man's cerebrum is the locus of his capacity to think, to make signs and symbols, and to communicate with other men in ways not known to the lower animals. His capacity to think has enabled him to adapt and survive in a wider variety of external conditions and social structures than other animals. Now, however, it begins to appear that man's fore-brain is also the seat of another capacity: that of experiencing a kind of anxiety which is unknown to other animals. The lower animals appear to experience fear and confusion, but these states of being seem to come in response to external conditions alone. Man, on the other hand, seems to be the only animal capable of creating internal images and responding to them as well as to external

71

stimuli. Man's fore-brain is, then, at one time a great asset, but at another can be a great liability.

Second, man has the longest period of maturation of any animal. Even animals close to him on the evolutionary scale need only a fraction of the time man needs to come to full maturity. His long period of dependency means that he has more time in which to learn a wider variety of responses to the situation he confronts. Again, man's uniqueness is often a blessing, but can also become a curse. The human being, with his large fore-brain and with his long period of learning, has been able to devise symbol systems with which he can accumulate and condense a great deal of knowledge. He is then able to transmit this knowledge to his off-spring so that the laborious findings of one generation become the easy assumptions of the next. On the other hand, however, man's ability to learn often leads him into difficulty. Though he has few, if any, instincts, he is so malleable during the early years of his life and his learned responses are repeated so often that they take on an automatic quality that is almost more inflexible at times than an instinct. And, to complicate matters further, man not only creates internal images and responds to them, which other animals apparently cannot do, but sometimes even prefers to respond to the images rather than to the reality stimuli from without. When this occurs he is, in effect, establishing and maintaining a self-contained internal "feed-back system." [1]

Third, man depends for survival upon his ability to make some sense out of his experience. Anxiety, as he experiences it, with its corresponding disorganization of the inner world, if unresolved and unrelieved over any length of time, is fatal. The present-day use of the newer drugs is usually effective in preventing what has been known as "schizophrenic exhaustion," but the author's own experience includes witnessing this phenomenon. Sullivan [2] has called anxiety the only intolerable emotion. Man apparently will do anything to relieve himself of this condition. In other words, then, he finds himself in the position of being able to experience what no other animal can experience, and he must, if he is to survive, order his experience around a meaningful core which is understandable and acceptable to him.

The fourth observation about man, and a most important one, is that he is capable of at least two distinct kinds of knowledge. The first is what has been called variously empirical, rational, intellectual, scientific. This is the kind of knowledge which can be transmitted orally or in written form through lectures, sermons, books, course of study, and the like. This is the kind of knowledge which can be accumulated in one generation and transmitted to the next. The second kind of knowledge is immediate, direct, and personal, and has been called variously experiential, phenomenological "existential." This kind of knowledge cannot be transmitted from one person to another through lectures or courses of study. Communication depends, rather, upon what has become known as the "I-Thou" encounter. [3] In this encounter, each "I," aware of his own state of being, approaches the "Thou" with an attitude of understanding, appreciation, and reverence for the state of being of the "Thou," and communicates this attitude in whatever way is adequate, appropriate, timely, and consistent immediately, directly, and personally. This kind of knowledge can neither be communicated in the usual way nor can it be accumulated and transmitted from generation to generation. It is available to each individual *only* through his own personal experience.

Perhaps an illustration is in order at this point. The author had an opportunity recently to visit Spain. Prior to the trip he had intellectual knowledge of the Spanish national sport of bullfighting. He had read about fights, had seen pictures, and was aware of some of the color, pageantry, and symbolism of the bullfights. But the actual *experience* of the bullfights was of a different order. He now knows "existentially" what a bullfight is. He has experienced what we have come in our training program, to call the "gut response." And, unless the reader himself has had this "gut response," he and the author are communicating on the rational level rather than the experiential level.

The author's visit to Spain was prompted by an invitation to present portions of this chapter to the Fourth International Congress of Psychotherapy in Barcelona. The theme of this congress was "Psychotherapy and Existential Analysis." The recent rapid growth, especially on the continent, of the movement known as "existential analysis" leads us to the following comments. It appears that the first seventy-five years of dynamic or depth psychology have been devoted primarily to the building up of a body of knowledge which is empirical, objective, and scientific, which can be accumulated in periodicals and libraries, and which can be taught to newcomers to the field in the usual way. True, the training of the psychoanalyst did include a "didactic analysis." One wonders, however, whether a personal encounter can take place between analyst and analysand under the rigid rules which usually govern that relationship. It would seem that this most recent development in psychiatry, the emphasis on "existential analysis," is a rediscovery by psychiatrists of the second modality of knowledge—the immediate, personal encounter—and an effort to integrate it into the theories and practice of psychotherapy.

Though man's interest in psychology is of recent origin, his concern with religion dates back to earliest recorded history. Even a cursory review of man's religious history reveals two seemingly unrelated emphases. There has always been the conflict between the "letter" and the "spirit' 'of the law. On the one hand have been the Pharisees and the Sadducees of every sect who have been the codifiers of the law and the "guardians of the Temple." To them religion means conformity to the "objective" requirements of the particular group to which they belong. On the other hand, in every religion there have been the "existentialists," individuals and small groups usually, who were intuitively aware and responsive. They experienced themselves and the world around them in unique ways, and their messages reflected the "spirit."

It now becomes increasingly clear that both kinds of knowledge are necessary in every field of human endeavor. In the study of man the structure—the bones, the nervous system and the functioning of the organs—can be understood only as the result of rigorous scientific research. The flesh and blood—man's thoughts, feelings, and his sense of meaning and value—cannot be understood without awareness, intuition, heart. "Man as a whole" cannot be comprehended by either the psychologist or the religionist unless he uses both kinds of knowledge.

A Point of Reference

It is now possible to develop the main theme of this chapter. Before doing so, however, it is necessary to state that it is not the purpose of the chapter to develop or to defend any dogma, theology, or religious group of any kind. It is, rather, to find, if possible, a point of reference from which to examine the dogmas, theologies, and religious activities and systems as we observe them, whether they be found in ourselves and our associates, or in another time and cultural group.

It is unnecessary to give any detailed or precise definition of religion for the purpose of this discussion. Almost any definition is acceptable. It is enough to recognize that man has feelings and thoughts, and that he participates in many activities. Some of them he calls "human" or "animal" or "secular"; some of them he calls "religious" or "spiritual" or "holy."

The Magic Level of Being

It is possible to make a clear clinical distinction among at least three different levels on which man as an individual and man as a race can order his experience. The earliest of these three levels is what we choose to call the magic level.[4] The central fact about man on this level is his complete helplessness. It is really true that if he does not have a mother or a substitute for her he will perish. Comfortable physical surroundings and sufficient food and water are not enough.[5] The human infant needs tender, loving care as well as food, and his need for this ingredient extends over a number of years.

Given the fact of the infant's complete helplessness, there emerges a psychic phenomenon which needs to be understood and appreciated. Most of the time the good mother anticipates the infant's needs: in other words, she reads his mind, and gives what is necessary for his well-being without his being called upon to become aware of his needs. If, for a moment or even for a longer period of time, she is a neglectful mother, all that is usually required of the infant is that he become aware of the fact that he has needs unfulfilled and that he is unhappy, and to let his unhappiness be known either by fretting or by crying. Eventually mother comes, meets the need, and all is well with him again. Within a few months the infant learns that he is the center of his universe. It may be a small universe, and may include only himself and his mother, but it is *his* universe and in it *he* is all-powerful.

If the experience of the infant and young child is couched in "existential" or experiential terms, we can formulate four basic propositions around which most of life on this level can be organized:

- I am the center of the universe.
- Mommy and Daddy are here to meet my needs; (they are not people, they are objects).
- Everybody is my friend; (everybody is an object, a source of need satisfaction).
- Things will not change.

The experience of life on the magic level is a wonderful thing, and no one in his right mind would want to change it. It is the Garden of Eden experience where man has only to reach into the closest tree or bush and pick what he will to satisfy himself. This state is so satisfying that every child is reluctant to leave it behind. It becomes the haven of refuge for older children, adolescents, and even adults when external conditions or internal disorganization are too anxiety producing and painful. Clinical experience reveals that a great many individuals who may have attained physical, economic, and intellectual maturity, and who may be thirty or even fifty chronological years of age, experience themselves predominantly on the infantile magic level of being. In other words, their empirical knowledge of themselves is on one level, and their "existential" knowledge of themselves is on another.

An illustration of the split between the two kinds of self-knowledge is found in a 39-year-old minister of one of the larger Protestant denominations who came for consultation after his wife had been undergoing counseling for some months. He was a graduate of a well-known theological school, and had had two years of graduate study at a large European university. He had been treated surgically for stomach ulcers and was for the first time in his life "able to eat anything I want." He had no use for psychiatry. During the discussion he revealed that he had two major complaints. The first was that his wife was a complete failure as a woman, as a minister's wife and hostess, as a mother (they had four children) and as a co-worker. She was sexually frigid, was raising the children "all wrong," and was a handicap and a burden to him in his work. When asked what he wanted from a wife, he replied, "I want absolute obedience, and a wife who will meet my needs without my having to tell her what they are." His second complaint was that he could not find the right parish. In his eleven years as a clergyman, he stated, he had accepted calls to five different churches, all of which had been "in blighted and dying areas." He had hoped that his efforts on behalf of the parishioners would be appreciated, but they had not been. Now he was beginning to wonder whether any congregation was worth his full time and devotion.

This man's wife reported a slightly different story. She stated that she acted as her husband's secretary, dropping everything and taking dictation whenever he had letters or a sermon to write. Each week he gave her his sermon topic and outline, insisting that she arrange the worship service around them, choosing appropriate hymns, scripture, and responsive readings. If all was not exactly as he wanted it, he demanded repeated corrections. In their family life, he left all the work to her. He never fed any of the children, had not changed a diaper in years, and whenever a baby cried during the night and his wife could not immediately quiet the child, he would move out of their bedroom to his soundproofed study to complete his interrupted sleep. Not only did she teach in church school and take part in some of the church group activities on his demand, but in addition was organist and choir director in a nearby church. This also she did at his request to supplement his rather meager income. She admitted her sexual unresponsiveness, but she wondered how she could be expected to be responsive when most of his requests for sex came immediately after he had heaped verbal, and occasionally physical, abuse on her. During intercourse he would speak of "breeding her like a cow," revealed his fantasy of being a human stallion who could impregnate all the women of the neighborhood, and complained of her response, comparing it unfavorably with the response of other women with whom he had had sex relations both before and since their marriage.

Regarding the churches and their responses to his ministry, the wife reported that he had accepted the calls to the deteriorated area churches because "he knew he could build them up singlehandedly and make them successful." In each church in turn, as soon as anyone questioned his suggestions he would begin to build up a dossier of information about his questioner which he would eventually be able to use "to get him out of the church." Anyone who thwarted his strivings for omnipotence "would be stricken off the rolls." Even now, in his present church, people were beginning to criticize him and disregard his advice.

How our young minister came to his position is understandable in the light of his early experiences. He was an only child, and a sickly one, and was raised on a farm consisting of several sections of land. His father's ambition was to make him his successor as owner and sole operator of the farm. He experienced his mother as anxious and oversolicitous, and he made his own her hopes for a career in the ministry. In the pursuit of this ambition he received no financial assistance from his father, but moral support from his mother. To put himself through college he first worked for a year at heavy manual labor. While actually in college he managed to survive by accepting any work, no matter how menial. He was successful in creating a world in which he was the center, and he was all-powerful. Everything that did not contribute to his goal was eliminated. He denied all his needs but one— the need to succeed.

This man illustrates the experience of self on the magic level. Confronted with a reality world in which wife and congregation do not meet his demands completely and fully, he creates out of his deepest needs a compensatory fantasy world in which he is God, the center of the universe. The God concept becomes an object, as do all the people in his world, there only to meet his needs. If circumstances do not meet his demands, he has a solution. It is to leave wife, children, congregation, parishioners, and to find a situation which will meet his needs. He pictures himself as an itinerant evangelist giving salvation to a sequence of expectant audiences, and giving love to a series of women responsive to his dynamic personality.

The Black-and-White Level of Being

Eventually the human being, if internal and external conditions are favorable, develops to the point where he has repeated experiences which point to two facts that are very important to him. The facts are, first, that he can do some things for himself and, second, that his parents are concerned (that they care) about him. Although he must give up the pleasure of the magic position, he now finds himself able to move about more freely. His universe has widened. He can now explore a world in which there are two positions. He can bargain for what he needs: do some things for himself and pay (with dependency) for those things he cannot do for himself, or he can fall back into the magic position. Again, the existential meaning of the "black-and-white" position reveals four basic propositions:

- The world is black and white (no grays), and I must stay on the white side.
- People are for me, or against me.
- If I stay on the white side, I will win (that is, I will get what I want).
- If I win, things will stay as they are.

Parenthetically let it be said that most of us are experiencing the black-and-white level of being most of the time. Politically, we belong either to the party that is in or the party that is out. Socially, we were born either on the right or on the wrong side of the tracks. Internationally, we are either outside of or behind the Iron Curtain. So it is, also, with our religions. Let one illustration clarify this level of being.

A 33-year-old nun was referred for counseling by the head of her religious order because she was in constant conflict with the rules of the order and with the authorities. She had once left the order for a year, and within a month of her referral she left again, this time permanently. She herself minimized her disciplinary difficulties, attributing them to "unreasonable requests and assignments" on the part of her superiors. Her complaints were that she was constantly depressed, and that she alternated between being overweight from constant eating and losing weight rapidly from "upset stomach" and diarrhea.

Religiously, our nun was completely devoted, performing not only the required devotions, but initiating many ritual duties of her own. She was letter perfect in her knowledge of the rules of the order, and often exposed her superiors in oversights or violations of them. She was always able to find some statement in the Scriptures or in the regulations of the order to justify her defiance of her superiors. She was living up to her part of the bargain. It was her superiors who were failing to do their duty.

How she developed her point of view can be understood from the events of her childhood. She was the first of three daughters in her family. As the first-born, she bore the brunt of her mother's complaints which were two. The mother's first complaint was that she was in an unhappy marriage, and would have separated from her husband had it not been for the pregnancy with this child. Thus, our ex-nun's existence (even in utero) kept the mother in an unhappy marriage. The mother's second complaint was that since this was the eldest of the three girls, all the misbehavior and mischief of the three girls was her fault. She experienced herself early as the unwanted child, while the second daughter was the mother's favorite, and the third girl the father's favorite.

In response to this situation our nun learned early how to survive. She conformed to the requirements of her parents until she sensed a threat to her very existence. Then she would clench her teeth and fight back violently. As she later put it, "I would rather die than give in." She quickly learned that although her parents might wish to break her spirit, they could not or would not destroy her. She may have been unwanted, but she was still their child and they were concerned about her. As a result she entered into a series of pacts, mostly unspoken, with her parents, but particularly with her mother (the father died when she was ten): she would do whatever was required of her (that did not threaten her existence) and in return she would be cared for. Though this was not a particularly happy world in which to live, it was a secure world in its own way. That is, it was secure as long as all involved kept their bargain. Her bitterest memories of her childhood centered around the occasions when her mother made a promise and did not keep it. Then, as in the convent later, she felt justified in verbal retaliation or acts of defiance.

One is reminded at this point of the pact between Abraham and Jehovah, and how the concept of being the "chosen people" has been both the strength of, and the major problem of, the Jews. It is more important, however, to keep in mind that the bargaining kind of religion is not only an historical phenomenon associated with a particular level of civilization. The black-and-white level of being, like the magic level, is a stage of development experienced by every human being when inner growth and external conditions permit. It is an ordering of experience which has its own meaning and value, which allows progression and regression, but which has another built-in seduction to maintain the status quo.

We have seen how man on the magic level has created a religion. He is actually helpless and frightened, and needs to be cared for. Out of his deepest need for tender, loving care he builds a fantasy world in which he is God with the power to command complete obedience to his will. So, too, the man who experiences himself primarily on the black-and-white level creates a religion out of his deepest needs. This time he does not delude himself into believing that he is God, but he knows who God is. He knows, because he has created a God in his own image, but he has created Him bigger and stronger than he is himself. He then attributes to God certain of his own qualities: jealousy, loyalty, justice, and perhaps even love. And, between this God and man agreements are created. Man lives up to certain moral codes, ethical systems, commandments. In return, God grants salvation.

Man will not die if he stays on the white side. Man is really a spirit, residing temporarily in a body. The spirit existed before his life, and will continue after this life. Unsatisfied wishes and frustrated needs are to be tolerated in this world, but in the world to come the elect will have bliss. There will be pearly gates and golden streets, and everyone will have shoes. That is, everyone who has kept his end of the bargain. For those who have violated the rules, there is purgatory, or hades, or hell. Violations of minor rules are punished with short periods of purging. Flagrant or persistent violators will be condemned with eternal torment.

Orthodoxy in most religious groups manifests itself primarily on this level, but a very clear example is the sect known as Jehovah's Witnesses. This rapidly growing group divides all mankind into the "saved" and the "damned," prescribes specific steps in the process of being saved, commands complete loyalty to its dogma to the exclusion of all others and envisions an imminent battle between the forces of good and of evil. The outcome of this battle is foreordained. The good will win. The "sheep" will be gathered into the arms of God to experience eternal joy, and the "goats" will be cast into outer darkness.

The Wholistic Level of Being

The key experience, it will be remembered, which allows the individual to progress gradually from the magic to the black-and-white level of being is the discovery that he has some strength, can do some things for himself, and that parents are concerned about him and so he can make bargains with them. So, too, there is a key experience which allows man to move gradually into what we have called the "wholistic" or "existential" level of being. It is that he no longer needs his parents, or any substitutes for them, in order to survive. He has then separated himself completely from those around him and experiences himself as a unique human being.

In the relatively rare moments when man experiences himself on the existential level, there emerge again four propositions which add meaning and value to life:

- I am Me: (I have discovered the boundaries of self).
- You are You: (I respect the boundaries of your self).
- We are human beings together: (We have similarities of experience and can communicate our understanding of each other; and we have differences and can tolerate those differences without seeing them as threats to each other).
- Things will change.

Man on this level of being accepts himself as he really is, accepts others as they really are, and knows that constant change is a necessary part of life. In the knowledge that whatever his present state of being is it will eventually change, man becomes more able to participate fully in the here and now. He can experience pain, suffering, and frustration in the knowledge that "these, too, shall pass." He can participate more fully in the pleasure, happiness, and satisfaction of the present. At the same time that he is living more abundantly in the here and the now, man on this level is aware that each state of being has its own value and meaning and that it will gradually merge into another state of being which in turn has its own purpose. He knows, too, that a state of nonbeing, or at least a state utterly unlike his own living experience, is possible. He knows that his body will die, and what happens to him thereafter is unknowable as long as he is alive.

Three Levels of Prayer

It will be remembered that the purpose of this chapter is to attempt to find a position, a point of reference, from which to examine some of man's religious activities. If the concepts of the three levels of being have any validity, they can then be applied to any specific religious ritual, dogma, or theology for the purpose of clarifying and ordering it. Let us see what happens, then, when we apply these concepts to a religious act, in this case prayer.

Prayer for the man living on the magic level is an act of magic. Whatever the words he uses, prayer is primarily petitionary prayer. If he exists on the more primitive levels of magic, man does not even have to pray. God knows what his needs are and is constantly at his side and meeting all his needs. He has achieved what the young minister who was described earlier wanted: a God (not a wife this time) "who will meet my needs without my having to tell what they are." If the man is functioning on a more advanced level of magic, the only thing required of him is that he become aware of his need and make the appropriate noises. He goes through a ritual of words, a ritual which has proved its effectiveness in the past, and God automatically takes care of his needs. On the more primitive level, then, man is functioning completely automatically as a nothing attached to a God who is everything, entirely satisfied by whatever his God gives him. On the more advanced level of magic man has created the delusion that he is God, and what he calls God is in reality a servant at man's beck and call. Man now is everything, and all else is nothing except as he makes something of it.

When man experiences himself predominantly on the black-and-white level, prayer is quite different in quality, although some of the words may be the same. Instead of being automatic or purely petitionary, prayer now becomes a request for guidance and intercession for others. Since the greatest virtue on the level of black and white is to be on the white (right) side, it is of utmost importance to ascertain what is the right thing to do, to say, or to believe. On this level, man creates his own God without realizing he has done so. He creates a God who is like his parents: that is, God is manlike, but he is bigger and stronger, and he is in control. Now the problem of the human being who must be on God's side to survive is to find out what this Being who controls the universe wants. Like parents, this God tells us that he will love us or approve of us only when we are good. But, like parents, he does not always tell us what being good is, and sometimes being good means one thing and sometimes another. With parents, for example, sometimes being good means being quiet, as in church or when they want to talk ("Children should be seen and not heard"). Sometimes being good means making noises, like saying "Goo" or "Dada" for the nice man, or "show the nice people how our little Johnnie can play the piano." And if this is the way things are with God, then we have to pray to him constantly for guidance. Each new situation may call for a new set of signals, and we must find out what the order of the day is.

Prayer on this level is also intercessory prayer. If it is important for man to get onto and remain on the white side, then it is just as important for all those who are near and dear to him to be on the white side, because he needs those particular people. He prays then not only for guidance for himself, but for guidance for all his friends: "Please, God, take care of Mommy and Daddy, and Aunt Mary, and Uncle Joe, and teacher, and Fido, and. . . ." All of them are necessary to the child, hence they must be saved too.

On the wholistic level of being prayer assumes another dimension. It becomes contemplative and thankful. It will be recalled that the man on the magic level is either completely in the hands of his God, or he deludes himself into believing that he is God. The man on the black-and-white level knows who God is, because he has created Him in his own image. The man who experiences himself on the wholistic level cannot know who or what God is. He has existential knowledge only of his own human experience. He cannot experience the Divine. He can say to himself, *"It may be* that some part of my human experience parallels the Divine. I think so. But, I do not know." For him, then, prayer becomes contemplation. This man, aware of his capacity for self-direction, withdraws temporarily from the constantly moving, action-reaction chain of psychic events. He observes and contemplates and, aware of his many potentials, chooses the direction which will give his own life the meaning and value he wishes. The result of the contemplation is guidance, but guidance from within rather than from without.

Let it not be thought for a moment that life on the existential level is comfortable or easy. It is far from it. Man on this level has relinquished the absolute certainty that is implicit in the fantasy world of magic living. He has come to terms with the false security of the bargains, explicit or implicit, of the black-and-white world. He has accepted fully the anxiety of living in a world of reality: of seeing himself as he really is, and of knowing what the world around him really is like. On this level man may have worked through much of what Tillich [6] has called neurotic anxiety, but he is constantly confronted with existential anxiety in all its aspects. The move from the other levels into the world of existence is truly a "leap into the unknown." [7]

The religious life on the existential level is a life of both knowledge and faith. Man can know the events of human history. He can know the facts about the world around him. He has the intelligence to order these two sets of data into meaningful wholes which have both aesthetic and practical value to him. In addition, man has the capacity of experiencing himself in many different ways. At one moment he is helpless and frightened, at another confident and serene. For a time he is the center of his universe, however small it may be, and for another period of time he can see himself as one small mite on one of the smaller planets of a solar system, which in turn is an almost inconceivably small portion of an inconceivably large universe. At nine o'clock in the morning he is a busy executive, making bargains with one and all; at two o'clock in the afternoon he is finishing a leisurely lunch with good friends (one of the boys); and at 7:13 P.M. he comes home hoping that his wife has read his mind and magically produced the food and drink he did not even know he wanted. And the net result?

The result can be gratitude. Man on this level often prays gratefully. He is grateful first for sheer awareness of himself and of the world around him. He was asleep before; now he is awake. Then, too, he is grateful for the fact that he has choices. He looks back at earlier times when he was an automaton, driven by his needs. And finally, he is grateful that his self-knowledge, even though limited, makes it possible for him to live meaningfully in the here and the now without being constantly threatened by some undiscovered destructive nook or cranny of his own being.

Man on the magic level prays petitionary prayers, asking that God will let him survive. Man on the black-and-white level also needs to survive, but he has a new dimension added to his experience potential. So he prays petitionary prayers, but he also prays for guidance and for those who are near and dear to him: prayers of intercession. Man on the existential level must also survive and needs guidance, but he experiences a third dimension of his being. He prays, not only petitionary prayers and prayers for intercession and for guidance, but also prayers of gratitude for self-awareness, self-knowledge, and self-direction.

One final comment: it is not the purpose of this presentation to discuss pastoral care or pastoral counseling. However, it is the position of the author that pastoral care is an opportunity for both the religious leader and his parishioner to experience the "I-Thou" encounter on whatever level is open to either. The pastor whose knowledge of himself has included all the levels of being which are described here is sometimes, not always, able to recreate in himself the state of being in which he finds his parishioner. When he is able to do so, the pastor knows two things: First, he is aware that each step toward self-knowledge is painful and anxiety producing: that it is often experienced as "walking through the valley of the shadow of death." He knows further that his parishioner's experience of being understood and appreciated, even revered, becomes "the rod and the staff which comfort." He knows, too, that he cannot walk through the valley of the shadow of death for any other human being, only for himself. But he can let the walker know that he, the pastor, has been through his own valleys and has survived. The communication of this kind of experience, when shared, can become the ground from which will come, in its own time and at its own pace, the new growth and the new integration which can lead to the life abundant.

In summary, then, the thesis of this chapter [8] is as follows:

- To recognize man's uniqueness among the animals, with special reference to his large fore-brain, his long state of dependence, his need to order his experience, and his capacity for both empirical and experiential knowledge, especially self-knowledge.
- To describe the three levels of being which can be illustrated with clinical material.
- To establish a point of reference from which to examine and understand man's religious life in all its complexity.
- To illustrate the use of the point of reference in relation to one religious activity—prayer.

REFERENCES

1. As developed, for example, in W. Ronald D. Fairbairn, *An Object-Relations Theory of the Personality* (New York: Basic Books, Inc., 1954).
2. Harry Stack Sullivan, *Clinical Studies in Psychiatry*, H. S. Perry, M. L. Gavel, and M. Gibbons, eds. (New York: W. W. Norton & Co., Inc., 1956).
3. Martin Buber, *I-Thou* (New York: Charles Scribner's Sons, 1958).
4. The concepts of "magic" and "black and white" are borrowed from Dr. Charles Odier, whose essays, as compiled in the volume *Anxiety and Magic Thinking*, translated by Marie-Louise Schoelly, M.D., and Mary Jane Sherfey, M.D. (New York: International Universities Press, Inc., 1956), represent an attempt at integration of psychoanalytic concepts with the findings of Jan Piaget, M.D., in the field of genetic psychology.
5. René A. Spitz, M.D., "Hospitalism: An Inquiry into the Genesis of Psychiatric Conditions in Early Childhood," *The Psychoanalytic Study of the Child*, Vol. I (New York: International Universities Press, Inc., 1945), pp. 53-74.
6. Paul Tillich, *The Courage to Be* (New Haven: Yale University Press, 1952), especially Chapter III: "Pathological Anxiety, Vitality, and Courage," pp. 72 ff.
7. A phrase used by Florence Powdermaker, M.D., psychoanalyst, and borrowed without her permission from meaningful personal discussions with her.
8. Though the specific formulations expressed in this chapter are those of the author, a great deal of credit goes to the entire training staff of the American Foundation. It is only as teachers and students alike have participated in continuous discussion of the concepts that they have become more clear and relevant. The author is especially grateful to Herbert Holt, M.D., psychoanalyst and associate director of training of the Foundation, without whose constant enthusiasm and stimulation this chapter would never have been written.

WILLIAM DOUGLAS ❧

William Douglas, a young professor at the Boston University School of Theology, combines thorough training in social psychology with his preparation in theology. After he was graduated as a Bachelor of Divinity, he became a doctoral student of Gordon Allport and received his Ph.D. on a study in the field of psychology of religion. In the footsteps of Allport's psychological orientation Douglas attempts the renewal of a psychology of religion which is sympathetic to the essence of the Christian faith and conscientious in applying proper psychological methods to its investigation.

His background allows him to combat the popular abuse of secondhand psychological ideas by ministers. He points out that psychology is a young branch of the social sciences and still needs quite a bit of patient research before it will come fully into its own and make its place between the natural sciences and philosophy, both of which have stood at either side of the cradle of psychology. That psychology should have become such a popular fad has its good reasons but not a good effect either on psychology or on those who believe themselves free-lance psychologists by using psychological terms incorrectly. Douglas is a strongly committed Christian and feels that the abuse of psychology by ministers is a cheap escape from facing up to the difficulties of their own mission in our time. He makes clear how psychology can be relevant, especially as a proper academic discipline within the theological curriculum or in connection with it.

This chapter contains a real contribution to the needed attempt to distinguish between secular psychology, pastoral psychology, and psychology of religion. Pastoral psychology calls for more conscientious work to discover its own nature and function, and to make it more useful to the pastor as counselor. Psychology of religion needs the competent help of experimental and social as well as clinical psychology if it is to offer a better understanding of religion to those within and outside of the community of believers.

Psychology in Theological Education

Psychology as a scientific discipline is generally acknowledged to be less than a hundred years old, a youngster which, as Henry Murray has observed, at times still has problems in becoming free from its possessive mother philosophy and its dogmatic grandmother theology. Like many young children, it has found it difficult to live up to others' expectations concerning its potential achievements. Likewise, in its effort to achieve status among peers it may have sometimes appeared brash and overly self-confident. Never sure whether it belongs with the family of the Humanities or the family of the Sciences and, if the latter, whether its middle name is Biological, Social, or Natural, it has struggled to find its identity, and at times has found others even doubting its legitimacy.

In this struggle, the main role figure has been an older brother, physics, and in recent years, brother has caused as many problems as mother and grandmother, for older brother has changed his ways, rejecting the "billiard ball universe" with its causal determinism which psychology had learned to regard as scientific. More-over, theoretical physics has established new bonds with mother (philosophy) just after psychology had valiantly striven to deny any association with her. So, the psychologist who yearns to be part of the family of the Sciences has new problems in determining conditions for membership.

It is in this context that one can best understand psychology's relations with grandmother (theology). In the early years of psychology's separate existence, the relations were in general cordial ones. Wilhelm Wundt, who founded in Leipzig in 1879 the first psychological laboratory, also wrote *Facts of the Moral Life* and *Elements of Folk Psychology,* a discussion of primitive religion. In America, outstanding psychologists such as G. Stanley Hall and William James were among the pioneers in the new subdiscipline of the psychology of religion.[1] But, despite a notable output of works bearing this title from about 1880 to 1930, it was never established as a branch of general psychology. Rather, those with

85

interests in both psychology and religion tended to move into religious education or "pastoral psychology."

Psychology, in name at least, came into the theological seminaries at quite an early date.[2] By 1899, there was a course offered at Hartford Theological Seminary entitled "Psychology of Religion," and Boston University School of Theology initiated a Department of Religious Psychology and Pedagogy in 1912. In 1927 Chicago Theological School established a program of clinical training for seminary students, with Anton Boisen, first Protestant mental hospital chaplain, as the teacher. By 1943, when Seward Hiltner reported on "Pastoral Theology in the Schools," 56 of 89 seminaries surveyed listed at least one course in the psychology of religion, with 11 of them giving additional courses as well. But, only four of the teachers of these courses had had graduate training in academic psychology, and most of them were required to teach courses in at least one other subject area.

Indeed, the "baptized and applied" psychology woven into theological school curricula appears to have only a tenuous relationship to the psychology taught in other settings. When I recently surveyed forty theological school catalogues, less than 10 per cent of those teaching courses entitled psychology were affiliated with the American Psychological Association. In general, courses involving psychological content were included under the general heading of pastoral theology, practical theology, or religious education, with one teacher responsible for a wide variety of offerings, and all of them having a practitioner rather than theoretical orientation.

Several factors are related to this situation. In the last twenty years, psychology of religion has been displaced in popularity in theological education by pastoral counseling, clinical training, or the broader (and more ambiguous) topic of pastoral psychology. This, in turn, has led to a decreasing interest in academic psychology, which like so much "pure science" is regarded as irrelevant, and an increasing interest in medical psychology, especially psychoanalytic psychiatry. There has been a booming market for "how to" books and journal articles, to help the parish minister perform more effectively his pastoral responsibilities, especially his counseling of those involved in the crisis situations of life.

Also, like church-related colleges, seminaries have tended, and on occasion with justification, to harbor a fear of antireligious psychologists who might undermine the faith of their students. The test of a psychologist, or psychological tradition, has often been: "Are you for or against religion, or more specifically, our religious viewpoint?" In this manner, commitment has often become a more discriminating criterion than competence. The tendency has been to add psychology courses to curricula, to make them more "practical," and impressive in an age of scientism. But, for such courses to be offered, theologians or religious educators have had to teach them, since psychology as a whole has had little interest in religion. Until very recent years, to evidence such interest and participation would bring disdain, if not active rejection, from one's psychological colleagues. Psychologists have, therefore, seldom entered into theological education, though psychiatrists have begun to enter in recent years, as part of an increasing joint concern of clergy and psychiatry for the relations between religion and mental health.

It would appear, then, as if psychology, as a scientific discipline rather than merely a set of techniques or insights isolated from their theoretical framework, has not yet found its proper place in theological education. There is still lack of clarity as to where it fits into the curriculum: in pastoral theology, religious education, philosophy of religion, systematic theology, or in a place of its own. It will find its place only when a climate of opinion is established within the seminaries which permits psychology to operate without the artificial limitations of doctrinal loyalty oaths. Likewise, for psychology to be a creative constituent of theological education requires that this youthful science cease boasting of an emancipated "soul-lessness," which has led it to conclude (on slim empirical grounds) that religion is "nothing more than" a phenotypical manifestation of more basic motivational processes. Fortunately, there is now real hope that both of these conditions may be met in the near future.

Psychology and Theology

Most who are concerned with "making the ministry relevant" regard the social sciences as important guides in establishing some of the conditions for such relevancy. There is much less agreement, however, as to how the social sciences may best be utilized in the service of theological education. As indicated above, there is presently a strong trend of opinion which favors adapting psychological and psychiatric insights and procedures to the work of the pastor. Thus, pastoral psychology has been defined as "that psychology which has implications for the pastor," which is neither a branch of psychology nor a form of applied psychology.[3] It is the understanding of man which arises out of pastoral work. The pastor not only applies it in his work, but he also "learns and corrects it through his work."[4]

In theory, this approach appears valid: psychology's contributions to the pastor's work are determined in terms of "the questions the pastor asks," with the test of relevance the extent to which the specific idea or method "illuminates the human psyche." Thus, what distinguishes pastoral psychology from other psychology is not so much content as point of view or perspective. In practice, however, the implicit test of relevance has usually been that of congruence with one's doctrinal position. What can be fitted into one's established system of ideas is accepted; what cannot is rejected as "irrelevant" or "un-illuminating." (One should note, of course, that psychologists have often suffered from this same limitation regarding "what makes sense." For example, despite convincing experimental results upholding the psi phenomena of parapsychology in rigidly controlled investigation by Rhine and his colleagues, most psychologists have disregarded these findings, since they don't "fit" in terms of our most cherished physicalistic presuppositions. Similarly, American psychology and psychiatry have been slow to take advantage of the most important theoretical contributions of Carl Jung.)

In the extreme, this "relevance" test can amount to a reductionism as severe as that often attributed to the psychoanalytic interpretation of religious experience, since only those psychological contributions are accepted which fit the biblical view of man. As prior generations of churchmen sought to turn the Bible into an astronomy textbook, and thereby attacked Galileo and Copernicus, or into a biology textbook, and thereby attacked Darwin, so some today would turn it into a psychology textbook. Thus, a seminary professor of psychology of religion recently wrote that "contemporary psychological material needs correction through Christian insights." [5] He thinks that churchmen must bring "the witness of Reformation theology to bear upon the presuppositions, the conclusions, and the therapeutic methodology of contemporary psychology of personality." Otherwise, the Christian may have his faith corroded through a psychology of personality which represents "the secularization of the religious life of man."

Contrasted to this testing of psychology by theology is the opposite approach of seeking to replace theology with psychology as the "more modern" form of the interpretation of man, his predicament, and his salvation. (One is reminded of John Baillie's comment: "That which is 'up-to-the-moment' only lasts a moment, and later will seem more antiquated than *De Civitate Dei, Summa Theologiae,* and *Institutio Christianae Religionis.*") [6] According to this viewpoint, as amenable to the theological liberal as Biblio-centrism is to the conservative, the Bible and theology must be judged against the latest pronouncements of the natural and social sciences. What fits can be accepted; what does not fit must be rejected as pre-scientific myth. Sermons thus become essays in popular psychology for the masses. Pastoral care becomes cut-rate psychiatry, with God the "third man," always hovering, therapeutically, in the background, though seldom called upon.

One must grant that this position is seldom found in its extreme form, except among theological students who are overreacting against a religiously conservative past, and overenamored of the newly discovered social sciences. [7] It is found more commonly in the form presented in a book written about thirty years ago entitled, appropriately, *A Psychological Approach to Theology.* [8] Here the tasks of psychology and theology were equated thus: "How may personality be unified, energized, and directed to worthful ends?" Theology was called upon to alter, amend, or cancel that which was contradicted by "new facts that psychology may reveal." Such an approach to theology, in the general tradition of Schleiermacher, Ritschl, Macintosh, and Wieman, would not have been possible before the broadening of theology fifty to seventy-five years ago, to include an empirical theology quite different from the dogmatic theology normative in the Christian tradition. This "brand" of theology, as Kegley and Bretall point out, is "based not on authoritative revelations or church councils and thus 'once for all delivered,' but on changing human experience and even on empirical, scientific knowledge." [9]

Besides the two extremes, of a conservatism which tests science in terms of revelation and a liberalism which rejects all revelation which does not meet the test of science, there is a third position. According to this viewpoint, in the tradition of American pragmatism, that is true which works. The truth claim neither of theology nor of psychology is self-validating; indeed, both theology and psychology are regarded as suspect since "so theoretical." Thus, this group, which is a growing one within theological education, would stress the "clinical approach." Only that theology or psychology which can prove its relevance in the existential confrontation of man to man is worth considering. The emphasis, therefore, is on proved technique, especially that derived from psychiatry, with a general disregard for the "whys" behind the "hows."

A fourth way of relating psychology to theology is to "correlate" them, showing how the Christian message provides the answers to the questions implied in the psychological analysis of the human situation.[10] Tillich, who developed this general approach, was concerned that theology move back and forth between "two poles, the eternal truth of its foundation and the temporal situation in which the eternal truth must be received." The "situation," as here defined, refers to "the totality of man's creative self-interpretation in a special period," including psychology as well as philosophy, literature, the arts and so on. To oversimplify, the existential "is" of psychology is correlated with the essential "can be" of theology; man's need is answered by God's saving action.

The problem with all four of these approaches, including the last one which has tremendous possibilities, is that psychology and theology are "adjusted" to one another, either through reducing psychology to theology, or replacing theology by psychology, or denying both in the glorification of technique, or selecting aspects of each which allow a composite pattern of understanding. (Tillich does not fall into this trap, since he clearly distinguishes between the functions of theology and science, but his followers who apply his theory do seem to produce a "patchwork quilt" of psychology and theology. They seek to fit together in as integrated a fashion as possible the joint contributions of psychology and theology to the understanding of a given problem—such as anxiety, guilt, love. But, they fail to keep "question" and "answer" as separate as Tillich would recommend.)

The task of relating psychology to theology is, of course, made more difficult by the ambiguity and variety of connotations of both terms, as well as the emergent character of the disciplines which the terms denote. Given these circumstances, a definition inevitably represents a condensed expression of one's own theoretical preferences. With this warning, I would define theology as the systematic rational formulation of the contents of a faith which always has a mystical a priori. In the Christian tradition, this formulation focuses on the interpretation and communication of the experience of salvation in and through Jesus the Christ.[11] In contrast, the task of psychology, like that of any other science, is that of understanding, controlling, and predicting more exactly than is possible with unaided "common sense" or "insight," with the field of investigation defined as human behavior. Some would narrow the definition to concentrate on "the responses which living individuals make to their environment" [12] but I would define human behavior to include elements of experience far beyond the limited confines of such opportunistic adjustments.

In a sense, psychology and theology are both defined by their methodology, by their frame of reference, and by the community of shared experience out of which values are derived. Theology begins from given premises, provided usually in the divine-human encounter, though such revelation need not be one's own firsthand experience. One's task is, then, to reason from these general principles to their necessary conclusions. Theology operates within a defined community of commitment, and seeks to explicate the meaning of these commitments, in relation to one another, and to the person holding them. It is based on a faith-relationship to One who is ultimately beyond theology's system of doctrines as much as He is beyond the empirical investigation of psychology.

Psychology, to oversimplify once more, deals with creation as theology deals with salvation. For the psychologist, the method is empirical, of seeking to find lawful relationships between individual events, either within one person (the idiographic approach) or among a variety of people (the nomothetic approach). The community of shared experience is that of science as developed in the past century or two—of a systematic, replicable method of investigation which sticks as close as possible to the observed facts. In collecting data, systematically organizing them, and seeking to find their dynamic relationships, psychology, like any other science, seeks as well-established information as possible, but realizes that the "laws" discovered must continually be tested and revised in the light of new data. Increasingly, moreover, psychologists are discovering that observing "facts" and discovering "laws" are not so easy as they once assumed. As Collingwood demonstrated with regard to history, fact and interpretation are almost inseparably blended together; as Heisenberg and others demonstrated in atomic physics, the observer affects the observation.[13] Thus, the psychologist now tends to say in more muted and hesitant terms, "All I want are the facts." Nevertheless, objectivity remains a prime value for the psychologist, and causation remains the general principle of explanation.

Each of these disciplines is complex, and seldom does one find a person who has devoted the time and energy requisite for mastering both. But, beyond the problem of competence, there are more severe difficulties involved for one who would utilize the procedures of psychology and theology in harmony with one another. Not only do the subject matter and the method differ between the two disciplines, and the standards by which work is judged as competent, but more important, the *relation* between scholar and subject matter is of a different order. By definition, psychology requires detachment, or at most participant-observation which involves "calibrating one's biases." Theology, on the other hand, arises from commitment, a commitment shared with a community of faith out of which the theology arises and to which it is directed.

When psychology, or the psychologist, enters the theological seminary, this therefore means entering what is in a sense an alien world. As an individual seeking for the meaning and direction of his life, he may share the commitments on which this community is founded and which it professes in all of its activities, including its theology making. But, as scientist, he must seek for all the relevant facts in their exactness. He must dare to have his commitments challenged, to accept all evidence no matter how well or how poorly it fits one's cherished assumptions. The goal of psychology is not man's salvation but his understanding, not "that truth for which *I* can live and die" but that truth which stands up under the canons of scientific method and which has high probability by statistical measures. Psychology as pure science seeks knowledge for knowledge's sake, though its findings may be applied to a variety of practical purposes, as evidenced by the growth of clinical psychology since World War II, to the extent that this subdiscipline now threatens to "swallow up" the rest of American psychology.

If psychology is to be most effective in theological education, it must be allowed, as I have indicated above, to work and speak on its own terms, no matter how heretical its findings may appear on the basis of the prevailing orthodoxy. On the other hand, psychology itself must beware of overstepping its scientific bounds, of falling into a "nothing but" pseudo-explanatory reductionism as easily as theology may fall into a "something-more" pseudo-scientism.[14] Psychology can no more prove or disprove the mystical a priori from which theology begins than theology can, using its specialized tool kit, find the lawful principles of human behavior. Each discipline has its defined task; each has its limitations.

How, then, are the two related? In a final sense, the integration is an individual one, in the student who seeks to master, or at least become familiar with, both disciplines. Ideally, the two are related in terms which do not deny the nature and purpose of either. From theology, the student gains a systematic knowledge of the doctrines which express his faith-relationship as adequately as possible in rational terms. He may, in fact, through the testimony to the faith contained in the theology of the Christian community, be *led to* this relationship of trusting dependence in God, so that he may gain the courage to accept his personal existence before God [15]; for theology not only interprets the contents of the Christian faith: it also communicates them. From psychology, he gains deeper understanding of the psychic processes through which God, as other influences, must operate. For example, understanding the "why" of saints' behavior involves both the doctrine of the Holy Spirit, the systematic exposition of how God operates in human lives, and the psychological understanding (inadequate though it still is) of the principles of human motivation.

There are, of course, no certainties in either psychology or theology, and therefore a combination of the two may well produce more, not less, uncertainty. Theology, as Pascal and Kierkegaard pointed out, deals in certitude not certainty, while psychology as an infant science still consists (to quote Murray and paraphrase Butler) of the art of drawing sufficient conclusions from insufficient premises. Moreover, it is unlikely that one will be able to relate psychology to theology in an adequate way until there is a clear notion of the whole of which they are but parts. To relate psychology to theology requires that one first define the purposes of the church and its ministry, and, on this basis, the nature and goals of theological education.

An Overview of Theological Education

Recent research by the Education Testing Service, H. R. Niebuhr, and others, and by Samuel Blizzard concerning the Protestant minister—his selection, training, and role in modern society—has indicated the tremendous complexity of the clergyman's task. He is called upon to perform a wide range of functions, with adequate training for all of them becoming an impossible task for an already overloaded theological school curriculum. In his work, he is apt to be pulled apart by the competing pressures, or to sink into apathy out of sheer frustration, unless he can find some uniting focus for his manifold activities. One definition of such a focus has been given by H. R. Niebuhr[16] in terms of the minister as "pastoral director" of a congregation which he not only serves, but which is itself a "ministering community."

This office of pastoral director involves being the efficient administrator-organizer of an institution, with buildings, budgets, and programs, as well as the dedicated and faithful shepherd of a flock.[17] It includes the traditional preaching, priestly, educational functions of the clergyman. Training men for such a ministry is a tremendously difficult task, which involves finding a proper balance between the so-called "theoretical" and "practical" courses, so that adequate preparation may be given the student for a truly relevant ministry, without the seminary's becoming simply a trade school. As far as I know, no theological school would claim to have solved this problem in anything approaching a fully satisfying manner.

Most would recognize, however, that an increasingly important part of such training involves the social sciences. As Niebuhr and others observe,[18] "The student who discovers the way in which psychology or sociology or literary criticism can function as a mediating discipline between the Gospel and contemporary man's search for faith has one of the prime requisites for a lifetime of fruitful reflection." As they point out, such considerations led more than a quarter of the theological seminaries to add psychology to their required curriculum in the twenty years from 1935 to 1955. The goal has been not only better training in pastoral care and religious education, but also a fuller understanding of the Christian faith itself, particularly concerning the meaning of sin, guilt, and redemption.

I would agree with Niebuhr and his associates that this does not imply that any secular discipline can be substituted for the theological "center" of the minister's study and work. The social sciences can contribute essential insights to the Christian minister, but they must be kept in an auxiliary position, so that they do not dominate theological education to the point that one forgets the distinctive contribution of the church and ministry of which he is a part. It is imperative as theological education evaluates the question of relevance—of ministry to the contemporary situation and of the social sciences to the training of ministers—that the minister's unique identity be maintained. To know what will help him in his work, he must first know *who* he is—the task to which he is called, and the resources available to him to fulfill this task. Otherwise, he may forfeit his identity, seeking to become like the psychiatrist or psychologist or some other secular model, because of the superior "know-how" which he assumes they possess.

That this is a real danger is apparent in the tendency of "pastoral psychology" courses to develop an implicit theology divorced from the theology of the normative Christian heritage, and from that taught in the rest of the curriculum. (Social ethics and religious education have previously manifested such tendencies, though both presently appear to be moving toward a much more solid theological grounding.) For the future minister's work to be "of one piece," his training must also be such. There must be a clear focus on the purpose of the church and its ministry, which H. R. Niebuhr has defined as "the increased love of God and neighbor," following the two commandments in which Jesus summarized the Law and the Prophets. To define love in psychological terms, quoting Freud's injunction that the healthy man is one who can love and work spontaneously and adequately, does not solve the problem. Even though there are parallels and points of intersection, salvation cannot be equated with integration or self-actualization or adjustment. The New Being to which the Gospel testifies involves a radical reorientation of man's relationship to God, as well as to himself and to his fellow man. And, seeing all life in this divine dimension changes each of its aspects.

The social sciences must, then, be kept in an auxiliary position in theological education, and not be allowed to redefine the nature of the faith itself. Moreover, they must be regarded as solid "content" courses, and not simply as "practical tricks of the trade." Courses in psychology, in which the student gains a deeper understanding of the lawful principles of human behavior, should be kept separate from courses entitled pastoral psychology or pastoral theology, and the fact that these terms are used almost interchangeably is illustrative of the confusion which presently exists. Indeed, it would appear preferable to drop the ambiguous term "pastoral psychology" altogether, and replace it with the more descriptive term "pastoral care," which includes pastoral counseling. This course could then deal with the pastoral responsibilities of the minister, parallel to other "functional" courses in homiletics, religious education, church administration, and worship. (It may be noted that following such a functional analysis, most seminary curricula are woefully weak in training the minister for one of his most important and time-consuming responsibilities—the organization and leadership of groups, involving a thorough knowledge of group process.)

Such a course in pastoral care should not, however, be expected, as at present, to instruct the student in basic psychological content, or to give him an integrated view of his ministry. Ideally, the student should have been given basic grounding in the social sciences in his undergraduate liberal arts curriculum. If he has not received this training—and there is a growing number of theological students who have not—the seminary, despite an already overloaded curriculum, will probably have to assume this responsibility. To provide him with a perspective in which he can fit the pieces of his ministry together a course on "The Minister and His Task" such as that offered for seniors at Boston University School of Theology beginning in 1959 would seem helpful. Without such a course, which at Boston University is supervised by an interdepartmental committee headed by the dean, there is a real danger of pastoral care's being regarded by student and/or professor as all-inclusive in itself.

For the student to gain the fullest possible understanding of the lawful principles of human behavior, it would seem necessary, also, that he be taught psychology in other than "clinical" or "applied" courses, though these serve real purposes in themselves. If the present artificial, and often dangerous, distinction between "theoretical" and "practical" courses is maintained, then the social sciences should certainly be included in the theoretical portion of the curriculum, as much related to biblical studies and theology as to pastoral care and religious education. Something more is required than the "baptized and applied" psychology presently found in seminary curricula, which when offered as pastoral theology does not have the respect of the theologians and when offered as pastoral psychology is disdained by the academic psychologists.

Potential Contributions

In discussing the contributions of psychology to theological education, the word *potential* should be emphasized, for seminary curricula are already so overloaded with "must" courses that it would be unwise to insist on others, if the line is to be held at a three-year training program. Also, as I have indicated, the exact place and purpose of the social sciences in the curriculum depend on the answers given to fundamental theological questions regarding the church and its ministry, questions which cannot be settled in general here or elsewhere. The suggestions given below are not intended as in any way exhaustive, since the defined problem of this chapter is not one of suggested courses but rather that of principles from which curriculum construction can then proceed. These recommendations do indicate, however, the general concerns of one who has been trained in theology and psychology, who has served as a parish minister, and who now seeks to teach psychology to present and future clergymen. To use an overworked word, the concerns raised here are existential ones, faced day by day by a seminary professor.

Perhaps most important, training in scientific method can be a creative ingredient in seminary education. Beyond any content communicated, it is helpful to the student to be exposed to a tough-minded realism which attempts to face the facts as they are, rather than as one would like them to be, and which builds into its approach methods for checking on the effects of personal biases. It can be of real benefit to be forced to evaluate the evidence for conclusions on grounds other than one's own theoretical preferences, or interests. The student will probably be better able to deal in the future with issues in a more objective way, and to realize that not everyone approaches matters in terms of the commitments which he holds dear. He may also learn to communicate more effectively with those whose frame of reference and value structure is derived from the scientific community.

Content-wise, it is most important that the student gain an understanding of the structure, dynamics, and development of human personality. This does not imply any particular personality theory, but rather an approach which includes: (1) the dynamic, "depth" emphasis of Freud, supplemented at points by the ego-psychologists and by Jung; (2) the field emphasis of Lewin, Murphy, Rogers, Combs and Snygg, including attention to the *experiential* as well as physical environment; (3) the interpersonal emphasis of Sullivan and other social psychologists; (4) the physiological emphasis of the learning theorists, the neurologists, and endocrinologists, Sheldon, and so forth; and (5) the emphasis of Allport on the healthy, mature, responsible, goal-oriented individual. At present, there are few settled issues in personology, and the student should be made aware of the wide variety of conceptual models possible, rather than being rigidly indoctrinated in any one of them. The goal is that of the fullest possible understanding of the mystery of human personality. To reach that goal, no one theoretical formulation or method is adequate.

Once the basic principles of human behavior have been mastered, the student should be helped to apply them to himself, so that they are not used simply to manipulate others more skillfully. Self-knowledge is still, as it was for the Greek philosophers, the first step for those who would guide others into wisdom; for only if the minister is able to understand and accept his own psychological and religious motivation will he be able to relate most fully to others and communicate his faith to them in vital and relevant terms.[19] Only when he is able to get beyond his own needs, will he have the full vision of the needs of others. Unless he, himself, has found forgiveness, he will not be able to participate in the dark valley of guilt with others in such a creative way as to lead them from darkness into the light of God's love. Whatever else the pastor is, he is first of all a person, and the basic instrument with which he must work in his ministry is himself.

On the basis of self-awareness and self-acceptance, he is then able to relate deeply and helpfully to others. He will be more able to love people as people, rather than treating them instrumentally as pew fillers, or pledge givers, or work doers. He will be able to relate to them at a feeling level, rather than responding simply to the surface manifestations of what is done and said. He will be able to operate more meaningfully in co-operation with the family and other social groups important in the individual's growth in faith, since he is aware of the psychological processes involved in that growth. Through training in the psychopathology of personality as well as its normal development, he will be aware of "danger signals," of his own limitations in pastoral work with individuals, and of specialized professional workers and community agencies available for referral.

These are the basic contributions which I would consider psychology can make to theological education, centering in a required first-year course on the psychology of personality, with emphasis on scientific method and self-understanding. Hopefully, psychology would also help to illuminate the rest of the curriculum, in terms of the meaning of the human situation to which the Gospel is proclaimed, and the most effective means of communicating it to modern man. That there can be a fruitful cross-fertilization at this point, without sacrificing the contents of the faith, is evident in the writings of theologians such as Tillich, Niebuhr, and Outler. There is available in psychology, too, theoretical grounding for the work of evangelism in knowledge of the processes of personality change, as well as for homiletics, religious education, and pastoral care. Though psychology cannot substitute for the biblical doctrine of man, it can illuminate it, and give the student fresh perspectives for his biblical studies, his church history, and his theology.

There are, moreover, psychological services which can be most useful to the seminary. Increasingly, the church has felt a concern for improved recruitment and selection procedures, centering in an analysis of a candidate's motivation for the ministry, as well as the skills which he brings to this calling.[20] Even more important, guidance and counseling can help the candidate to wrestle with and work through his personal problems during seminary years. If necessary, psychiatric and other counseling services can be made available to him, so that he may help parishioners with *their* problems, instead of visiting *his own* problems upon them. Through vocational guidance, he can be helped to find the place in the church for which his aptitudes and interests best fit him.

Now, who is to do all this? Ideally, psychology should come into the seminary in the form of a competent psychologist, rather than a theologian or pastor or psychiatrist, since the scientific rather than pastoral or therapeutic emphasis is what is required in terms of the goals listed above. Credentials and training are not so important, however, as the teacher's general empirical approach to problems, and that he keep in contact with the psychological community, both by reading and by personal contact. Perhaps most important, he should do research, at a level of technical competence respected by other social scientists, and if possible, some counseling as well. Otherwise, he will simply be reworking secondhand materials. Here, indeed, is one of the greatest potential contributions which a social scientist can make in a theological school, in a vital research program which aids not only the individual but religion as a whole to grow in self-understanding, and thereby in effectiveness.

I would hope, then, that the youngster science psychology will be able to establish, in the near future, creative, friendly, and mutually beneficial relations with grandmother, theology. Each has much to learn from the other, if each grows to the point of respect for the other. There is a real place for psychology in theological education—*if* it can be determined in a manner which is faithful to the purposes of psychology as a science and to theological education as grounded in the central purpose of the church and its ministry.

REFERENCES

1. It is not the purpose of this essay to discuss psychology of religion as such. For a survey of the history of psychology of religion, see P. E. Johnson, *Psychology of Religion* (revised and enlarged) (New York: Abingdon Press, 1959) or W. H. Clark, *Psychology of Religion* (New York: The Macmillan Company, 1958). A forthcoming volume by Orlo Strunk, Jr., tentatively titled *Readings in Psychology of Religion* gives historical perspectives.
2. The summary presented in this paragraph depends upon material collected by Francis Strickland, Paul Johnson, and Seward Hiltner, some of it not available in published form.
3. This quotation, and the sentences which follow, are taken from an article by Seward Hiltner in *Pastoral Psychology* magazine, which was later reprinted in *Religion and Human Behavior,* Simon Doniger, ed. (New York: Association Press, 1954), p. 179.
4. *Ibid.,* p. 191.
5. Quotations in this paragraph come from W. E. Oates, *The Religious Dimensions of Personality* (New York: Association Press, 1957), pp. x, 24, and 298. For a further critique of Oates' position, see my review in the September, 1958 issue of *Contemporary Psychology*. Oates, who would probably represent the "majority position" in American psychology of religion and is one of its leading figures, writes *as a theologian* from a "frankly apologetic" viewpoint. He follows an eclectic approach, out of the conviction that psychologists are not the only professional people who have dealt with the problem of personality, and that the scientific approach needs to be supplemented by the contributions of classical Christianity. Unlike many who follow the approach presented in its extreme form in this paragraph, he has solid knowledge of the methods and findings of academic psychology.
6. John Baillie, *The Interpretation of Religion* (New York: Charles Scribner's, Sons, 1928), p. 405.
7. Antireligious or areligious social scientists would tend to follow this approach, also. Thus, James Leuba wrote in his *Psychological Study of Religion* in 1912 that theology bears a relation to psychology "similar to that of alchemy to chemistry" and that when theology becomes fully scientific "it will become a branch of psychological science."
8. By Walter M. Horton (New York: Harper & Brothers, 1931). Horton, who was then strongly under the influence of his teacher George A. Coe, has undoubtedly changed his position in the succeeding years.
9. C. W. Kegley and R. W. Bretall, *The Theology of Paul Tillich* (New York: The Macmillan Company, 1952), p. viii, from the introduction to the series of volumes which will constitute the "Library of Living Theology." Note the redefinition of the purpose of psychology involved in this adjustment of theology to psychology.
10. For a discussion of the "method of correlation," see Paul Tillich, *Systematic Theology,* Vol. I (Chicago: University of Chicago Press, 1952), pp. 8, 59-66.
11. This definition, which in general follows Tillich, has a different emphasis from that made by liberal theologians such as Harold De Wolf. See De Wolf's *A Theology of the Living Church* (New York: Harper & Brothers, 1953), p. 18.
12. G. Murphy, *Introduction to Psychology* (New York: Harper & Brothers, 1951), p. 2. N. L. Munn says basically the same thing on p. 16 of the third edition of his *Psychology* (Boston: Houghton Mifflin Co., 1956).
13. For further discussion of this point, see my review of Carl Jung's *Collected Works* in the March, 1959 issue of *Contemporary Psychology*.

14. Cf. Herbert Feigl's address to the 1958 annual meeting of the American Psychological Association on "Philosophical Embarrassments of Psychology," reprinted in *The American Psychologist,* Vol. 14, No. 3, March, 1959, pp. 115-128.

15. Cf. Homer L. Jernigan's discussion of *The Meaning of Faith—A Theological and Psychological Study,* an unpublished doctoral dissertation, Northwestern University, 1959.

16. In *The Purpose of the Church and Its Ministry* (New York: Harper & Brothers, 1956).

17. For a fuller treatment of this point, and others raised in this section, see my unpublished doctoral dissertation, *Predicting Ministerial Effectiveness,* Harvard University, 1957. Samuel Blizzard found in his recent research on the role of the minister in modern society that the average parish minister spends about 50 per cent of his working time as administrator or organizer.

18. H. R. Niebuhr, D. D. Williams, J. M. Gustafson, *The Advancement of Theological Education* (New York: Harper & Brothers, 1957), p. 102. Subsequent references in this paragraph are from pp. 81 and 87.

19. This sentence and the remainder of the paragraph come from an article written for the February, 1958, issue of *Nexus,* the Boston University School of Theology alumni magazine. Material presented here, and elsewhere in this essay, has been worked out in discussions with Professors Paul Johnson and Homer Jernigan of Boston University and Professor James Dittes of Yale University.

20. Cf. my dissertation, referred to in reference 17 above. Niebuhr, in *The Purpose of the Church and Its Ministry* (*op. cit.*), discusses most creatively the concept of "the call to the ministry." Current research by the Educational Testing Service on "Improving Selection for the Ministry," results of which have not yet been published, should bring considerable clarification of these issues.

GOTTHARD BOOTH &

The physician has his bag of instruments and drugs with him which in the popular mind gives him status and allows him to rely on this practical help. The lawyer has the law and its interpretation at hand whenever he is asked to give advice or pass a judgment. For the minister the Bible is not a textbook, a reference book to answer personal problems, or at least it should not be used that way. The wealth of tradition in the Christian faith has to be alive in the minister's mind and existence whenever he acts professionally. But in pastoral counseling the transformation of Christian insights into responses to personal need has to come through the personality of the minister himself. For this reason it is essential that the minister be a mature, stable, and outgoing person sensitive to other people's problems but not swayed by them to the point of merely catering to the whims of the parishioners.

Theological education and pastoral training, therefore, is adequate only if it develops the personality of the prospective minister at least as much as it passes on to him academic knowledge and practical instruction. But even before this can be faced the applicant for theological training has to consider whether he has at least the potentials for such personality growth. The experience of theological schools in the past was increasingly that many applicants were choosing the ministry as a career for neurotic reasons. They exchanged the emotional dependence on the physical mother for the dependence on mother church. The inability to come to terms with appropriate independence from their father at home made them rely immaturely on the father in heaven. Theological education today is limited to three short academic years into which a startling amount of education and training should be pressed. It is practically impossible that the student should have enough time to himself to allow him to grow through the last part of his puberty, called the intellectual phase. Many a young man marries just before he enters seminary or during his seminary years. The concentrated effort of studying and the usual necessity for the wife to procure the financial means for their survival create a very unsatisfactory situation. These two tired young people under strain are expected to deal constructively with the period of marital adjustment, which can often be complicated by the arrival of the first child.

For all these reasons it is essential that the screening process for applicants to ministerial training be of the highest possible quality. The goal is not to eliminate everybody who does not live up to the boring standard of the normal average American all-round boy. But for the sake of the ministry, of the quality of theological education and especially of the applicant himself, the psychological potentials have to be scrutinized. Dr. Booth, a leading psychiatrist in New York City, has done this specific work for many years. His acquaintance with the problems involved is immense. The editor is grateful to Dr. Booth that he was willing to share the account of his experience and reflection with all those either who are thinking of the ministry as a career, or who have to do the screening for entrance to theological schools. Certainly, the ministers who are already on duty will themselves have second thoughts upon reading what Dr. Booth has to say. Perhaps they will ask quietly whether they could profit by reflecting about the problems discussed by Dr. Booth and see to it that their ministry is not hampered by their still lingering personal problems.

The Psychological Examination of Candidates for the Ministry

Introduction

In recent years an increasing number of denominations have been demanding that candidates for the ministry submit to a psychological examination. This practice has presented psychologists and psychiatrists with a task for which they were not prepared by their previous experience. In ordinary practice they are required to provide psychiatric diagnosis and psychodynamic evaluations of individuals who are suffering from some manifest psychological or somatic disability. Only in rare instances are candidates for the ministry definitely sick and can they be "screened out" on the basis of serious pathology. The majority of the candidates come from the segment of the population which is considered "normal" from a statistical point of view. They have been able to meet life's demands without a psychological breakdown, or, to use psychiatric language, their neurotic or schizophrenic ego defenses have proved adequate for practical purposes.

If one examines an average "normal" candidate, one is bound to find weak spots in his personality structure which can be labeled as hysterical, obsessional, or schizoid, mechanisms. Such findings are compatible with adequate or superior functioning even under conditions of considerable emotional or occupational stress. Whether a given individual is going to become sick depends on the particular correlation between his personality and the specific demands he has to meet. The ministry not only makes demands, but also provides for certain personalities a way of living in which they can function usefully and creatively in spite of limitations such as have broken individuals engaged in a different type of work. The psychological examination of candidates for the ministry demands, thus, consideration of the following two points:

101

- An understanding of the specific psychological situation of the minister in addition to an awareness of the problems of personal life which the candidate has not faced already in the past, such as marriage.
- An evaluation of the strengths and weaknesses in the individual personality structure.

The present communication is the result of observations made by the writer in the course of the past nine years in his capacity as psychiatric examiner of candidates for the Protestant Episcopal Church, the first year on behalf of Bishop Washburn of Newark. He, like doubtlessly some other bishops, had moved ahead of the decision of the House of Bishops in 1949 which made it mandatory that all candidates for the ministry should undergo a psychological examination and "urged examiners to use, whenever possible, psychological and psychodiagnostic tests as part of their examinations." Up to the present the writer has seen 350 candidates, most of them first-year students of General Theological Seminary in New York and postulants of the Diocese of Newark. The procedure followed has not been changed significantly since a detailed study of the first 163 candidates in 1953 indicated that it yielded satisfactory results.* [1]

Psychological Problems Involved in the Ministry of the Protestant Episcopal Church

In order to understand the point of view from which the present investigation was conducted it appears necessary to clarify the most significant psychological problems inherent in the ministry of the Protestant Episcopal Church. Some time ago President Eisenhower observed about this denomination: "It is too darned dignified." This critical remark points to a very essential characteristic. Dignity, like most qualities, can be either good or bad according to the context. In its positive sense, the dignity of the church to Episcopalians is derived from the fact that according to its faith, the church as a corporate body has divine character: it is the Body of Christ. This puts the church as such on a higher level than any of its individual members and organs, but, at the same time, the individuals belonging to it derive from this membership a feeling of personal dignity which is independent of personal achievements and failures. This is particularly true for its priest. Outwardly he represents the church in public places by his distinctive clerical vest and collar, in services by elaborate ritual vestments. Inwardly he is reassured of his particular dignity by the doctrine of the Apostolic Succession. This means that much as in the Roman Catholic doctrine, the priesthood is endowed with supernatural grace, received through ordination to the priesthood from the bishop, who again has received the power of imparting it in an unbroken sacramental succession from the original apostles of Christ. Particularly in the frequent celebrations of the Mass,

---

* All superior figures such as this refer to the Notes at the end of the chapter. Numbers in parentheses throughout the text in this chapter indicate references in the Bibliography which follows the Notes.

the priest experiences again and again his intimate relatedness to God. The conviction of his mystic function provides him with strength for his varied practical tasks as a counselor to individuals in difficult personal situations, as a preacher and as a leader of his congregation in spiritual, economic, and administrative matters. In all these rational issues the Episcopal Church is by no means static: historically this was expressed in the revolt of the English against the Roman Church under Henry VIII. Regarding the particular problem of this chapter, Episcopalian priests have been among the pioneers of the recognition and practical application of modern psychological and psychiatric findings.

The ministry of the Episcopal Church, as is apparent from the preceding description, demands most of all a capacity for *identification with a spirit* transcending the material world of the senses, but at the same time it demands capacity for group identification on account of the emphasis on the church as the corporate Body of Christ. Protestant emphasis on the intellectual and practical achievements of the individual is apt to create difficulties in the Protestant Episcopal Church. This means that the Episcopal minister is expected to have a stable spiritual foundation and to be at the same time capable of dealing in a flexible, intelligent manner with the temporal issues of his position.

In the ideal case the candidate would be attracted purely by the ideal aims of the Episcopal Church, but in reality all candidates are influenced in varying degrees by nonspiritual needs for which the Episcopal ministry holds out satisfaction. As long as a reasonable balance between spiritual and egotistical motivations exists this natural human condition does not exclude a candidate for the priesthood. Each year, however, a number of men seek to enter the ministry who are, consciously or unconsciously, attracted to an excessive extent by the worldly ego gratifications offered specifically by the Episcopal priesthood.

First of all, the *conspicuous social dignity* of the priesthood attracts men who have suffered in their childhood from feelings of inferiority: either because their families had been socio-economically underprivileged, or because they themselves had been in an inferior position within their families because they were only children or less promising than their siblings, and similar situations. The child who feels the desire to rise above his inferior status finds that the Episcopal Church is interested in helping promising boys through college and seminary. It is obviously very difficult for the parish priest to weigh justly the motivations of a boy in his teens, the age at which so many form a decision for the priesthood; neither is the boy himself capable of being objective. In particular, the boy will find it difficult to face reasons for changing his mind once he has declared himself publicly, and may find himself committed furthermore on account of economic aid received.

A second source of complications stems from the fact that the church takes its responsibilities toward its priests very seriously: it provides *security* which is by no means of a purely materialistic character. There are many candidates who enjoyed very little parental affection as children and for whom being in church meant from childhood the only experience of being "in my father's house" or "being at home." These expressions recur again and again in the autobiographical sketches of the candidates. The family atmosphere of the parish adds so much emotional value to the economic security of the ministry that it often compensates for the generally low income level. Many of the candidates have proved that they have excellent capacities for earning money and that they have no reason to shun the competition of business or professional life.

Emotional insecurity of candidates in relation to women sometimes leads to a third specific problem, *homosexuality*. The latter is not always overt, often not even conscious. Overt homosexuals are sometimes attracted by the fact that celibacy in a dedicated priest is less likely to be considered suspect as sexual maladjustment than this is the case in any other occupation. Unconscious homosexuals sense in the church the possibility of sublimated satisfaction: the aggressive types are made secure in wielding power for the good of the church and of the individual parishioners; the more passive types are able to enjoy affectionate relationships without fear of being exploited by sexually aggressive individuals. Obviously the latent homosexuals may become victims of seduction, the overt homosexuals may lose their rational control, if at some point in seminary or later in the ministry they find their idealistic expectations seriously threatened.

A fourth cause of potential complications, again related to the previous points, is the *emotional and aesthetic emphasis* of the church services. This appeals to men who are more interested in the receptive than in the aggressive side of life. In American culture the priesthood represents the only occupation which is socially fully recognized and makes it a man's duty, not an "escape," to participate in emotional experiences mediated by aesthetic forms. In an unbalanced person, the aesthetic side of the ministry may become an escape from its other demands.

Method of Examination

The procedure followed by this writer has three main lines of approach which mutually supplement each other in the final analysis of the candidate:

- The written *self-evaluation of the candidate* regarding his biographical background and regarding his attitude toward the ministry.
- The reaction of the candidate to the standardized stimuli provided by four so-called *"projective personality tests,"* each of which brings out a different dimension in the functioning of the individual:
  a. The Szondi method (16) * reflects the relative strength of the basic need systems: in the sexual sphere, the tender, the yielding, and the aggressive components; in the sphere of superego control, the handling of aggression and of affection, respectively; in the sphere of ego function, the tendency toward self-sufficiency and toward fusion between ego and environment; in the sphere of object relationships, the tendency toward pleasure seeking. The method is based on the experience that individuals show various

* Numbers in parentheses throughout Dr. Booth's chapter refer to numbered items in his Bibliography at the end of the chapter.

degrees of like, dislike, indifference or ambivalence toward the pictures of patients whose respective illnesses represent extreme manifestations of one of the above-mentioned needs: homosexuals, murderers, epileptics, hysterics, catatonics, paranoics, depressives, and manics.

b. The Rorschach method indicates the way in which the individual experiences certain basic life situations as they are symbolized in the ten inkblot pictures.

c. The drawing tests of Kock (7) and Machover (8) in which the drawing of a tree in the first, of a man and a woman in the second test, indicate in various ways how the individual places himself actively into his environment by the way he uses the circumscribed field of the sheet of paper for his drawings.

● The *interview* in which the examiner discusses with the candidates the discrepancies between the image which the latter has of himself and the image which the examiner derived from the psychological tests and personal contacts.

The *first session* with the candidates usually takes *two hours* and is devoted entirely to the psychological testing. To provide some basic orientation he has been asked to send in, prior to the interview, an *autobiographical sketch* which is expected to cover the age, health, occupation of parents, siblings and wife or fiancée, if any; furthermore, the candidate's schooling, military service, and occupational experiences as well as his health record. Gaps can usually be filled in by the examiner without much loss of time, so that the testing begins without any significant "warming up" period. This makes some candidates anxious and limits their productivity, but this writer considers the anxiety reaction to a "cold" testing approach more significant than more material obtained by means of a winsome attitude of the examiner.

The first test administered is the *Szondi test*. In recent years the "latent profile" (17) has been added, because it gives a great deal of additional information in very little time.

Second, the *Rorschach test* is administered. Detailed inquiry and "testing the limits" are used, only if the red blots in cards II and III or the "popular" animal in card VIII have not been mentioned spontaneously. Finally the candidate is asked which two cards he liked best, which two least.

Third, the *drawing tests* are administered, and the candidate is asked to give a description of what he has drawn without imposing the systematic inquiry suggested by Machover (8). The examiner has to use his own judgment as to what features of the drawing need clarification.

At last the *Szondi test is repeated* without the "latent profile," but the candidate is asked for the reasons why he picked the particular pictures as liked or disliked after he has first been told that he may change his mind on seeing the pictures for the second time. The personal associations with the pictures afford usually a great deal of information along the lines of the TAT, but in much shorter time.

After the testing is finished, the candidate is given the *printed instructions for the examiner* [2] and is asked to write a self-evaluation with respect to the same points which the examiner will have to answer. He is told that the next session will be devoted to a discussion of points of disagreement between the candidate's statements about himself and what the examiner concluded from the tests and other observations. This procedure informs the candidate of the very specific nature of the questions which the examiner is asked to answer and which some men would otherwise consider unwarranted prying into their private affairs particularly when it comes to sex. Furthermore, the candidate is asked to give a short *description of the personalities of his parents, siblings and fiancée or wife.* The next session is then arranged with the understanding that the self-evaluation and personality descriptions will have to be in the hands of the examiner at such time as he requires for a preliminary evaluation of the whole material.

The *second session* takes an hour usually, but an occasional candidate may bring out so much disturbing material that an additional session is required to clarify the issues and make some therapeutic plan. In general, the hour is sufficient for giving the candidates some psychological perspective on his particular problems. This is made easy for the examiner and impressive for the candidate if the material from the psychological tests is used as illustration. The Rorschach lends itself most frequently to this use, if the symbolic-demand character of the individual plates is used as basis for the interpretation. This will be explained in the following section. In some cases the drawing tests provide more self-evident material; in others the associations to the Szondi pictures reveal a haunting problem. The examiner must obviously keep the psychoanalytical and other technical cues in the back of his mind while trying to make the candidate aware of significant *facts* in his biography and plans.

Interviews of this type are usually helpful to the candidate and often encourage him to bring out important additional information which had been held back for conscious or unconscious reasons. In case of need, the way to some therapeutic measures can be eased.

The Rorschach Method

INDIVIDUALISTIC AND CONFORMIST TENDENCIES

The method which has given this writer the greatest amount of verified information on ministerial candidates has been the Rorschach test. It has been used, however, in a more comprehensive and systematic way than taught in contemporary psychological schools and textbooks. The next concepts underlying the present approach were developed on the basis of the experience that the personality types predisposed toward chronic somatic diseases cannot be differentiated by means of the methods which differentiate between neurosis and psychoses. Just as these different psychiatric disorders can combine themselves with different somatic disorders, the different types of personality organization in somatic illnesses express themselves in ways of perceiving the inkblots which are independent from the ways characteristic of neurotics or psychotics. Whereas the psychiatric illnesses seem to be functions of the more recently developed cortex of the brain, the dispositions toward somatic illnesses seem to be functions of the older stages of cerebral evolution. This observation was made originally in a Rorschach study of chronic somatic illnesses: arthritis, Parkinsonism, and arterial hypertension, which have been recognized by an increasing number of researchers as related to personality (2). More recent unpublished investigations of cancer and tuberculosis of the lungs confirmed the validity of the hypothesis that very deeply unconscious layers of the psyche are reflected in specific tendencies of perceiving the inkblots. The psychological conclusions drawn from psychosomatic research have been applied to the interpretation of Rorschach tests by the writer in his psychotherapeutic and consultative practice where they proved equally applicable to cases free from somatic illness. The evaluation of candidates for the ministry have thus a wide background of experience made with very different types of personalities: over 200 somatic cases, most of them ward patients, and over 900 patients observed in private practice, during the last twenty-two years. A full account of the clinical observations and theoretical background of this writer's approach can be given only in the form of a comprehensive monograph which will be completed in the near future. Because the results, in the experience of the church authorities, have proved practical validity, the present publication was undertaken in the expectation that other psychiatrists and psychologists will consider the following suggestions of use in their work.

Certain features of the Rorschach observations accessible to the classical system of scoring and interpretations will not be discussed in the present publication, because they are self-evident to anybody familiar with the Rorschach method. Of the elements of personality revealed only by the new approach, one of the most important concerns the *basic identification of the individual* in meeting other individuals and his collective environment. This central aspect of the self became first manifest in a comparative study of arthritic and of hypertensive patients. Arthritics identify themselves from childhood on with the dominant parent and endeavor as adults to live according to their upbringing and make minimal concessions to the ways of their social environment. The hypertensives identify themselves since childhood with the submissive parent and endeavor as adults to live as much as they can according to the standards and demands of their social environment. In a pragmatic way, one may label the first group as "individualistic," the other as "conformist," although the difference in attitude may become apparent only at a time when the congregation, or the wife, for that matter, opposes the set of values with which the minister has been raised. As long as there is continuity of values, the minister may have given a conformist impression, but in case of conflict, he will prove rigidly set on continuing his original course. The really conformist minister may suffer from conflict between the values to which he is committed as a member of his congregation on the one hand, and the values of the community in which he lives, on the other hand. Social and racial conflicts in the town can become a source of anxiety for him although he is likely to get along with his own congregation. In general the two types described are not encountered in pure form, but the classification is based on the prevalence of one of the two tendencies over the other.

The most reliable indication for the relative strength of the two tendencies was found in the manner in which individuals perceive the vertical axis of the symmetrical inkblots: [3]

- The *"individualistic" personality* tends to make the axis of the inkblot coincide with the spine of a warmblooded organism or with the line along which some dynamic emphasis is directed—for example, arrows, drills, airplanes, Eiffel tower. This type of response is scored as "L," because it was found to prevail in patients bent on locomotor self-expression such as arthritics and Parkinsonians.
- The *"conformist" personality* tends toward the following two ways of perceiving the symmetry of the inkblots:
  a. The axis is made to coincide with inanimate objects which *symbolize* collective values—for example, totem poles, emblems, crosses, crowns —but are not used as means of physical action.
  b. The axis appears as unstructured material (air, water, fire) which is enclosed by some hollow organ or object—such as womb, cave, chimney, lake, valley.

This type of response is scored as "V" because it was found to prevail in patients bent on vaso-motor self-expression such as arterial hypertensives.

In the whole group of Episcopalian candidates the "conformist" responses prevailed over "individualistic" responses at the rate of 2:1. It is my impression that the presence of "conformist" responses is a very important consideration in the evaluation of individuals who, in terms of other Rorschach criteria, appear ill-equipped for stable and responsible work—for example, on account of emotional instability or intellectual rigidity or schizoid thinking. The "conformist" tendency allows them to use the clerical setting as a stabilizing and directive force which compensates for other limitations. One may say that for some the clerical dress provides a portable sanitarium, a sanitarium in which the individual accomplishes constructive work of which he would be incapable in a worldly setting. It should be clear from the preceding remarks that the term "conformist" does not mean necessarily a person who indiscriminately follows the crowd, but one who conforms with a group subordinated to impersonal values. The connection between this group attitude and the identification with the submissive parent is provided by the common denominator of submission to a dominant value-experience in a person or in a superpersonal organization such as the church.

In general the "conformist" personality proved better fitted for the ministry, but there were enough "individualistic" candidates and ministers to prove that this orientation is not only compatible with the ministry, but may provide original and firm leadership. It depends on many internal and external contingencies whether the conviction of one's leadership will prove more constructive or destructive in a given congregation.

Specific Life Situations

Some of the contingencies affecting the relationship between individual and environment can be envisioned by the systematic use of the ten Rorschach cards as symbolization of *ten specific demands of life*. This approach was first mentioned to the writer casually by Dr. Hector Ritey who had developed it in Italy before coming to this country in the late thirties. Unfortunately he could not be prevailed upon to publish his ideas, thus only his interpretation of Cards I and X stayed in mind. After completing the study of "individualist" and "conformist" types, this writer became interested in the demand character of the individual cards. The result turned out to be remarkably similar to the independent findings of Franz Merei (9), although Merei arrived at his results from a very different theoretical starting point and a Hungarian population (cf. 4, 15, 18). Recently the work of Minkowska (10) confirmed that in a French population and with a different theoretical approach the significance of the individual cards is defined in a manner similar to the findings in Italy, Hungary, and the U.S.A. In the following, the demand character of the cards will be described to serve as basis for the interpretation according to established Rorschach principles. Examples will be given specifically from the records of the 27 who proved failures in Seminary out of the first 163 candidates tested. They should serve as illustrations, but not as "signs" to be counted statistically. The latter type of evaluation may have its place when only rough approximations for mass purposes are needed—for instance, the large-scale Rorschach experiments of Harrower during the war (6). In ministerial candidates the complexities of individuality and vocation are so great, the number of promising applicants so small, that only a careful weighing of all available psychological information will do justice to the candidate and to the church. In the practice of the writer, "poor" Rorschach responses are singled out for amplification in the subsequent interview. Often the analysis of one such response provides the key to the special problem of the candidate and changes the picture completely. Many of the "poor" responses could be found also in promising candidates; they are noted simply because they should receive special attention in the interview and in the report to the church authority. The following observations have been made about the demand character of the individual cards:

CARD I

Rorschach planned the card to make all kinds of responses equally easy: as form or as movement, as a whole or as a number of details, large and small. As a whole it can be seen as a primitive unit, as relatedness or conflict between two halves, or as two sides related to a central figure (cf. Roemer 12), the center figure as one or two human figures, as an organism or as a symbolic object. The balanced manifold possibilities of this card symbolize the situation of the infant into which it is born. At this point the inherited vitality and strength of genetic drives (Szondi, *Fate Analysis*) play a decisive part regarding the effect of nursing, toilet training, and the emotional impact of the parental personalities. After the basic infantile pattern has been established, it is brought into play whenever the individual faces a new and strange situation as symbolized by the Rorschach examination, particularly because the first Rorschach is least of all weighted in any specific direction. Merei describes its demand character as "The presenting of one's own self. The inner situation."

In the light of this characterization it is understandable that three candidates who proved excessively handicapped by their bad childhoods saw severely damaged objects in the first card: a battered piece of tin, a worm-eaten leaf, a badly beaten-up butterfly.[4] It also proved significant that six candidates for the ministry started with what this writer considers preoccupation with face saving: projections of human masks and animal heads as whole response.

Card II

The card is most potent for bringing out *conflicts over aggression* by the following features:

- It makes the projection of one integral organism as a whole response impossible; there are inevitably "two sides" to the situation unless the whole situation is not faced at all.
- The situation is characterized by the violent red color as a situation of defenselessness, because as long as the physical defenses of the organism are intact, the blood color is veiled by the blood vessels and the skin.
- The running of the red color into the black makes it difficult to separate it from the rest (see Card III) and give an unemotional response to the black alone.

Merei considers this card as bringing out the relationship between sexuality and affectivity. Although this formulation applies in many instances, it does not distinguish clearly between primary and secondary qualities of the situation symbolized in this card. Primary for the understanding of this card is the threat of disintegration under aggression. Secondary is the specific way in which the individual reacts to this threat. The question is whether the individual may defend himself successfully against this threat by humor (for instance, the clowns), conventional behavior (dancing, greeting, toasting), counteraggression (fighting). An inadequate system of ego defenses is indicated by failure to see the human figures or to accept the red color, implied in responses indicating unintegrated counteraggression (explosions), genital anxiety (sex organs), flight into dependency (womb, cave), or into withdrawal from reality (white space as ballet dancer).

In the group of inadequate seminarians, ten saw neither human nor animal popular forms; three of them, inanimate destruction; five saw the popular forms engaged in a bloody fight.

CARD III

This card tests particularly the capacity of *controlling aggression in a conventionally structured social situation*. This meaning of the card is achieved by the following features:

- It is made easier than in any one of the other cards to see two human figures facing each other. This corresponds to the function of social customs: they facilitate human relationships without demanding individualized efforts.
- The figures are given a sexually ambiguous character. Suggestions of both sexes are made so discreetly that either sex can easily identify with the figures.
- The dark center connecting the two figures lends itself easily to interpretation as an implement of co-operative activity or as an object torn apart by two competitors, or as two objects handled individually.
- The red color as symbol of aggression is clearly separated from the human figures. This makes it easy to keep aggression "in the back of one's head," and to avoid "seeing red."
- The red color is given outlines which make it easy to give them a purely formal interpretation and to avoid emotionally "colored" responses—for example, the lateral reds may be seen as monkeys or cherubs, the center as a butterfly or a bow tie. On the other hand the color may dominate the impression as gay decorations, as blood, or as fire.

Merei comments on this card that it is critical for schizoid personalities thus singling out one of the personality types which have limited capacities for meeting conventional social situations.

All individuals in the group of inadequate seminarians responded to Card III in a revealing manner, suggesting feelings of inferiority; three failed to see human beings at all and saw a "primitive whole" (Roemer) instead (bug, crab, pelvis). Of the other 24, ten saw the figures as women, others as waiters, cannibals, or as "holding on to something in the middle." The response "cannibals cooking a missionary" is a particularly plain expression of what inadequate sublimation of aggression does to the vocational aptitude of these men. (It may be mentioned in this connection that schizoid personalities are often doing surprisingly well in the ministry because they derive strength from their symbolic identification with spiritual powers most easily. This clinical group is not represented among the seminarians who had to withdraw.)

CARD IV

This card symbolizes a situation in which the individual has to *face the world alone*. Merei characterizes it as evoking "childhood and anxiety." This effect is produced from the following features:

- The concentration of dark color is associated with the childhood situation of being alone in a *dark* room in which no familiar supporting person or object can be seen.

● The outlines suggest a *single* human being or animal with human traits (apes or bears); furthermore the organs of the intellect and acquired skills (arms and head) are weakly suggested, and the feet as organs of the power of standing up alone are exaggerated. A good image of interhuman relatedness cannot be projected into the whole inkblot.

These two main features facilitate two contrasting reactions: the individualistic. self-assertive person will see a warmblooded animal or human figure. There is obviously a difference whether a person sees a marching giant or Charlie Chaplin sitting on a tree trunk.

The isolated person who seeks support is likely to see an animal skin; some may be quite specific about a "doormat" quality of the inkblot. The card has been called the "Father Card" (Phillips & Smith, 11) because Western culture expects fathers to stand securely on their own feet. The self-sufficient and independent Swiss seem to consider this card beautiful, although difficult, as Rorschach observed (14). The French, according to Theodora Abel, tend to see foreign invaders in it. They have certainly stayed individualists in spite of their long history of being alternately invaders and invaded (1).

In the group of *successful* seminarians the situation "alone without emotional support" produced in only 23 per cent a kinesthetic response suggesting a self-assertive attitude, but 45 per cent reacted to the "fur" aspect of the card suggesting a strong tendency toward falling back on support. In view of what was said above about the security needs of many candidates these data may be interpreted as meaning that many of the successful seminarians find their security needs satisfied by living close to the church.

In the *failing* group the tendency toward self-assertion (popular kinesthesis) appears somewhat higher (33 per cent), but often the responses indicate the lack of strength behind it: the figure is seen as sitting down, the weak arms are emphasized, the feet are seen only in the dark part of the popular feet so that the person seems to stand on his toes. A related symptom of insecure self-assertion appeared in 33 per cent of the failing group: the "feet" are seen as shoes or boots. In other words, in affirming a stand they are more concerned with a protective layer and with what meets the eye than with the live power behind it.

CARD V

This card is extremely simple and uninteresting. It seems to test the individual, whether he can accept the flat, humdrum aspects of daily life. Certain people cannot accept the boring "bat or butterfly" aspect of this inkblot. Merei calls it "relationship to reality" and claims that in all cases in which the popular response is missed, the reality function is disturbed. "Reality," however, is too wide a concept. It is a better definition to say that failure regarding the popular answer indicates a lack of common sense, conscious or unconscious difficulties in leaving a simple situation simple.

In the *failing* group seven missed the popular response, all because they used the simple situation for the purpose of showing off after the intimidating experience of Card IV. Such showing off took the form of aggressiveness (eagles, vultures, "Superman," man in riding breeches and hat) and suggested weak personalities seeking in the church a boost for their aggressive needs.

CARD VI

Psychologists discovered early that this card tests the attitude toward sexuality. Again, as in Card III, the suggestion of male and female anatomy is not made explicit because in the well-integrated personality masculinity and femininity are part of the total personality. A person who sees only sex organs is likely to express gender only on the level of direct genital activity.

Generally, the sexual symbolism remains unconscious, even though the onlooker may betray concern with the balance of power between the sexes. This happens when a person cannot see anything in this card before having turned it so that the male part is below the female part.

Aside from the symbolism of the two distinct male and female parts, the total configuration of this inkblot suggests the problem of peaceful coexistence between male and female: it is very difficult to see this inkblot as a unit. We know from anthropology that humanity has developed an amazing number of experimental solutions for the puzzle that both sexes partly need each other, partly need autonomy in order to function effectively. Most Episcopalian seminarians are poorly prepared for dealing with sexual relationships. Even omitting the overt and latent homosexuals, they usually are in their middle twenties and have grown up with the intention of entering the ministry. This, in most cases, has discouraged early marriage as well as premarital sex relations, although they have been subjected to a good deal of temptation in college and in the Armed Services.

In the group of *failing* seminarians the records showed a few types of frequent responses:

- *Phallic part.* Ten were unable to respond to this part at all, whereas seven gave it strong dynamic emphasis (man with hat, tiger head, lighthouse, radio station, TV antenna, bullet), three saw penises and only three saw totem poles which are a frequent response among seminarians who have fitted their sexual role into the moral pattern of their social group.
- *Feminine part.* Indications of frustration regarding their affectionate needs were frequent in the inadequate group; in fact only four saw the popular animal skin. Three could not respond at all, and twelve gave R-responses of the "map" and "canyon" type of which the most striking was "two cement walls with only a small crack between them." Seven used the outer edge of the feminine part in order to display a forced masculine front toward the outer world: the profiles of kings, longnosed or bearded men, for example. Most expressive of this fake "masculine" attitude was "two lions nailed with their backs to the part in the center."

CARD VII

This card tests the attitude toward a situation which the individual cannot dominate. This purpose is achieved through the following features:

- The broad expanse of white space in the center and the split in the base makes it impossible to project oneself into a dominating center. The frustration of this need may lead the subject to turn the card upside down and to discover the head of Napoleon or George Washington in the space. It is hardly necessary to say that such a would-be Napoleon is not likely to tackle the world realistically because we cannot turn the real world upside down.
- The separate halves of the inkblot make it fairly easy to project two human figures into them, which face each other. Contrary to Cards II and III, the interpersonal relationship is not structured, either by aggressive emotions or by forms of cultural relationships. Instead of any emotional or rational tie, the two halves appear precariously balanced, and the centrifugal projections point in opposing directions.
- The problem of concern with domination is further suggested by the fact that if the onlooker discovers the people facing each other, he finds them equal in size, and both precariously balanced. Both have, furthermore, clearly something on top of their heads. Headgear throughout the world seems to be closely associated with the desire for social distinction and superiority.

All these features put the subject into a situation that he must identify with one of the two figures which are exactly of the same height. If he is sensitive to a situation in which he cannot gain any advantage over his fellow man and in which he does not get any visible support from him either, anxiety is produced. This makes the two popular figures appear hostile if they are perceived at all. Merei calls this card the one which brings out the "ego and aggressive tendencies," having had obviously experiences similar to mine.[5] This writer feels, however, that the problem of aggression is secondary in this card, contrary to the situation in Card II. It is due to the competitive emphasis in our culture that statistically aggression appears so often.

This card has acquired the reputation of being the "Mother Card." This is probably due to the fact that the child-mother relationship represents the basic human experience of being unable to control the other person. This is essentially true for both sides: the child cannot control the mother physically, but the mother cannot control the emotions of the child. Certainly the age of "momism" produces numerous Rorschach records in which the domineering and possessive tendencies of the individual mother are revealed by the reactions of Card VII, but it may be hoped that the current trend in parent education will diminish substantially the number of subjects for whom "mother" and "domination" are synonyms and Card VII the "Mother Card."

With respect to the Episcopalian students I found no difference in emphasis between successful and failing groups. In both, preoccupation with the "headgear" part (33 per cent) was frequent. This finding bears out what I said in the beginning, that a certain preoccupation with prestige is compatible with adjustment to the Episcopal Ministry.

CARD VIII

This card tests the individual attitude toward a harmoniously balanced situation. This function is accomplished by the following characteristics:

- The simple, rounded, and closed outline of the whole inkblot suggests a finite and rational world.
- The three chromatic colors and the gray are harmonious. The red color is not weighted aggressively as in Cards II and III.
- Although not all details are easily interpreted, a four-legged animal is very obvious. It represents the organism which symbolizes all the basic needs of physical existence.
- The different colors are separated by white spaces. This makes it easy to ignore those parts the subject cannot cope with. It symbolizes an important condition of rational existence: we must be able to exist physically without understanding everything about ourselves and our environment.
- The gray, peaked top suggests that the subject may leave the emotional complexities of the subconscious and rise above them to the height of cool, rational ego control. Some subjects feel the need to turn the card by 90 degrees in order to feel on top of the situation. Even then the gray is ahead, leading the situation in a precise manner.

One may consider this card as a deepened presentation of the situation in Card V: even in its rationally ordered and undramatic aspects, life is full of emotional complexities. The latter may be consciously integrated (all details are interpreted) or may be ignored by those who live simply by their "healthy instincts." The sick only are apt to be disturbed by the appearance of several colors or by the lack of perfect harmony. This characterization agrees with Merei's designation as showing the "affective attitude toward the environment." In view of the following two cards, however, this should be made more specific: *the affective attitude toward a rational, reasonably harmonious environment.*

There is no significant difference of trends between the successful and the failing groups of seminarians. It may be mentioned that in both groups about one-third of the subjects saw beasts of prey. This may illustrate that the choice of the ministry is motivated in many by an aggressive disposition which, however, requires the backing of the church. In the failing group, one saw a charging bull; another, a dog straining at the leash. What forced them to withdraw was the inability to subordinate their aggressiveness to the demands of the seminary.

CARD IX

This card is most difficult to interpret. It seems to test the ability for coping with the full impact of the complexities of life. This effect is achieved by combining some of the particular difficulties of Cards II, VII and VIII.

- The colors are running into each other as in Card II. This makes it difficult to ignore the fact that our emotions are not so clearly defined and so easily dismissed as we wish to think.
- A central white space is placed as in Card VII. This has again the effect that a situation is symbolized which the subject cannot control. The pointed heads on top repeat the "headgear" motif, and the figures facing each other are again in a poor state of balance. They cannot even get away from each other, but send unpleasantly pointed projections toward each other. The coloring is part and parcel of the implication of this card: if our emotions are involved we cannot get away from the situation. As long as the controversy is merely rational we are able to dismiss our opposite number and imagine that we have won our case. In the colorless Card VII the arms pointed away from each other.
- As in Card VIII the coloring is again not weighted in the direction of aggression, but, on the other hand, there is no escape from emotions into rational gray. This escape would be particularly desirable since most people experience the colors as disharmonious. There is also not the chance of Card VIII to turn it 90 degrees in order to put oneself on top of the situation. There is a fairly obvious human head at the bottom of this card, flat on its back. Even when we turn the card, the head is still surmounted by a green blotch.

Summing up all the form and color symbolism of this card, it may be be said that it evokes, in a concentrated form, *the complexities of life which surpass human understanding.* Successful interpretation of this card suggests ego strength. This agrees with Merei's finding that Card IX tests the capacity for work and achievement.

In the *failing* group of seminarians, altogether 19 gave responses indicating their limited capacities for dealing rationally with uncontrollable situations. Only one failed completely, but 10 reacted with a definite *throwback into infancy*: the pink turned into baby heads, babies just born, still hanging from the umbilical cord. Others expressed the regression induced by the card on a poorer form level as pelvis, sex organs, buttocks, caves. Another group of nine showed anxiety in the form of aggressive and self-assertive responses; three turned the card around and discovered the mushroom of the atomic bomb; the others gave the popular human character of famous people (Mark Twain, Roosevelt), or haughty looks or turned the whole blot into one gigantic headgear. Although this card proved most sensitive in eliciting blatant symptoms of anxiety, it does not prove fitness for theological studies if the subject deals with it adequately. The subject may very well prove successful in a different environment. Conversely, the group of successful seminarians had by no means a good record in this card, but the compensatory powers of the church exclude for many the unsettling effects of an unsupported, competitive situation.

CARD X

This last card follows appropriately the experience of existence in its most trying aspects. It tests the *attitude of the subject toward the future*. This effect is achieved by the following means:

- The card offers all the chromatic and achromatic colors in a great variety of sharply separated shapes. This symbolizes the freedom of choice among many possibilities which is a condition for our interest in going on with life.
- The card makes it nearly impossible to interpret it as a unified picture. All the preceding cards had a certain integration of form which created an illusion of a comprehensible wholeness. Like classical art, they conveyed a feeling that life has a meaning, even if it may be a tragic one. It is significant that the only satisfactory whole interpretations of this card are nature scenes. The many wide gaps between the single blots suggest the fact that we must make our decisions in a world which we perceive only in a fragmentary way. The practical-minded person accepts this fact pragmatically; the philosophically-minded person bridges the gaps by faith in science, economics, or God. To the seriously disturbed person, this last card represents a most distressing chaos of meaningless blotches.

That the best whole responses to this card are nature images suggests that the mysteries of nature convey most strikingly the idea of the incommensurability between the insight of God and man as expressed in the great speech of God to Job (Job, Chapters 38-40) and nowadays in the works of scientists like Eddington and Einstein. Card X then, tests that aspect of health which means the capacity for *making decisions in a world which is presented to us in a fragmentary way only,* in which life builds up to a gray top which is cut off abruptly, contrary to the rounded or pointed natural forms of all the other inkblots—an apt symbol of the seemingly arbitrary way in which our conscious lives end.[6] Thus, the last card seems to pose the question of what attitude the subject takes toward his future in the face of a reminder that it is based on a present which we cannot figure out and which ends in a gray mist, where finally our thread of physical life will be cut off.

The preceding analysis of the symbolism of Card X is given as an explanation for the similar conclusion about the meaning of it which has been reached independently by Ritey and Merei. Ritey called it "The Future," Merei, "The organism-environment field" (*der Lebensraum*) which in Lewinian terms is expressed as "the sum total of potential events ...: practical people ... give popular responses and like this card ..., those who dislike it have turned away from the world. In states of depression and blocking, the organism-environment field is contracted. People who fear life express this in the contents of their responses" (9).

In the group of inadequate seminarians more than half indicated clearly that they looked toward a future with the expectation that it would provide an opportunity for indulgence in oral dependency (12) and/or aggression (8). The aim of self-aggrandizement appeared in six seminarians who saw headgear in it. The basis of the underlying infantile anxieties was symbolized in seven cases by interpreting the usual blue "crabs" as spiders, praying mantises, or scorpions, although not all of them knew about the peculiar sex relationship in these animals: that the male plays a very inferior role and is devoured by the female as soon as the mating is finished, in case the female should be hungry. (The rationale of animal symbolism in the Rorschach has been discussed by this writer previously and cannot be gone into at this point.) (2)

It may be said in conclusion that I have found the Rorschach analysis on the basis of the symbolism of each card more enlightening than the classical method of scoring which is unsystematic about the meaning of the individual cards. This does not mean that the classical methods and rules of interpretation can be ignored. They underlie the preceding observations. The total score will continue to provide the basis for integrating individual personality traits into the broad categories of clinical diagnosis and typology. The latter, however, does not provide a specific enough description of the attitude of the subject toward the important issues of existence which are likely to affect his conduct as a minister.

Szondi and Drawing Tests

This examiner found the Rorschach test particularly illuminating because it tests the type of action and inaction with which the individual responds to a sequence of ten basic life situations. As was shown in the preceding chapter, this is accomplished by the feat of symbolizing such situations by nonrepresentational structuring of inkblots. This distinguishes the Rorschach from the so-called "projective techniques" which reflect individuals in their reaction to "unstructured material," a rather unfortunate expression since some structure is inherent in all "projective tests." Since in the Rorschach responses both personality structure and the structure of the individual plates are equally involved, it provides the most differentiated answer to the practical question: what can be expected from the candidate in those ten situations?

For a fuller understanding of the dynamics behind the candidate's behavior, its genesis can be clarified by the two other types of tests employed.

- The Szondi test indicates the relative strength of the constitutional needs forcing the individual to make choices between definite objects limited to eight distinct categories.
- The drawing tests give the candidate literally "carte blanche" for choosing how he wants to express himself as an organism, leaving all individualization of the basic forms: tree and human being, to him.

The two variables of approximately maximum and minimum freedom of choice provide information which adds significant perspective to the behavioral character appearing in the Rorschach; for example, in a case of aggressive behavior manifest in the Rorschach, the Szondi provides information whether the aggression is the result of strong drive or of lack of control, and the drawing tests indicate the acting-out tendencies when no specific environmental demands are made beyond the basic acceptance of a limited *Lebensraum*.

In proportion to experience and theoretical knowledge the individual examiner can gain a great deal of insight from the tests used by this examiner in an auxiliary function. It is suggested, however, that even an examiner with limited experience can benefit from taking the most obvious features of the Szondi and the drawings into consideration.

As far as the *Szondi test* is concerned, the pattern of the average candidate for the ministry was found by Harrower (5) and this examiner to tend in the direction of the following:

$$\pm h, \ -s, \ +e, \ -hy, \ -k, \ +p, \ -d, \ +m.$$

This suggests that this group attracts men with inner conflict about their strong affectionate needs, tendency to sublimate aggression, to keep it under moral control, and to repress exhibitionistic needs. Their ego is characterized by inferiority feeling due to the opposing forces of repressed egocentricity and need to become part of something greater than their ego; they are holding on to their old love objects and they find gratification in this limitation.

Of the 27 candidates who were asked to leave the seminary for personality reasons or because they themselves found that they had misjudged their fitness, only one had the above-mentioned "typical Szondi profile"; the other 26 showed the following distribution of deviating choices:

	h	s	e	hy	k	p	d	m
plus		2		3	3		1	
plus-minus		5	1	3	3	2	2	2
open	2	9	7	2	2	5	7	5
minus	1		10			4		
	3	16	18	8	8	11	10	7

The frequency of deviations seems to fit well with the type of prevailing problems found in the Rorschach and Machover tests. Aside from the formal evaluation of the profile, the self-revelations in the associations to the likes and dislikes often prove very valuable. This means that the unsatisfactory group deviated little from the average group with respect to their needs for affection and control of self-display, their repression of narcissistic ego needs and of object enjoyment. *The deviations occurred definitely in the direction of aggressive needs, resentment of moral strictures on acting out, weak or ineffectual need for fusion with something*

greater than the ego, and indiscriminate reaching out for objects for enjoyment.
The spontaneous associations with the Szondi pictures enhanced further the impressions gained from the formal profiles.

In the *Machover tests* of the failing group of seminarians, the frequency of gross disproportion in size between the pictures of the two sexes was particularly striking. This fact and the different nuances of the sexual image are best appreciated by placing the two drawings on top of each other and holding them against the light, so that the spontaneous placement of the two sexes in space as well as the actual sizes (by bringing the feet on the same level) can be compared. In this group it was particularly striking that 13 drew the male at least one head taller than the female, 7 drew the female at least one head taller than the male. In many the disproportion was even more emphasized under the influence of oral fixations: 6 of the males and 4 of the females were drawn with their nipples exactly on the level of the mouth of the opposite sex, and two males with their genitals on the level of the mouth of the female. On the other hand, there were 5 candidates who expressed their narcissism by drawing the two sexes practically identical in outline, features, and size.

It may be mentioned that the procedure described did not include *intelligence tests,* because most Episcopalian candidates are college graduates. This omission appears justified still, although 8 seminarians had to withdraw on account of academic failure. In going over the tests of these men, the conclusion was reached that their failures were due to their being inadequate personalities, more concerned with their personal needs than with the interests of the church. What inhibited their studies was the result of more or less conscious guilt feelings over trying to get something they did not deserve. The fact that they impressed the Dean and Faculty as "good personalities" supports this interpretation. Apparently they had a conscience about what they had been trying to accomplish.

Evaluation of the Candidates

First of all, it should be pointed out that this examiner has been extremely cautious in his conclusions about the potentialities of candidates. He confined himself to a description of the personalities, leaving it to the Bishop and the Dean, respectively, how much weight they would attach to his evaluations. This caution stems from the fact that in the ten years preceding the obligatory examination of all candidates the writer had the opportunity to examine 46 priests and 35 seminarians because they required psychiatric consultation. He became very much impressed by the fact that many of them had distinguished themselves before and after his contacts with them, although their personality limitations were clear from the psychological tests as well as from the difficulties which had brought them to a psychiatrist. This incongruity is due partly to the special conditions of the ministry discussed in the second section of this chapter, partly to the fact that psychological tests do not give any clear indication of one of the most important qualities of the "ideal" minister: his *spirituality*. The projective techniques used indicate the organization of the personality, but not the spiritual values for which this organization is used. We know from psychoanalysis that any one of the primary instinctual processes can lead to the integration of spiritual values into the personality. This may be considered an empirical fact even though the interpretation of such developments as "sublimation of sexual libido" can be questioned. Persons are found in the ministry who are in one or more respects seriously handicapped in their human development, but they are capable of being inspired by the values of the church to such an extent that they literally "surpass themselves" in their functions as ministers. For instance, some may appear under close scrutiny so narcissistic about their gifts that they do not seem likely to be inspired or inspiring, but experience has taught this writer that the church and its individual members owe a great deal to narcissistic ministers. There are certain indirect conclusions one may draw from projective tests regarding the spiritual potential of candidates—for instance, the positive "p" reaction to the Szondi found very often in this group by Harrower (5) and this writer; but it is by no means a reliable indication. On theoretical and empirical grounds the best psychological method to appraise spirituality appears to be graphology, but the lack of trained graphologists in America makes this an impractical suggestion.

The evaluation of the candidates was informed particularly by the findings in the 27 seminarians who had to withdraw from General Theological Seminary one or two years after the psychological examination, during the first five years of the program. In addition to the eight who were considered inadequate personalities by the Faculty, and eight who were academic failures, five proved to be overt and uncontrolled homosexuals,[7] two agreed that they had no vocation, one left because he developed a functional heart condition, two became Roman Catholics, and one withdrew for financial reasons.

Of the results of this investigation of postulants for the Episcopal ministry it may be said: on the positive side, the methods used establish the importance of balance between the introversive and extratensive sides of the personality, the control of aggressiveness, and the capacity for collective identification.

On the negative side, it was found that the following characteristics occurred frequently in a group of 24 seminarians who were found psychological failures:

- Insecure but ambitious men who expected to attain prestige and power through the supporting medium of the church.
- Emotionally frustrated men who had known the church as a source of security which they had not found in their childhood homes. This group often has problems of overt or latent homosexuality.

The difficulty of evaluating this group for the church authorities stems from the fact that the undesirable traits mentioned occur also in those who prove satisfactory. Except in extreme cases, it is not possible to measure reliably the *strength* of the undesirable tendencies in any statistical way as resultants of plus and minus points in the four different tests used, since the different levels of psychological functioning are mutually interdependent.

In comparing the evaluations of the withdrawals made by this examiner with those made by the Faculty of General Theological Seminary, fair agreement was found in most cases, excepting seven in which I found by hindsight that I had not considered certain features of the tests subsequently found to be of considerable significance for the adjustment of Episcopal candidates and discussed in the second section. Furthermore, these cases had been examined before the present procedure had been fully developed: three were blind diagnoses taken by a tutor at General Theological Seminary in clinical training (altogether 55 seminarians were diagnosed during the first year without personal contact), and none of the seven had been given the task of a written self-evaluation which forms now an essential part of the psychological examination. Obviously no personality evaluation can be made foolproof. Yet, in the opinion of the Bishop and the Dean involved, the method followed has provided valuable enough insights into the personalities of the candidates to warrant the considerable financial investment of the church and to encourage the publication of the experiences made.

In communicating the results of the evaluation to the church authority, the current practice of evaluating candidates in terms of psychodynamics and clinical diagnosis is not useful. Psychiatric statements about the "case" may be theoretically correct, but they may be practically misleading because the psychiatrist or clinical psychologist is inclined to draw conclusions on the basis of symptoms in tests and biography which he is used to encounter in patients seeking therapy. He has generally no experience with the intimate history and psychological tests of the many individuals who fulfill important social functions in spite of impressive psychological distortions. The purist may feel that all "sick" personalities should be kept out of the ministry, but this writer is convinced that screening out candidates on the basis of psychiatric classifications would deprive the church of some of its most valuable ministers. As was pointed out earlier: there is no way of evaluating the spiritual strength of a person which may decide the outcome of the specific problems.

The task demands from the examiner careful weighing of the psychiatric mechanisms and their influence on the ministry in each individual case, taking into account the basic personality and the demands of the family and of the ministry. How this can be done is not likely ever to be caught in a formula. The best the examiner can do is to describe to the church authorities the way in which the candidate reacts to certain basic situations of existence. For this task, the symbolic demands of the ten Rorschach cards and the quality of the candidate's self-evaluation provide a valuable base. In discussing with the candidate his particular problems and the discrepancies between his self-evaluation and the judgment of the psychiatrist the examination assumes a therapeutic function and actually improves the likelihood that the candidate will live up to the demands of the ministry. In presenting the candidate to his clerical supervisor as a functioning human being, not as an instance of psychiatric mechanisms, the task of the pastoral relationship is often helped by focusing the attention of the candidate and pastor on the significant problem areas. Often the candidate is helped to risk a sincere relationship with his superior and not only does he benefit personally, but the experience gives him also the basis for his own future work as a pastor.

REFERENCES

1. The present report is based on a paper read at the meeting of the New York Society for Projective Techniques on October 15, 1953. I am greatly indebted to Bishop Washburn of Newark and Dean Rose of General Theological Seminary in New York for having provided me with reports on the later developments of the man examined; furthermore to Beatrice Booth, B. A., for having tabulated the many data underlying the report. The latter was not published in the *Journal of Projective Techniques* because the editor felt that the new approach to the evaluation of the Rorschach should not be presented to the profession without statistical validation. This writer is convinced that it would be more in the spirit of Rorschach's original presentation to explore the clinical usefulness of additional formal concepts than to engage in premature statistical experiments. The whole accomplishment of present-day Rorschach psychologists rests on Rorschach's lead in psychological thinking about the meaning of various types of form perception. In the course of the last four years the new approach suggested has proved its usefulness in the analysis of many other clinical problems. A thorough presentation of these observations is in preparation. As will be pointed out in the following, concepts similar to those used by this writer have been discovered independently by the research workers in three other countries: Hungary, Italy, and France.

2. What traits or characteristics of the applicant's personality would make for, or tend to lessen, his effectiveness in the ministry of the church? (In answer to this question, the Examiner is requested to report such information, or impressions, as he is able to obtain concerning the following matters:

   - Rigidity of thinking and particular areas where it appears.
   - Potential intelligence and ability to use it.
   - Attitudes toward those in authority and the applicant's own use of authority.
   - Feelings about men, about women, about sexual aberrations, about his past sexual experience, his present situation, his expectations.
   - Uses of aggression, creative and destructive.
   - Capacity for group relationships, and sense of community or of collective values.
   - Types of situations that create anxiety and his reactions to them.
   - The place of religion in his emotional life.
   - His psychological motivations for desiring to enter the ministry.
   - Insights into his own strengths and limitations.
   - Special abilities or outstanding qualities of leadership.)

3. For technical details and theoretical explanations see my previously mentioned paper on axial responses, specifically pp. 373ff. and 376ff.

4. All figures refer to the 27 out of 163 seminarians who were asked to withdraw during the first four years of the testing program. The figures were not brought up to date because the following years confirmed the conclusions drawn from the first group and no statistical use of the data is contemplated.

5. Merei's explanation that the conspicuous white space "provokes responses to it and thus aggression is provoked" seems unconvincing to this writer. Primary aggressive

tendencies are manifest in the Rorschach test either in the reactions to red color ("extravert type") or in the movement responses projected into the black parts ("introvert type").

6. This treatment of the gray appears particularly relevant if one compares it with the crowning gray in Card VIII. There it ends organically as the "top of a tree or mountain." Sometimes the top small detail is even elaborated into a "monument" or "castle." This fits with the general optimistic character of Card VIII. Only a very few people notice that the top is split, in other words, are conscious of the tragic limitation of human consciousness, even when it is made easy to forget about it.

7. Homosexuality as such is not a reason for rejecting a candidate. Those with homosexual problems are expected to recognize the need for psychotherapy, as well as to exercise the same self-control in their human relationships which is expected from heterosexual seminarians.

BIBLIOGRAPHY

1. ABEL, THEODORA, "The Rorschach Test in the Study of Cultures," *Journal of Projective Techniques,* 1948, 12, 79. See also *Themes in French Culture* by RHODA METRAUX and MARGARET MEAD (Stanford, Calif.: Stanford University Press, 1954).

2. BOOTH, GOTTHARD, "Organ Function and Form Perception," *Psychosomatic Medicine,* 1946, 8, 367.

3. ————, "Objective Techniques in Personality Testing," *Archives of Neurology and Psychiatry,* 1939, 42, 514.

4. ————, "Art and Rorschach," *Bennington College Alumnae Quarterly,* 1956, 7, No. 2, 3.

5. HARROWER, M. See Susan Deri: *Journal of Projective Techniques,* 1954, 18, 33.

6. ————, and STEINER, M. E., *Large Scale Rorschach Techniques* (Springfield, Ill.: Charles C. Thomas, 1954).

7. KOCH, KARL, *The Tree Test* (New York: Grune & Stratton, Inc., 1953).

8. MACHOVER, K., *Personality Projection in the Drawing of the Human Figure* (Springfield, Ill.: Charles C. Thomas, 1949).

9. MEREI, FRANZ, *Der Aufforderungscharacter der Rorschach-Tafelen,* trans. by Dr. Stefan Neiger (Innsbruck, Austria: *Institut für Psychodiagnostik und angewandte Psychologie,* 1953).

10. MINKOWSKA, F., *Le Rorschach* (Brussels, Belgium: Brouwer, 1956).

11. PHILLIPS, L., and SMITH, G. S., *Rorschach Interpretation,* Advanced Technique (New York: Grune & Stratton, Inc., 1953).

12. ROEMER, G. A., "Vom Rorschachtest zum Symboltest," *Zentralblatt f. Psychotherapie,* 1937, 10, 310.

13. ————, *Die Vortrage der 4. Lindauer Psychotherapiewoche* (Stuttgart, Germany: G. Thieme, 1954).

14. RORSCHACH, H., *Psychodiagnostics* (New York: Grune & Stratton, Inc., 1942).

15. SPITZ, CHARLOTTE, *Rorschachiana III* (Bern, Switzerland: Hans Huber, 1947).

16. SZONDI, L., *Experimentelle Triebdiagnostik* (Bern: Hans Huber, 1947). See Susan Deri, *Introduction to the Szondi Test* (New York: Grune & Stratton, Inc., 1949).

17. ————, *Trieb-Pathologie* (Bern: Hans Huber, 1952).

18. ZULLIGER, H., *Einführung in den Behn-Rorschach Test* (Bern: Hans Huber, 1941).

ROBERT C. LESLIE ॐ

Time and again the editor and writers of this book have pointed out the essential significance of the personal development which alone helps the minister to be a real pastor to his parishioners. Robert C. Leslie, of the Pacific School of Religion, has made this task the central focus of his chapter. Far from promoting a closed-in spiritual exercise which would transform a young human being into an efficient but stoic functionary he would bring to this educational process the fullest possible experience. Since the minister will have to serve in this world he should grow into understanding his environment. Moreover, he should understand it better than his fellow men since he can recognize the deep-seated religious aspect of all that which otherwise may appear trivial and burdensome. But whether he can render this service of interpretation depends on whether he can open up his spontaneous potentials of innate curiosity.

Leslie is careful not to detach personality growth from the rest of the student's studies. Only after he has begun to marvel about the intricacies and wonders of life at large will he gain respectful attention for the way past generations have marveled at the same life and the same faith with which he is concerned today. The concern for the student as a human being leads Leslie to emphasize the Socratic teaching method. To teach the student "something" fills him up with a content which he possibly neither digests nor therefore can ever put to use. All the wealth of traditional Christian thought will never enable the student to meet as minister the unpredictable complexities of unique lives and situations. To teach how to learn is perhaps the most difficult task in any education. But to teach to keep wondering and asking for new solutions in the light of what the past had to offer is a still higher task.

Leslie comes to the real core of the problem in theological education. The student can be taught successfully only if he is taught to question and search. This can be taught only by a professor who himself is still open-minded, searching, and questioning. The question of why theological students seek the ministry as a career above all other professional opportunities leads to the question of why theological teachers have chosen their career. Leslie is right in his assumption that sometimes a theological teacher has escaped the direct struggle with the world by becoming a scholar and the representative of a discipline in knowledge which is not to be questioned on the basis of mere human reason.

The conclusion from Leslie's chapter is simple. The faculty in theological schools should not waste its time by discussing all kinds of curricular questions and possibilities of student activities before it is clear that the professors themselves are capable of preparing young men for the ministry. Helping the theological student to dare to be himself is the approach and aim of Leslie's suggestion. No technical changes will do the job before the faculty dares to face its own personal involvement in the constant growth above all scholarship and teaching methodology.

Helping the Theological Student
Dare to Be Himself

ROBERT C. LESLIE

The mood of the times is often presented more accurately in the theater than in any other area of life. Thus it is not strange that Archibald MacLeish's "J.B." has evoked a response on Broadway which, although astonishing the religious world, has only verified MacLeish's contention that man is eager to consider the ultimate questions of life. However unsatisfactory "J.B." may be in its humanistic solution to the problem of suffering in the love of a woman for a man, there is no doubt that the playwright has raised the questions about the meaning of existence with which the religious world has to come to terms.

But it is not only the message of "J.B." that interests us: we are also attracted by the method of its staging. As presented on Broadway, the entering audience finds the curtain already raised with the stage in full sight. The play begins with two vendors of popcorn and balloons (God and Satan) making their way down the aisle, sauntering onto the stage, talking as they go. The audience is carried with them onto the stage and never loses its sense of personal involvement. In a similar way a recent presentation [1] of "Lost in the Stars," the musical drama based on Alan Paton's Cry, the Beloved Country carries the chorus out beyond the stage on either side of the orchestra seats so that the audience feels more like participants than like spectators. And in like manner the production of "The Caine Mutiny," using no scenery and a minimum number of props, declares implicitly that it is the interaction between people that counts whereas the details of the surroundings are unimportant. So the theater speaks loudly to the world at large to stress the significance of personal involvement in a day when alienation and separation are characteristic of the culture.

This same stress on personal involvement is creeping more and more into psychological thinking. Harry Stack Sullivan's interpersonal theory, Martin Buber's I-Thou relationship, and Moreno's spontaneity theory have all made more articulate

127

the need for the therapist to be participant as well as observer, to enter into a relationship with persons as subjects rather than objects, to be free enough to permit natural spontaneity to override calculated strategy. Ferenzi's insistence on a more active therapist has been underscored by Jung and most recently by Carl Rogers. An increasing segment of the therapeutic world is declaring that the heart of the healing relationship lies in a genuineness on the part of the therapist that permits his own unique person to become involved in the therapeutic task.

That the matter of personal involvement is a major concern for theological students can be testified by every teacher of pastoral counseling. No topic arouses more heated discussion in my classrooms than this; no topic demonstrates more clearly the personal rigidities of the individual students than this. Because the question is so basic and because so much of method and attitude hinges upon one's convictions at this point, I have chosen to focus the major attention in this discussion on the question of personal involvement.

One student at the end of a significant period of clinical pastoral experience evaluated his progress with this summary statement: "I can now dare to fail." The insight shown by these words strikes me as being quite tremendous. Here is a man who has found the freedom to be himself, even though the attempt at self-realization may lead to failure in some specific tasks. He has sensed that more important than following any prescribed method, more significant than the application of proved theory, is a free and natural exposure of himself in a genuine relationship with another person where manipulation is rigorously avoided but spontaneous interaction is invited. This student's statement carries some of the same overtones that Carl Rogers has been writing about recently. Rogers' words are: "I launch myself . . . ; I risk myself . . . ; I let myself go. . . ." A fuller statement of his words reads as follows:

> I am not consciously responding in a planful or analytic way, but simply in an unreflective way to the other individual; my reaction being based (but not consciously) on my total organismic sensitivity to this other person, I live the relationship on this basis.[2]

One of the ablest teachers I have ever known, the clinical director of a great psychiatric institution, reinforced the emphasis of Rogers' thinking as he asserted to a young chaplain that the chaplain's effectiveness in work with psychotic persons would not be dependent on his role as a parson but on his ability to relate as a person.[3]

Yet to dare to be a genuine person is to present the average theological student with a formidable task. For the most part his professional training tends to depersonalize him into a theologian who knows the true view, or a scholar who recognizes the right theory, or an educator who demonstrates the proper technique. And if he fits the cultural pattern of the "organization man," as most seminarians do, his sensitivities as an other-directed person are radar-sharpened to fit into the group with a loss of individuality in the interest of a superficial togetherness.

Moreover, if the seminary curriculum itself does not work against the free developing of selfhood, the experience in the field often does. One student, for example, who had scarcely ever attended church school, found himself teaching a church school class of adults who expected him, as a minister-to-be, to have thought through all the questions of faith which were bothering them and to be able to articulate his position with clarity and persuasiveness. No wonder that he felt driven back to traditional orthodoxy and away from free inquiry! The more fortunate student is introduced more gradually to the role of prophet and priest, but even he feels the pressure to arrive at beliefs he can articulate in the first sermons, and this very pressure tends to solidify his thinking into traditional patterns whether they make sense to him or not. The price of certainty not only is the loss of the open mind [4] but, as Carl Rogers points out, leads easily to attitudes that are socially destructive for those who follow.

> If, out of fright and defensiveness, I block out from my awareness large areas of experience—if I can see only those facts which support my present beliefs, and am blind to all others—if I can see only the objective aspects of life, and cannot perceive the subjective—if in any way I cut off my perception from the full range of its actual sensitivity—then I am likely to be socially destructive, whether I use as a tool the knowledge and instruments of science, or the power and emotional strength of a subjective relationship.[5]

The loss of free individuality may not only be destructive in relationships with parishioners but also be deadly in family interaction. Many of us in the seminaries are beginning to sense a responsibility to assist in the growth and development of the wives that more and more of our students are bringing with them to school. If the pressures of school and church are in the direction of the loss of unique personhood for the ministerial student, they operate with even greater force on his wife. One commentator, writing on this predicament under the caption "Why Young Ministers Are Leaving the Church," declares:

> Forced by convention to play the role of the man who thinks he must be God to his family, his church, and his society, the minister in far too many instances dominates the private, intellectual, creative, sexual and spiritual life of his wife until all that is human and alive and beautiful is crushed within her. . . . She is expected to say the "right thing" and to do "the nice thing" if it kills her. And it often does kill her—the real self God gave her.[6]

Desiring to emphasize the aspects of his role for which he feels himself best suited, but feeling compelled to fit the role-expectations of society, the minister often capitulates and in so doing loses his zest for his work. How to keep free to remain an individual in the presence of expectations of the role established by the slow-moving tradition of the religious society is a constant problem for him.

Even if the minister manages to maintain his unique individuality in his parish and in his home, the cultural expectations of society work toward fitting him into a mold. Take, for example, the decision to enter the ministry itself. In the study entitled *The Advancement of Theological Education* James Gustafson points out that a significant number of men are coerced into the ministry by pressures from home and/or home church.[7] Any counselor of theological students knows how strong the pressures are on such a man to stay in the vocation even though by personal inclination and aptitude he may be better fitted for other work. Or consider the discrepancy between the minister's perception of his task and the role-concept held by the parishioner. Whereas most ministers (and theological students) stress the tasks of preacher, teacher, and priest (counselor), the parishioners place first emphasis on administration with the organizing and pastoral functions all preceding the work of preacher, teacher, and priest.[8]

The task, then, that confronts a department of psychology and counseling in a seminary, is clearly set forth. Its major thrust is to help the theological student dare to be himself, to develop the God-given uniqueness that makes him distinctively himself, even as he strives to sharpen his skills in pastoral relationships. How the task can best be carried out is the concern of the remainder of this discussion.

If the task of the department of pastoral psychology and counseling is perceived as being concerned with helping the student to develop his own uniqueness, then it is apparent that creating an experience becomes a more significant part of the teaching task than does imparting knowledge. If the growth of the student toward greater selfhood is involved just as much as the acquisition of knowledge, then, as in the therapeutic endeavor, something different from presentation of fact is needed. When Frieda Fromm-Reichmann declares that "the patient needs an experience not an explanation"[9] she is asserting that self-discovery cannot be taught but can only be learned in self-appropriating ways. Carl Rogers cites Kierkegaard regarding this kind of learning:

> Kierkegaard regards this . . . type of learning as true subjectivity, and makes the valid point that there can be no direct communication of it, or even about it. The most that one person can do to further it in another is to create certain conditions which make this type of learning *possible*. It cannot be compelled.[10]

To create the conditions that are proper for self-discovery in increasing measure is a major concern of pastoral psychology.

To be sure, experience in field work moves toward this same goal of growth through experiential encounter. Where field work placement is able to meet the student's growing edge, where adequate opportunity for supervision is provided, where the assignment is conceived of more as an educational experience for the student than as cheap help for the church, and where the student is related to other students struggling together with similar problems under guidance—where these conditions are met the opportunities provided by field work are very genuine. But even so the focus of attention remains on the problems in the field and not on the attitudes within the student. In capable hands, field work can assist in providing the desired experience that encourages self-discovery, but by itself it seldom completes the task.[11]

A closer approximation to the task is found in programs of clinical pastoral training, especially as these programs are of twelve weeks' duration in a setting where close supervision is provided by a capable chaplain and the full resources afforded by the group experience are utilized. Reuel L. Howe gives what is now a classic statement of the expectation that the seminary holds for clinical training:

> As a result of these experiences in training, I want my students to be confronted by themselves, by other people, by the needs of men, and the great questions growing out of existence. I want them "dunked"—plunged deeply into life, brought up gasping and dripping, and returned to us humble and ready to learn. Until all students are faced by the tragedies, the contradictions, and the stark questions of life, they cannot understand the need for redemption or God's redemptive action.[12]

That most students taking clinical training *are* plunged deeply into life and come up with a renewed appreciation of themselves is quite clear from the testimony that is readily available. So one student writes:

> I am gradually coming to a whole new depth of understanding and, consequently, a whole new order of experience. I have always been aware that my defenses and those of other people are strong determinants in interrelationships, but till now I have come only to halfhearted, indefinite grips with that fact. I feel that at least I'm grasping the problem and that already it's making a difference in my relationship with others. It will make a profound difference in my Christian witness.

To help the student in facing the "whole new order of experience" is obviously the task of the entire seminary; the seminary needs to be related to the clinical training center program in a vital and reciprocal way. But even though clinical training provides the best opportunity for growth in self-knowledge, it is not easy to relate this specialized training to the ongoing seminary curriculum, and so further approaches need to be explored.

There is a sense in which self-discovery is involved in all the course work of a seminary, since the subject matter of the theological school curriculum can be conceived of as contributing to (or standing in the way of) deeper self-knowledge. In actual fact, however, it is the rare class which sees itself as involved in both an educational and a therapeutic task. Indeed, all too often the creating of a climate conducive to learning is overlooked under the pressure of accomplishing the information-gathering task. Thus, even though real learning may be thwarted by "selective inattention,"[13] it is seldom that real effort is made either to ascertain the emotional climate of the classroom or to eliminate barriers to communication.

Indeed, the seminary would do well to examine the relationship between the practices of the classroom and the nature of the church. If we are correct in assuming that more real learning takes place in the experiential situation than in any amount of talking or preaching, then it would follow that the nature of the church is being *demonstrated* in the classroom more clearly than it is being expounded through lecturing. Ross Snyder who develops this concept at some length declares:

> ... While a class is not a church, it must partake of the essential nature of a people of God whose nature is ministering. ... There are ministries to be performed in the class enterprise. ... These ministries are performed and experienced in the encounter between professor and students, between student and student.[14]

Snyder's point is not only that it is in the varied relationships that go on in the classroom that the nature of the church is taught, but that both professor *and students* carry the responsibility for the enterprise.[15] The direction of Snyder's stimulating thinking is indicated in his descriptive titles of the ministries performed in the seminary classroom: the ministry of (1) authentic existence, (2) personal revelation, (3) understanding and midwifery, (4) the great conversation, (5) the pulse of tradition, (6) acting as corporateness.[16] In a summary discussion Snyder defends his position in these words:

> I ... have a deep feeling that you must be dealing with your central core of a person and not just the intellectual dimension. ... I think I'm feeling that deep down inside man is not different things such as will and intellect and so forth, but there is some kind of primeval stuff, at the core and at the heart of ourselves as persons.[17]

In order to implement the encounter with the authentic person both in the professor and in other students, the class obviously needs to be broken down occasionally into smaller units for complete communication, and needs to employ periodic feedback devices. Whether or not such an approach is deemed feasible or desirable in classes in the seminary in general, it is especially appropriate as a consistent emphasis in the pastoral psychology courses.

Having considered the importance of creating in the class the conditions that represent the church at work, we turn now to a specific consideration of course material in the department of pastoral psychology and counseling. If the focus of attention is on material to be covered, then it makes little difference when the basic courses are introduced, but if the emphasis is on the developing person, then the course work comes ideally in the first year when the question of the student's identity as a part of the professional religious world is being raised constantly. As the student is immersed in the seminary and as he is compelled to look at himself as a part of the world of professional religious workers, he needs to face the prior question of who he is as a person. His religious role may very well reflect the picture that he has of himself as a person. Our first task, then, is to help him to become better acquainted with persons in general and with himself in particular. And since we cannot assume prior knowledge in the psychological world, our task is to introduce him to the study of personality development with special attention to the religious encounter at each level of growth. Such a course easily becomes the basis for further work in religious education as well as in pastoral counseling and might be listed under a title such as "Personality and Religion."

Because of the wide diversity in background among those who come to the seminary, any basic course must be prepared to meet students at several different levels of sophistication. One way of meeting this situation is to rely heavily on case material,[18] since such material, when fresh and current, can be helpful both for the beginning student in psychological study and for the student who has an undergraduate major in psychology. The introduction of major personalities in the world of psychological thinking enriches the study of personality growth and at the same time introduces the student to original writings of those who have shaped current psychological thinking. Thus Freud may be cited for the biological start, Lewin for developing social relationships, Sullivan for the beginnings of altruistic love, Allport for the challenge of young maturity, Horney for cultural impact, Jung for middle age and Kierkegaard for ultimate concerns.

The real value of such a course, however, does not lie in the introduction of new concepts as much as it does in the relating of an individual life to the common problems of growth. At least two means are employed to accomplish this end. The first involves the use of a battery of tests given after admission as a part of the orientation week [19] and the second is the writing of an autobiography, drawing upon the deepened understanding from classwork and reading of both conscious and unconscious factors affecting personal growth (for example, unconscious motivation for the ministry). Although many students have already taken advantage of the opportunity offered to examine openly all the test profiles and to have the summary evaluation (written by a clinical psychologist) interpreted to them, others are motivated to look at their profiles by the emphases of the course and as preparation for writing the autobiography. An additional test is introduced at this point in the Edwards Personal Preference Schedule [20] with the plan of having the student take the test, then give himself a score on the 15 "needs" measured, then have his wife (or a close friend) give him a score on the "needs." His perception of his own needs is then compared with that of his wife's and both are examined in the light of the objective scores as seen in norm groups of the general population and of seminary students. When the same process is carried out by the wife, then a fruitful basis is laid for illuminating discussion. The use of the findings of this test (and the orientation battery) is encouraged in writing the autobiography, and the instructor encourages personal conferences to discuss any or all of this.

Although the focus of attention is on self-understanding in this basic course, a beginning attempt is made at understanding the self in the pastoral role by requiring at least one clinical pastoral contact with a verbatim interview write-up, evaluated and discussed by a graduate student (with role playing and other devices as seem appropriate). Indeed, throughout the course the context of the pastoral ministry is constantly referred to, and the psychological concerns are constantly related to theological issues with ample opportunity for the discussion of both.

It is to be noted that considerable resistance is encountered from some students in this introductory course. On the one hand, the resistance may be due to preconceived prejudices about psychology or, on the other hand, the facing of the determining influence of unconscious factors in personality growth may prove so upsetting that resistance develops. Moreover, the struggle for identity in the new and often confusing world of biblical scholarship and theological concern may be so great that the ego is not strong enough to consider its psychological make-up as well, and so a barrier to self-investigation is erected. By the same token, however, the plowing up of preconceived religious notions makes fertile soil for a reconsideration of personality factors and helps to make more possible the development of a mature self with a more developed religious sentiment.[21]

When the student has completed the basic "Personality and Religion" course he has laid the foundations for subsequent work in the pastoral psychology department and has had at least an introduction into self-discovery. Further courses keep both theoretical concepts and practical personal application in focus. We have already referred to the value of clinical pastoral training but emphasize now that the student comes to it best with at least this introductory basic course and, indeed, preferably with an additional thorough course in pastoral counseling. Recognizing, however, that full-time clinical pastoral training (as in a summer program) is not always possible, we sense a need within the regular curriculum for a somewhat similar experience. We attempt to meet this need with a course called "Clinical Experience."

Central in the "Clinical Experience" course is the student's growth in interpersonal relationships. As we utilize the clinical situations of general and mental hospitals, of state prisons and juvenile detention halls, of alcoholic clinics and of children's homes, the emphasis remains not on the patient or inmate or counselee but on the student counselor. In a sense the clinical setting itself is not significant; the weekly clinical contacts are used to make possible an investigation of the student as he reaches out to relate himself in therapeutic ways to others. His verbatim interview write-ups give him opportunity (in the analysis which follows the verbatim account) to evaluate himself in the actual encounter, and the supervisor's marginal comments push his thinking farther. The weekly seminar session with other students involved in a similar program provides further opportunity for evaluation of the developing relationship and, indeed, provides a group setting in which the interaction within the student group itself can be utilized as a further indication of habitual patterns of relating. The unique opportunities for self-understanding that emerge in the clinical training group, even in the one-day-a-week setting, are still only partially recognized.[22]

There is still another kind of experience which extends the opportunity for deeper self-understanding. This is the student group planned specifically for its therapeutic impact. Such groups may be purely voluntary on an extracurricular basis, introduced as "Human Relations" courses or as "Discussions in Interpersonal Relationships" (as our groups for wives and for couples are), or they may be courses carrying regular credit as a part of the curriculum.[23] Let us consider in some detail a four-unit course called "Interpersonal Relationships."

The hypothesis upon which the course "Interpersonal Relationships" is built is that knowledge about the self and others in group relationships comes best through participation in and critical evaluation of a significant group experience. Because of the well-established fact that therapeutic progress is dependent upon adequate motivation, this course is designated as an elective and is clearly defined as having a therapeutic orientation. The catalogue listing is as follows:

> The meaning of interpersonal relationships in individual and group counseling; an experience of group therapy for exploring the therapeutic opportunities in the group setting.

Enrollment is limited to ten, and the permission of the instructor is required in order to give further opportunity to make clear the nature of the course. The basic course, "Personality and Religion," is normally considered prerequisite, but diversified membership is desired, and so occasional persons, including women, are encouraged to participate from outside the seminary community. The intent is to provide a realistic laboratory in which personal involvement in a group can be experienced and evaluated.

In order to provide a variety of group experiences the course is set up with two dimensions: the first and major emphasis is the interacting group with the instructor serving as group leader-therapist; the second is an investigation of leadership technique with each student in turn participating as the discussion leader, thus having opportunity to demonstrate a leadership approach. Although these two dimensions are kept separate by assigning one day (a two-hour session) each week to each approach, the second tends to blend into the first. Both sessions are observed by a student-observer with the observation task rotating so that each student observes the group operating on the two levels and brings in a report (limited to seven minutes) to begin the therapeutic session.

The observer's report focuses on the emotional climate, on interaction on the feeling level rather than on the content of material discussed. This device in itself serves to sensitize the group to the tone of its meetings by identifying interaction (as perceived by the observer) as hostile, or supportive, or unemotional.[24] Moreover, by rotating the observer's role each class member has opportunity not only to sharpen his sensitivity to what is going on but also to have his perception of what has happened checked by the participants. In addition, the very nature of the observer's report (whether open and spontaneous or reserved and calculating) gives good insight into the typical approach of the observer and provides an immediate topic for consideration. Experimentation in the form of the report is encouraged with the result that statistical graphs and sociograms of interaction are often included.

The heart of the program, however, lies in the interacting group under the instructor's leadership. The instructor, perceiving his role as that of group therapist, refuses to play the usual authoritarian role of one who instructs but instead serves as catalyst for deepening communication on a rather personal and intimate level. He establishes two ground rules and enforces them but is otherwise quite permissive and accepting. The ground rules are that the group will focus on the expression of feeling and that the feelings dealt with will be the ones being currently experienced. That is, no agenda is provided, but the focus is on the feeling about the interaction going on in the immediate present, in the "here and now." Whenever conversation tends to move toward theory or toward impersonal ideas or toward irrelevant discussion the leader reminds the group of its primary task and invites a discussion of what led to the diversion. Personal reaction to group relationships is encouraged, including especially feelings felt toward the leader. Some biographical material is inevitably introduced, but it is encouraged only when it is relevant for an understanding of present feelings or reactions. An excerpt from one of my former students may clarify the leader's role:

> . . . I want to thank you for what I learned: how to keep quiet and listen to others; the whole concept of what you termed "unfinished business" . . . which meant that there was an interpersonal relationship in the group which had not been worked through; the surprising truth that there is no conflict that does not disappear if both people will go into the encounter and face the negatives and articulate them in terms of actual *feelings*—the road to a *yes* that leads through a *no;* your emphasis on the significance of nonverbal behavior . . . how we reject or accept each other by bodily movements, attitudes, posture; the confidence you gave each one of us by never stepping out of your role . . . always you were the leader and sat in the status position . . . (remember the time you were asked to pour coffee and you explained that you were not functioning in that capacity . . . even though you often did in your own home); your refusal to discuss any of us behind our backs . . . your continual emphasis on *getting rid of the things that keep people from loving each other.* . . .

It is obvious that participation in such a group experience is difficult for many. Our culture so trains us to mask our feelings that spontaneous participation in a group with a freedom of expression is seriously curtailed. When the training of the Christian community with its repression of angry and other negative feelings is added to the cultural trends of the secular world, then real resistance to free release of emotion is encountered. Yet, until each person dares to see himself as he is, dares to face the feelings that he has, dares to express the emotions that are present, the opportunity for true growth into emotional and spiritual maturity is denied. Within the context of the therapeutically oriented group, and under the leadership of a competent instructor-therapist, the opportunity for real personal growth in interpersonal relationships is tremendous. That the personal rewards are well worth the pain experienced in the growing efforts is the well-nigh universal testimony of those who open themselves to the group.

Recognizing, however, that some are not ready to enter into the life of the interacting group, a second dimension is added to the group experience. On this level the emphasis is on group leadership with a book of case studies serving as the point of departure. The book currently in use is called *Human Relations,*[25] a two-volume work with one volume devoted entirely to case studies in a variety of leadership problems and the other to readings in related theory. We have found that these cases taken from the secular world provide better opportunity for discussion than studies involving religious leaders since the secular cases give opportunity for identification with a wide variety of personalities. Considerable role playing is used to amplify the case material presented, thus providing opportunity for the kind of emotional interaction that the "make believe" of role playing creates. Discussion of both the leadership described in the cases and the leadership demonstrated by the student chairman for the period quickly involves the group in a very personal way and leads to further exploration of the group members themselves as they interact.

Up to this point we have been stressing the importance of helping the theological student to see himself as a unique person. We have implied that the task is complicated by the particular role which he will play as a minister, but we have only touched on the uniqueness of this role. Convinced that finding himself as a person is the first task, we have chosen to hold until now a consideration of the uniqueness of the ministerial task. When, however, the fledgling minister has dared to see himself as he is, has dared to risk himself, even inviting failure in the interest of integrity, he is then confronted with the special aspects of his role which define the uniqueness of the ministerial task.

To begin with, the ministerial role carries with it an exceptional status from the very beginning. Even the very young seminary graduate is accorded the respect and esteem of the community as he assumes leadership of his first church. His position puts him in a special relationship with his parishioners which no other professional person in our society enjoys; it gives him *entree,* uninvited, into the homes of the parish with a reasonable expectation of a warm welcome. It puts him in the position to receive privileged communication under the "seal of the confessional" at the same time that it places him in professional standing among the leaders of the community. The crises of life provide an opening for him into the personal lives of his parishioners, and in the common ventures of life he has a unique role as mediator of the faith (birth-baptism, growth-instruction, marriage-matrimony, vocation-commitment, adulthood-holy communion, illness-prayer, bereavement-grief work, death-faith). His routine contacts with his parish make possible the recognition of incipient problems which he learns to detect and work with before they develop to rupture the fabric of relationship. The fellowship of the concerned of which he is the leader provides group support for those who falter, and consecrated laymen multiply his efforts in supportive ministry.

This very variety of opportunity, however, carries with it some very special problems. For one thing, the role in which he functions always lacks clarity. Unlike the secular therapist who sees his patient in one structured relationship in an office setting, the minister seldom sees his parishioner in a structured counseling relationship and more often than not sees him in the context of two or more conflicting roles. To preach on social justice one moment only to step into the administrator's role the next with the prospect of serving as personal counselor to one who has sat under the preaching and worked co-operatively in the administrative task takes a very high degree of emotional maturity. As if the multiple role which he plays were not enough, every minister has to make the difficult decision about how far to go in his social contacts and at what point to become therapeutic. Given the opportunity to be the well-liked minister, he has to decide how committed he really is to the task of helping people in their growth (the therapeutic task), knowing full well that growth is never easy and that it usually involves suffering. Having the same need as his parishioners for intimate personal relationships, he nevertheless faces the question of how far he can go in meeting his own needs for socialization with his parishioners and when he must seek gratification for personal needs in contacts outside the parish.

But even if he manages to resolve these problems, he still faces the most basic demands of his role. He works not only within a human context of people in need, but he stands for the "supreme context" [26] within which the answers to life's deepest problems can be found. Tempted to adopt the premises along with the methodology of secular psychotherapy, he is compelled to re-examine his own beliefs about the nature of man and the nature of the universe. Preaching and teaching of a God-oriented world, he is compelled in the interest of avoiding a schizoid view of life to conceive of his counseling within a framework that sees purposive striving in life. Trained in the exact discipline of contemporary counseling, he is now required to relate his counseling task, and his therapeutic orientation, to a frame of reference larger than that conceived by any of the current schools of counseling.[27] Convinced through demonstration of the value of acceptance and the setting aside of judgment and condemnation, he is nevertheless confronted by the fact of the dual nature of the God he proclaims, of His justice as well as His love. Reading the Gospel records with new care he discovers that whereas Jesus always approached the searching questioner with loving acceptance, Jesus also did not stop with mere acceptance but invariably added a challenge to higher living.[28] The Christian counselor, then, is never unbiased; he stands within a tradition that seeks commitment to the highest values, to a life lived in a responsible way under God.

This very tradition, however, needs constant re-examination. In a theological age that stresses God's power and man's impotence, that declares man to be caught up in sin so thoroughly that the only way out is through the grace of God, clinical evidence seems to say that man, even mired down in sin, can find the way out. The testimony of the counseling room is not that man needs to be denounced as a sinner so much as it is that man needs help in seeing the source of power to rise above sin. The orthodoxy of theology needs to be challenged constantly by the existential situation which the clinic reveals.

Indeed, if the clinical study of man has any validity at all in the seminary course of study, it must constantly challenge the most orthodox positions of the faith. Recognizing how easy it is for the minister to retreat from the arena of conflict with secular views of life into the sanctuary of traditional ideas, the seminary has a special responsibility to impress upon the student that "there are no irreverent questions" [29] and that the movements of our time that seem to threaten the faith can serve as instruments to sharpen our understanding of certain weaknesses and oversimplifications characteristic of much religion, and at the same time help us see more clearly the truth of our own faith by pointing up the inadequacies of any single approach to truth.[30]

To introduce the student to the sharpest criticism of the faith (for example, Freud's *The Future of an Illusion*) is a significant part of the task. And to uncover the secularized distortions of religion that our culture endorses, whether it be the peace of mind cult or the religious community as the locus of social identity [31] is an equally significant task. To challenge dogma in the light of clinical observations, rather than to retreat into it or give lip service to it, is the special task of the clinically oriented person.

There is still one final word which needs to be said. Just as in the therapeutic task the burden of responsibility falls on the therapist, so in the educational task the teacher sets the pace that determines the outcome. Even though the student shares responsibility for what takes place in the classroom (as we have indicated above), it is the instructor who makes possible creative growth or who blunts the growing edge. Just as in a therapeutic group it is the therapist who establishes the climate of acceptance that encourages growth into new patterns of behavior, so it is the instructor from whom the students take the cue as to the nature of the class and the classroom procedure. One discerning senior described his experience with one instructor:

> The professor bore all things, our feeble attempts to think, to find ourselves, our anxieties and hostilities, in such a way as to help us transmute them into wisdom and into power to love people.[32]

But to fulfill the role of the therapist is not enough; to play a supportive role is only a part of the task. To become a genuine person in his *own* right the student needs to find in the *instructor* a genuine person, not only a scholar highly trained for his technical field but a man, a person struggling to clarify his perception of life, honestly facing his uncertainties, openly sharing his growing understanding of the faith. How can the student be expected to "risk himself" if the instructor never does so? How can the student dare to keep growing, sometimes in unorthodox ways, unless he finds his instructors growing? How can the student witness to his faith except as he finds his instructors witnessing? So a discerning senior student writes in evaluation of one of my classes:

> I believe that you are able to enrich my life and that of others far more if you would express your convictions concerning . . . how your Christian faith compels you to witness. . . . In your Christian conviction I might find a way to come closer to God.

And a graduate student, rejoicing in the freedom granted in an advanced seminar, speaks of what it means to strike out creatively even in areas which take him beyond the competence of the instructor. So the educational task proceeds, not in authoritative instruction but in a real meeting of minds, in a grappling with fresh insights, in a discarding of old prejudices, in creating a climate which fosters growth. And out of such an experience emerges the student who dares to be himself and so is able to help those whom he serves to become more truly themselves. And as each encounter is more genuinely real, the encounter with the eternal Thou takes on deeper and more personal dimensions.

REFERENCES

1. Festival Theater in Berkeley, California, August, 1959.
2. Carl R. Rogers, "Persons or Science? A Philosophical Question," *The American Psychologist*, X (July, 1955), 267-268.
3. Dr. Elvin Semrad at Boston State Hospital.
4. Cf. Allen Wheelis, *The Quest for Identity* (New York: W. W. Norton & Co., Inc., 1958), p. 232.
5. Carl R. Rogers, *op. cit.*, p. 278.
6. James B. Moore in *Harper's Magazine*, CXV (July, 1957), 68.
7. See the chapter "Theological Students: Varieties of Types and Experience," H. Richard Niebuhr, Daniel Day Williams, and James M. Gustafson, *The Advancement of Theological Education* (New York: Harper & Brothers, 1957), pp. 145-173.
8. Cf. Wesley Shrader, "Why Ministers Are Breaking Down," Life, XLI (August 20, 1956), 95-104.
9. Quoted by Rollo May, "Contributions of Existential Psychotherapy" in May *et al.*, eds., *Existence* (New York: Basic Books, Inc., 1958), p. 81.
10. Carl R. Rogers, *op. cit.*, p. 269.
11. Cf. Carroll A. Wise, "The Relationship Between Clinical Training and Field Work Supervision," *Journal of Pastoral Care*, VIII (Winter, 1954), 189-194 for a thorough treatment of this subject.
12. "The Role of Clinical Training in Theological Education," *Journal of Pastoral Care*, VI (Spring, 1952), 5-6.
13. Harry Stack Sullivan's term. See his *Conceptions of Modern Psychiatry* (New York: W. W. Norton & Co., Inc., 1940).
14. "Teaching-Learning the Nature of the Church Through Student-Professor Encounter," *Report of the Fifth Biennial Meeting* (Association of Seminary Professors in the Practical Fields, Boston, 1958), p. 98.
15. Snyder points out that 100 senior students in twelve different seminaries all failed to see that making a good class is a responsibility of the student as well as of the professor. *Ibid.*, p. 99.
16. *Ibid.*, pp. 100-106.
17. *Ibid.*, p. 107.
18. Cf. Robert White, *Lives In Progress: A Study of the Natural Growth of Personality* (New York: Dryden Press, 1952). This book contains three detailed case studies. See also Paul E. Johnson, *Personality and Religion* (Nashville, Tenn: Abingdon Press, 1957) for four briefer case studies.
19. Our battery includes: (1) *Academic Achievement:* School and College Ability Test (Scat) for a general academic ability index, quantitative and verbal; Nelson-Denny Reading for a speed of reading index; Terman Concept Mastery for an index at the upper limits; (2) *Vocational Interest:* Strong Vocational Interest Inventory; (3) *Personality Inventory:* California Psychological Inventory (CPI); Self-Rating Index; Background Information Blank.
20. Available through The Psychological Corporation.

21. Gordon Allport uses the term "religious sentiment" as he talks of maturity in religion. See his *The Individual and His Religion* (New York: The Macmillan Company, 1950).
22. Cf. Robert C. Leslie, "Growth Through Group Interaction," *Journal of Pastoral Care,* V (Spring, 1951), pp. 36-45.
23. For a discussion of a two-hour (once a week) course see Robert C. Leslie, "The Therapeutic Group Experience as a Course in the Theological School Curriculum," in Helen I. Driver, ed., *Counseling and Learning Through Small-Group Discussion* (Madison, Wis.: Monona Publications, 1958), pp. 346-349.
24. See an adaptation of Bales' Interaction Process Analysis in Helen Driver, *op. cit.,* p. 84, for a method of charting interaction.
25. Hugh Cabot and Joseph A. Kohl, *Human Relations: Concepts and Cases in Concrete Social Science* (Cambridge: Harvard University Press, 1953).
26. Gordon Allport's term. See his *The Individual and His Religion* (New York: The Macmillan Company, 1950), p. 142.
27. An exception to the current schools is Viktor E. Frankl who writes in *From Death Camp to Existentialism* (Boston: Beacon Press, 1959), p. 111: "... if psychotherapy and education aim to cope with existential frustration ... they must free themselves from any nihilistic philosophy of man and focus their attention upon man's longing and groping for a higher meaning in life."
28. Cf. Mark 10:17-22 (Rich Young Man): "And Jesus looking upon him loved him, and said to him, "... Go, sell ..., give ...,... come, follow ..." (10:21).
29. J. Wesley Robb (University of Southern California) in an address on August 29, 1959.
30. *Ibid.*
31. Cf. Will Herberg, *Protestant-Catholic-Jew* (New York: Doubleday & Co., Inc., 1955), especially p. 52.
32. Snyder, *op. cit.,* 106.

JAMES E. DITTES ໄລ

Yale Divinity School has taken up a new approach to the area of psychology of religion, pastoral counseling, and the supervision of the practical experience of its students. Through the appointment of one of its own graduates who afterward received a doctoral degree from the Yale Department of Psychology on a study in experimental psychology, both the practical and the theoretical facets of theological education are being dealt with and enriched in terms of psychological insights.

Professor Dittes recognizes among contemporary ministers a temptation to use pastoral counseling as a mistaken way of rendering the ministry relevant to the world. Instead of trusting the Protestant principle of justification by faith, these ministers appear to be struggling to justify their exisence through a heavy load of work which often deals merely with quite secular problems of their parishioners, problems which secular experts are far more qualified to handle.

He suggests, therefore, that ministers and prospective ministers seek rather to understand and to be true to their faith, making full use of psychology to this end, and hence permit their parishioners to open up their lives to the high potentials of the Christian faith. The all too few pages on which Dittes demonstrates the psychological significance of justification by faith, based on his own experimental study, promise in themselves a future to this specific approach in psychology of religion.

Dittes writes at length and with conviction on the problem of psychology in the curriculum of a theological school. Psychological studies as a part of the total theological enterprise make two different contributions. Psychological concepts of the personality, for instance, derived from empirical studies, are bound to revitalize the doctrinal and ethical thinking of theology. According to Dittes, they belong properly within theological studies as a means of asking constantly for the relevance of theological thought.

The second way in which psychology can be helpful to the prospective minister is to make him aware of the different and diverse loyalties which his profession will bring upon him. The minister is a man who is burdened by multiple loyalties which he has to integrate into a total unity in his work. Dittes is able to focus sharply on one of the most painful problems of the modern ministry which heretofore has often been so painful that the minister himself did not want to be aware of it. But to close one's eyes before reality does not solve problems, and the man who has to pay for it with his health and happiness is the minister himself. Dittes finds the average minister much too dependent on the satisfaction of being effective. He asks the disturbing question whether the ministers themselves have not enough faith on which to depend.

Although the concept of loyalty integration may not be so helpful as Dittes seems to hope, he certainly is to be commended to the readers both for his sensitive appreciation of the ministry and for his pointed suggestions.

Psychology and a Ministry of Faith [1]

◄§ JAMES E. DITTES

"A couple in my church has just been divorced," a recent graduate wrote me. "I wish I had taken more training in counseling in seminary." ("I could have prevented it with the right help from you," he implied.)

"Thank you for the course in counseling," another told me on a recent visit. "It's been an important part of my ministry. Just last week a man who had attempted suicide five months ago went back to work." ("See what I did with your help," he meant.)

A recent survey among several thousand ministers, typical of many such studies, discovered such facts as these: [2]

- Eighty per cent of the pastors want additional training in counseling.
- Counseling is the skill they most want to improve through special training, ranking well ahead of other skills such as preaching, training of lay leaders, leading of groups, worship.
- Counseling provides pastors with the greatest "personal enjoyment and sense of accomplishment" of any of their pastoral activities.
- Pastors feel that counseling is their most effective activity—although the average pastor spends just five hours a week counseling.
- Over one-half of the pastors feel that their seminary education was deficient in counseling, a far greater percentage than feel inadequacies at any other point in their seminary training.

Such testimony is overwhelming. It is in personal counseling that these ministers feel the hint or the hope of an effective, relevant ministry. If a seminary is truly responsive to such pleas, can there be any doubt or hesitation about the direction of curriculum developments? More and better courses in personal counseling seem to be the answer, including provision for supervised clinical experience in counseling, the necessary supporting courses in basic principles of psychology, and some provision for individual or group therapy for students as a necessary prerequisite to their own effectiveness as counselors.

143

Indeed, there *can* be doubts that this is the answer. Grave doubts. In fact those most sympathetic with the plight of these ministers and those most informed in the area of counseling will perhaps have the most doubts of all, the most doubts that training in personal counseling, however proficient, can provide a real resolution of the distress experienced by these ministers and enhance their actual "effectiveness."

This plea for more and more thorough training in counseling is—as counselors learn to say—largely but a symptom. It is a cry for help, for relief from distress. It is couched in the only terms they know, but these terms do not necessarily provide an adequate analysis of their situation. The situation is perhaps like that of a sick man begging his doctor for a dose of a new wonder drug. The drug may be effective for many things but not necessarily for this man's illness. The doctor must take seriously his patient's cry of distress but may not trust his diagnosis and prescription. Such resounding pleas for counseling must be taken as serious evidence that something is amiss and help is needed. But more training and proficiency as personal counselors may not necessarily provide so much help as these ministers now think. Let us attempt to look behind the symptom to learn more about the kinds of distress from which it originated.

Ministries of Good Works and of Faith

Personal counseling is resorted to by many theological students and ministers because it seems to offer a sense of purpose, relevance, and achievement which they crave for their ministry. The relevance is, in most instances, illusory and false: personal counseling is not nearly so effective as it frequently appears to the counselor to be and, when it is, its achievements cannot automatically be identified with aims of the Christian ministry. The fact that in spite of this so many men have turned so eagerly and so unquestioningly to counseling gives evidence of the powerful, even desperate, desires for "relevance" which lie behind this particular postwar rush. To analyze this situation in some detail may help us better to define what we should mean by making the ministry relevant.

Theological students—most of them—are distressingly perplexed. They feel powerful and emotionally deep attraction, even commitment—but they are not sure toward what. They hold highly general, often inarticulate, convictions and aims, but the translation of these into words and actions is tormentingly difficult. What Mark May wrote twenty-five years ago is just as true today. "Entering the ministry is like entering the army, where one never knows where he will land or live or what specific work he will be called upon to perform." [3] And we might add, one does not know quite why he is there in the first place.

We should add to this uncertainty two other factors, inadequacy and something like embarrassment. Theological students and ministers are painfully and sensitively aware—though again perhaps vaguely so—of the needs, even the yearning of their people for spiritual help. There are prescribed forms and procedures for the ministry, but somehow these seem inadequate and confining. How can the minister break through these and actually reach the persons where their need is? They don't easily see the way. In addition the students and the ministers are likely to feel more or less implicit demands on the part of family, friends, and society in general, to justify their profession. "Look at all these other professions, but what good do ministers do?" is the persistent challenge of college roommate, professor, and summer employer.

If something like this is the perplexing plight of many ministers, we can better understand the attractiveness of personal counseling. Counseling offers a relatively precise definition of goals, which appear to be consistent with the general ideals to which the minister has committed himself. Counseling provides the helpful specification of those ideals for which he has been searching. Counseling offers relatively concrete procedures, a formula for action, and moreover, a formula which the minister finds himself capable of following. Counseling offers the minister a well-regarded role. Psychology, especially in its clinical forms of healing, is currently in high popular regard. The skeptic and the layman can accept this activity as understandable, legitimate, and perhaps even helpful. To a minister, then, who may despair of ever knowing very clearly what he is doing and why, counseling appears to offer a way of making an effective impact on persons' lives of a degree and quality which he may otherwise never experience. The minister may sigh at the end of the day that at least those hours which he spent counseling accomplished something. Here, at least, he was able to enter meaningfully into another person's life with a relevant ministry. It makes little difference whether the minister achieves visible signs of improvement or relief from distress in the life of his counselee—though these can usually be found if it means enough to the minister to do so. The chief rewards are not in the long-range effectiveness but in the immediately available evidence within the interpersonal relationship that the minister feels he is understanding and being understood, dealing with important issues in a person's life and in turn being taken seriously.

Counseling is by no means the first, and probably not the last, specialization to hold out to ministers the hope of relevance. Its most immediate predecessor was the range of activities marshaled under the banner of social action. Specification of goals, formula for action, and popularly understood and accepted roles—social action provided the minister with all these and with the same general satisfaction of making his ministry relevant. One even may hazard the guess that personal counseling could not have achieved its popularity until that of the social gospel and social action had declined, and left ministers, many of them, again adrift. One may also hazard the guess that just as social action has now become well baptized, better integrated into the existing structure of churches and better grounded in theological and ethical soil, so may pastoral counseling be moving into the church.

Other contemporary resorts to relevance can be noted. Much of the current trend toward liturgics and sacraments can be understood in these terms; here are specific goals, formulae, and roles of another sort. A similar feeling of security comes to the minister who plunges too avoidingly into the organizational machinery of his church, either that which he supervises in his local church or the lattice work of committees along which he climbs in his ecclesiastical structure. Here again are the specifics and the tangibles offering rewards and satisfactions for which the minister thirsts. Heavy moralistic and pietistic emphases also provide some of these same rewards, the feeling of reaching into another person's life and apparently having an effect. For those ministers who found special comfort and satisfaction in their theological studies, there is the possibility of organizing adult study groups and of acquiring—as such discussions move over familiar grounds—a sense of impact and effect: "these people are learning, they are becoming more like me; soon they will know so much that I shall be able to have a bull session with them as I used to enjoy in school." Some of the ministries to specialized groups offer advantages of specification that a more general pastorate does not have. Here we must list campus ministry to students, inner city parish work (an interesting combination of social action and personal counseling), and, of course, college and seminary teaching.

Personal counseling, or any one of these other special forms, offers the appearance of relevance. But there is a real question whether such apparent relevance can stand up as genuine or whether it is largely an illusion which makes the minister and theological student feel better and more comfortable. Here we get to the main point of this discussion. Perhaps by examining carefully the possible deficiencies of personal counseling as an attempt to make the ministry relevant we can better define the actual relevance which we seek.

Counseling, as generally practiced, provides a ministry of self-justification and of good work, but not a ministry of faith. The minister feels both responsible for and capable of arranging, managing, and guaranteeing the spiritual—and, as this is usually interpreted, also the psychological and social—well-being of his parishioners. The conception of the ministry which is governing here is the call to build the kingdom—with construction targets, production quotas, precise engineering specifications, efficient mobilization of all resources, and frequent progress reports. To be relevant means to undertake careful and precise motivation and market research, to discover what the potential residents of the heavenly city want and/or need. Perhaps then the product is modified accordingly, or perhaps scientific methods of "education" and "communication" are employed so as to prepare properly the potential consumers and to guarantee that the product will receive the endorsement which it deserves. To be relevant means intricate job analysis and precise aptitude testing so that each worker in the kingdom can be assigned to that exact task and place in which he can derive maximum job satisfaction.

Or, if this conception of the ministry is not modeled upon that of modern industrial and commercial manipulation, perhaps it is modeled upon the image of a doting (heavenly) father, anxiously overindulgent, constantly hovering, supervising, directing, and interfering—all, of course, for the child's own welfare.

A recent film report on some new developments in physiological psychology includes a brief demonstration that may represent the essential orientation many ministers have toward their ministry. In the film the psychologist sits on one corner of a table. A rat is cautiously sniffing and moving around on the table, aimlessly at first. But the psychologist holds in his hand a control button connected by a wire to a tiny electrode planted permanently deep inside the rat's brain. As the psychologist begins to operate the button the rat begins to move toward a particular corner of the table (which we may label for our purposes "the good life"). As the rat gets to the corner the psychologist stands up, chalks a tally on the blackboard and announces, "I wanted him to go to that corner." The psychologist's electrode is able to administer sensations in the brain which apparently the rat feels as rewarding and satisfying. The psychologist in advance selects one corner of the table as "right," then carefully watches the rat's behavior, and every time the rat takes a step in the "right" direction he gets a rewarding sensation from the control button. Soon he is taking all his steps in the "right" direction. This may seem to many the ideal model for the relevant ministry, the ability to direct each person along the right paths for him. All that is missing perhaps is a separate electrode and control button which can deliver punishment for wrong steps.

I have also shown to my classes a longer film which seems to get across in a different way these alternative conceptions of the ministry. The film actually reports on recent developments in the treatment of mentally ill persons, apparently a profession in which both these orientations, self-justifying good works and faith, also prevail. In part of the film, busy, precise, white-coated scientists are describing new drugs capable of having important tranquilizing and other influences on patients' behavior. We are provided exact pharmacological names and formulas and precise statistics on the ways the patients are affected by each drug. At the climax of one scene a hospital official boasts happily, "We have greatly reduced the number of pillows and mattresses damaged by patients." Magnificient triumph of modern scientific medicine! But also an uncomfortably close parallel to the notion of the ministry held implicitly by many of us. To be relevant, just learn how to diagnose and prescribe, and all will be well.

Another part of the film begins to suggest an alternative orientation. It shows the pipe-smoking director of Warlingham Park Hospital in Croydon, England, leaning back in his chair and explaining how the hospital has removed all locks from its doors and all fences from its grounds. All mental patients in the area are admitted, no matter how severe, and treated according to this same open-door policy. More conventional forms of therapy are also used, but a critical factor in many recoveries appears to be the basic attitude of trust communicated through this policy. The director does not appear to know, or even to care very much, how and why this policy works. It simply seems to "bring out the best in people."

This, then, begins to suggest an alternative orientation toward the ministry. Opposed to the kingdom-building, electrode, syringe-needle conception, there is a view of the ministry based on trust. "The kingdom of God is not coming with signs to be observed . . . the kingdom of God is in the midst of you" (Luke 17:20-21). The minister is not responsible for knowing everything and arranging for the satisfactory outcome for all his flock, nor is he capable of it. He has limitations and turmoils and miseries, and so do his people; and redemption from these rests with God. There are resources for healing and salvation whereof the minister knows not. And even whatever healing flows through his ministry is probably neither due to nor enhanced by his own or his seminary's self-conscious efforts to make his ministry relevant. The minister has a role, but it is very different from that of social engineer or brain washer. He is simply to represent his basic confidence in these healing resources and to communicate this confidence through word, deed, gesture, posture, and whatever mode of interaction he as a person has with others. This may or may not happen in a counseling interview, in a sermon, an official board meeting, a ministerial association meeting, in his home, or any place else. The formal situation makes little difference; it is neither guarantee nor barrier. Through such grace, trust, faith, acceptance, other persons are set free, in large ways and small, to make use of resources of healing within themselves, within their community, within their church, and elsewhere.

This understanding of the ministry turns the problem of relevance around. Now it is not a matter of making a man's ministry relevant to the people but rather making sure his ministry is relevant to his faith. One must analyze his product for purity not his consumers for motive. It is not a matter of knowing when and where to insert the electrode or syringe needle and what kind of charge to load it with. It is a matter of appraising whether one's total mode of dealing with persons is consistent with, and communicates, the basic verities on which the ministry is founded.

Does this mean that the minister remains insensitive to and uncaring of the plights of his people? Hardly. On the contrary, he is more deeply and more selflessly concerned. He is concerned with a person's plight for what it means in its deepest dimensions, for the individual himself, not for the satisfaction he as minister can, perhaps unconsciously, derive from a busy manipulation and working for effect. The minister simply lives and acts in the trust that by making his own ministry relevant to his faith he can provide his people with the most effective possible help. This may open up to them all manner of healing resources which they could never find if the minister scrambled around looking for just the right answer to their problem. As in so many other things, he who seeks to save a life, often in that very seeking loses it. The self-justifying type of ministry, scrambling for effects and "relevance," so often defeats its very purpose. When the minister focuses on the things he can manage, he focuses on the trivial and secondary—the mattresses and pillows, the jot and tittle—and is distracted from the central and the important. Furthermore, the more or less frantic effort to probe and to analyze, to control and to manipulate, easily communicates to persons the anxiety and unrest which underlie it in the minister's own life and thereby denies the faith he claims to represent. But the minister who feels content to sit quietly by the hospital bed of a weeping man or to remain unruffled by the wrangle of an official board debate because he does not know what to do to stop the weeping or the wrangle, can in his very quietness become an instrument of healing—if his presence conveys to people the basic current of assurances and demands which underlie their lives.

To deny himself, then, the quest for a "relevant" ministry in terms of discernible impact and effect, the minister does not abandon his people but, on the contrary, holds up for them what he has both reason and faith to believe is the most adequate and effective type of ministry.

Consider this report from a person who, at a time of grief, happened to receive the attention of two ministers. "I found one intent on probing my feelings and making comments. He seemed self-consciously determined to apply to me a heavy dose of Bible, theology, psychology, and prayer. He made every effort to make these doses appropriate. But somehow I resented it. I found myself much more aware of the minister than of myself or of the deceased. The other minister seemed a bit distraught by the death, just as I was. He was new to the community and wasn't quite sure himself about which cemetery and which funeral director to recommend, or how one made arrangements with the cemetery. But he got on the phone and then drove around to the cemetery with me and helped me find out. I don't remember what we talked about, a little about the deceased, I guess, a little about the church, the weather, whatever seemed natural. I found myself deeply comforted and spiritually refreshed by this minister, although I can't recall anything that he said or did that was comforting or religious."

Aims of Psychology in the Theological Curriculum

The minister of faith is concerned with the study of psychology for two important reasons, and these define the proper role of psychology in the theological curriculum. He does not study psychology so as to see more clearly a target toward which he is taking careful aim. Primarily, he studies psychology so that he can better comprehend the fundamental realities of the universe in which he ministers, the dis-ease within and between persons, the yearnings for forgiveness and freedom, the conditions and terms in which these seem to be accessible. Second, the minister investigates psychological disciplines because he is concerned that he himself represent the ultimate verities as well as he can and because he knows that the degree and form of his representation are subject to psychological principles.

These purposes coincide with the twofold goal of theological education in general. Traditionally in the curriculum the two goals are recognized in the distinction between "content" and "skill" courses. The distinction, of course, is a false one. Theology and ethics are nothing if they do not well up out of and become reflected back into the experience and life of the minister. Similarly, study of the Bible and church history becomes a futile, abstract exercise except as it engages in a constant dialogue with the currents and concerns of the minister and his people. The task of making these "relevant" belongs squarely in the "content" classroom and may not be delegated to some other stage along the assembly such as that labeled Pastoral Psychology. Pastoral arts, on the other hand, is nothing if it is not the discovery by the individual of how he, in his unique individual ways, can internalize, represent, and reflect the "contents" of his faith and heritage.

It happens that psychology, of all parts of the theological curriculum, most obviously spans these two aspects of the curriculum. It is generally recognized that psychology is involved both in "content" and in "skills." But psychology is not unique in this respect. In principle every component of the curriculum should serve a similar spanning function until these two frequently isolated domains are in fact linked as one. The lines between theology and Bible and church history and other content areas are much more defensible than the lines, perpendicular to these, between content and skill. Theological education cannot be divided up into wholesale and retail departments with miscellaneous middle men in between, a status often ambiguously reserved for psychology. If theology is not made relevant to a man's ministry, no amount of counseling or study groups or other peculiarly psychological gimmicks will make it relevant. Psychology is a co-ordinate part of the theological curriculum with responsibilities for relevance no greater and no less than any other part of the curriculum.

However, if the distinction between these two stages of knowing—the cognitive and the behavioral—is a false one for actual practice, it is still a useful one for purposes of analysis and definition. The fact that psychology spans very easily both these foci has frequently led to confusion and ambiguity in the definition of psychology's role in the theological curriculum. Rather than performing both functions deliberately, psychology sometimes has blurred the distinction and performed one when it thought it was performing the other or fallen completely between. It will keep the exposition clearer if we look separately at these two functions of psychology, first at psychology as part of the theological discipline, broadly conceived, and second at psychology's role in the internalization and personalization processes traditionally associated with the teaching of the pastoral arts.

Psychology takes a place co-ordinate with other social sciences, history, biblical studies, theology, and philosophy as part of the enterprise of comprehending the fundamental realities of the life and the world in which a man ministers. Each of these disciplines is a partial one and each supplements the other. As psychology looks at the intimate dynamics of personal life, it may find itself in the position of telling the theologian what he really means by such things as sin and grace. On the other hand, theology will alert the psychologist to dimensions and ranges of personal functioning which he might overlook if he were oriented only to the perspective available from contemporary American psychology. Each of the disciplines also serves a corrective and critical function toward the others as methods of investigation. Theology and philosophy remind the psychologist of the limiting, restrictive nature of some of his presuppositions and the consequent limitation he must necessarily apply to his generalizations. On the other hand, psychology can remind the theologian and the philosopher of some of the limiting behavioral laws to which they are subject in their very act of theologizing and philosophizing.

There are beginnings here and there of the relationships between these disciplines being worked out in formal systematic intellectual fashion. But such systematic integration is an arduous process. For the moment we must still rely on those mysterious personal processes by which one person can put together in his own life various strands of insight and experience into a more or less unified personal outlook and mode of behavior—bypassing an intellectual rationalization. We shall give further consideration to this process when we return to the role of psychology in the personalization phase of theological education.

Among all the forms and labels by which psychology now appears in theological curricula, one form which is now relatively neglected deserves a central place, if we are to follow the implications of the assertions above. This is the psychology of religion. This is not the place to review the sixty years of this field except to note that its rise and decline were largely due to its close symbiotic alliance with religious education. It borrowed its problems and insights in great part from the concerns of religious educators. But the self-conscious and easily identified religion of children can be a largely peripheral and external thing. And as religious educators became more and more concerned with what was really happening inside the child, they found psychology of religion unable to keep pace. But the psychology of religion properly is not limited to the obvious phenomena of religion, worship, prayer, mysticism, and the like. Rather, psychology of religion takes as its object of study the deep and universal religious strivings and searchings of man. Sometimes the predicament and its various resolutions is termed religion and sometimes it is not. The strivings and the resolutions may frequently seem indistinguishable from the needs and processes that other psychologists study under such labels as anxiety, guilt, defensive adjustments, and the like. Indeed, they may be indistinguishable, except that the psychologist of religion comes upon them with a somewhat more comprehensive perspective and a potentially integrating theory. It may be that the psychologist of religion should define his field as being concerned with the deepest currents of human personality.

In its search, psychology of religion looks at miseries and torments of persons, at their aspirations and at their reminiscences of a more adequate state of affairs potentially within them, and at the many different processes by which persons are seeking, consciously or not, to move toward these aspirations. If some of the torments which the psychologist looks at under such labels as anxiety and guilt, or compulsion and phobia, or the depersonalization and desocialization of schizophrenic symptoms seem continuous with and related to conditions described in more conventional religious terminology, this increases our confidence that we are dealing with something fundamental and important. But we do not necessarily wait for such correspondences to appear before pursuing the investigation. Similarly, many of the "adjustment" processes which persons adopt may seem continuous with activities and outlooks which are conventionally regarded as religion. General processes, for example, of social group identification, or of rationalization and intellectualization, or of self-punishment, or of sublimation, all seem to have their counterpart in explicitly religious behavior. But we define our problem and look not only for illumination in terms of these overt phenomena of personality which provide dynamic for this religious behavior but for much else as well. These deeper processes rather than the overt phenomena appear to be the more proper subject matter of the psychology of religion.

Other psychological courses in the curriculum would derive their focus and rationale from this understanding of the psychology of religion, as the principal contribution of psychology to the theological curriculum. The psychology of religion, thus conceived, depends heavily upon general, "secular" psychological understanding of personality and of groups. Basic work in personality and in social psychology should be presupposed and regarded as a prerequisite to a course in the psychology of religion, and since it is unrealistic to expect most theological students to have had adequate work in college in this field, suitable provision should be made for such prerequisite courses in a theological curriculum. Psychology is a legitimate and useful science. In some respects the charge may be true that psychology only puts into words which nobody understands things which everybody understands. But very frequently the apparently slight difference between scientific psychology's way of putting something and common sense may represent a precision and a level of insight which make the difference between a useful comprehension of personal functioning and a frustrating inarticulateness. Everybody knows, for example, that personal insecurity breeds all kinds of behavorial aberrations. But this knowledge is so general as to be useless. On the other hand, the designation with some precision of those conditions of family environment or of group processes which define personal security and insecurity makes it possible to understand particular personal plights with sensitive insight. The term anxiety is in such common parlance as to be meaningless and useless. The attempts to specify rigorously the characteristics, the antecedents, and the consequences of anxiety provide the student with an important and useful working tool. There is no substitute for precise attention to definition and validity of psychological concepts and theories. It is in the demand for such care and precision in observation and thought about persons and in the sharing of the results of psychologists' previous careful deliberation and research that a course in basic personality psychology makes its contribution.

A course in personal counseling has a particular place in this curriculum scheme which deserves careful attention because it differs from the usual conception of such a course. It happens to be an historical fact that much of the present understanding of personality derives from psychotherapy. This is true for two reasons. In psychotherapy we have an unparalleled compilation of intimate reports by persons of what they feel is happening in their own lives. Also, in the process of psychotherapy itself, we have an instance of two persons interacting in a situation simple enough to allow some study and understanding but intimate and complex enough to make us believe that we have here an important sample of interpersonal relations in general.

Some characteristics of personality and its functions show up much more clearly in psychotherapy and in personal counseling than in any other situation. The understanding of repression and of its clue to the unconscious life in general was first detected by Freud in the phenomenon of resistance to free association and is perhaps still best demonstrated by this phenomenon. The efficacy of love, forgiveness, and acceptance has been most clearly demonstrated by psychologists such as Carl Rogers, who have seen its effects in the situation of personal counseling. The analysis made earlier in this chapter of alternative conceptions of the ministry, labeled as self-justifying good works and as a faith-orientation, depends in large part upon analysis made by others of the distinction between relatively directive and nondirective approaches toward counseling.

A course in counseling then is perhaps best regarded as a special or an advanced course in the understanding of personality. It provides both the advantages of richness and the disadvantages of limitation which accrue from restricting one's investigation to a particular arena of behavior. Among the advantages is the not inconsiderable one, to be discussed in more detail later, that it is relatively easy to arrange for students to get involved in more than an intellectual way and to garner some actual experience of the phenomena being studied.

In principle, at least, other special arenas of behavior could serve the same function, if the same wealth of study had been already brought to bear upon any one of them so that we could present to students the same conceptual understanding that we can now supply about persons in counseling. We might look, for example, to such special areas as parent-child relations, other interactions within the family and between marriage partners, relations between teacher and pupil in the process of education, patterns of friendship, or behavior in small groups. Indeed, we do already in some curricula use these arenas of behavior as foci of study. It just happens that we know less about personality functioning in these than in psychotherapy and counseling, little as we know about the latter. But it seems to me that the legitimate excuse for any such especially focused course is not in what we may learn about child rearing or about counseling or about conducting small groups, but rather in what we may learn in general about personal functioning. For what we are still primarily interested in understanding is the general quest of persons for "salvation"—under whatever labels they seek it—and the study of personality, including the special courses, is but a means toward that end.

This is often implicitly recognized in the teaching of counseling, especially when the course is called something like Pastoral Psychology. There is frequently much emphasis in such courses upon generalizing from the dyadic situation of counseling to more general pastoral activities and to personality in general. This, to some extent, represents some of the confusion mentioned above when the two roles of psychology are not kept distinct, at least in conception. Such fairly casual generalization may run risks of thinness, invalidity, and inappropriateness.

One additional course found in some curricula needs to be considered in relation to the discussion above. This is a course which can be described as one on the relation between psychology and theology, though it goes under many fancier names in catalogues. This is the effort to make the systematic integration between psychology as a set of theories and theology as another set of theories. This is a task for which little help can be offered the student because very little of this relationship has yet been achieved. It is undoubtedly a useful exercise to make the student push to his limit the possibilities of his own intellectual integration of these conceptual systems. But he runs the risk of becoming preoccupied with the exclusively intellectual and therefore of becoming distracted from what may be regarded as the more primary task, the behavioral and the experiential integration of these perspectives within his own person. The achieving, after many pages of exposition, of some of the preliminary rules by which "anxiety" and "sin" may be used in the same sentence offers some satisfaction. But this is no substitute for a more important kind of integration. Such a course carries a special responsibility to insure that some relevance is provided for within the content course itself.

Making Psychology Relevant

How can the psychology of religion and these supplementary courses be taught so as to foster the maximum "relevance"? Whether we allow the assumption that the primary responsibility for relevance—for personalization and integration within the life and behavior of the student—is reserved for a separate course in pastoral arts, or whether this is the final responsibility of the psychology and other content courses themselves, the first responsibility for these courses is the same. It must be the goal of the psychology of religion—and any other content course—to get the "understanding" lodged in the experience of the student where it will be accessible to those mysteriously effective processes of personal integration and appropriation within the student. What we aim for is a full experiential, not merely a cognitive, kind of knowing. In this first stage of making relevant, we want the student to be sensitive to cues within the actual behavior and personal functioning of persons, himself and others, not just to the verbal concepts used to apply to behavior—just as in the second stage, we want the student's response to be appropriate reactions within his own behavior and not merely verbal reactions. We want an emphatic awareness of the emotional range and intensity of personal experience. The psychologically sophisticated patient undergoing psychoanalysis generally reports an astounding kind of vivification as familiar psychological concepts suddenly come to life in his own life. Concepts once thought fully comprehended emerge as though from misty veils with a new rich meaning and usefulness. Something like that is probably the aim here, although we cannot depend exclusively upon discovery within a person's own life. Toward that end some suggestions will be made here. If some of these suggestions seem very obvious, it is not obvious that such procedures are in wide use.

We need "clinical material." We need actual samples of human behavior which the student can begin to feel his way into and against which he can try out his gradually acquired conceptual tools. For this we customarily turn to the hospital, because here are persons to whom our ministerial students have ready access in the role of ministers and because here are people who are under stress and therefore willing to expose themselves in a way which we can exploit. But need we limit ourselves to hospitals? Can we not devise other conditions in which we can go to people and ask them to talk with us intimately about some aspects of their personal lives? Need we necessarily—though such a well-defined role makes an interview less stressful for the student—go in the guise of counselors and chaplains? May we not frankly say that we are interested in understanding and learning from our subject, not pretending that our primary purpose is to help him? It is often assumed in psychological research that unless a person is under stress, he is not sufficiently motivated to speak revealingly about himself. But this is not necessarily true, and "depth interviews" are actually a standard and important part of the psychologist's research equipment.

Professor Ross Snyder of the University of Chicago has made one notable attempt to make use of such "normal" subjects. Members of one of his classes pursued a set of six intensive interviews with high school students. The interviews were moderately structured, especially the early ones, including some pictorial "test" material to which students were asked to give response. This was frankly interpreted to the subjects as a kind of research project in which the interviewers were interested in finding out about how young people understand the "meanings of life." Subjects of such research may or may not derive any incidental benefit, therapeutic or otherwise, but it seems almost certain that under such circumstances they cannot be damaged, as is not always true in dealing with hospital patients. Persons are not nearly so unwilling to talk about themselves as we sometimes suppose, and it would seem to require not much imagination to devise other pretexts and circumstances of the kind used by Professor Snyder with which to approach persons.

Without approaching other persons directly, we may still find useful secondhand case material. We have fictional character sketches, we have biographies, we have clinical case histories, and we have film.[4] These materials offer both the advantages and disadvantages of having been screened through another person's eyes. The data are not raw but are already selected and arranged to represent particular theoretical reconstructions. We cannot, therefore, use these materials to test whether particular concepts are valid and the most appropriate way for interpreting experience. But because the materials are arranged so as to highlight and focus particular aspects, they are especially suitable for getting an empathic "feel" of particular characteristics and processes. Written case histories and film offer this advantage over live subjects: there is more guarantee that the student will be able to detect and experience coherent, intelligible patterns.

Films in particular offer another important advantage over live cases, either other persons or oneself. Personal identification and empathically aroused emotional response is easy. There is not the resistance encountered in using oneself as the case. Nor is there the anxiety or other impediments involved when one is interviewing another person and feels "on the spot," obligated to respond in some way, or otherwise preoccupied with one's own emotional involvement to the point of missing something in the other person. We should not overlook the possibility of finding still other and more indirect ways of bypassing resistance in order to lodge understanding in the experience of a person. Using subject material less similar to the student himself may help to lower resistance, though it also runs the risk of reducing the learning impact as well. There are films, for example, on rats and on mental patients which may actually represent important personality processes but in a somewhat more removed and therefore safely assimilable form. Two films mentioned earlier in this chapter regarding alternative conceptions of the ministry are examples. Or cases can be found located in remote situations—as Shakespeare located such threatening tragedies as Hamlet and Othello, perhaps to enhance identification.

The most easily available and potentially most valuable subject, of course, is the student himself. This, however, raises difficult problems. There is the student's resistance to insight. There is the student's strong need to understand his behavior and experiences according to certain interpretations and not others. There is the risk of raising material once satisfactorily handled but requiring new therapeutic help once opened up for "exploratory" purposes. This may be especially true when group processes, generally accorded a safe, silent treatment, are exposed; an individual can use repressive processes much more effectively alone than in a group. There is a wealth of valuable experience in any of the interactions of the classroom itself. But it is not easy to know how to employ this for the profitable educational experience of the student.

If a specially defined situation with known limits and safeguards can be offered to students, they may be more inclined to let themselves go and to look at themselves. The usual kind of role playing is not the only form this safeguard method of instruction can take. One can arrange an experiment or demonstration, announced as such. The students know that there is something staged and artificial and that they will not be held fully accountable for their behavior. Presumably they trust their instructor to know they will not be led up a too risky primrose path. Even if they are a bit on guard, they do not know in advance the exact nature of the demonstration, and so they do not know at what point to pull themselves in and retract. In general, they let themselves go according to the rules of the demonstration and produce genuinely illustrative material which can be subsequently examined with considerable insight and benefit, not the least of the benefit being that they have themselves experienced it.

Many familiar group processes can be so demonstrated. An example follows in which the class is used for a slightly different kind of demonstration, that of the powerful process of rationalization. A class is divided into two teams and instructed to debate the two sides of some issue, which may be one of religious interest such as adult versus infant baptism. To decide which team will take which position, a coin is flipped. Excited planning conferences are then held and a heated debate proceeds in which students find themselves employing biblical, theological, psychological, social and *ad hominem* arguments with dexterity and vigor. Time is called, and many of them are amazed at the energy with which they have defended a position in which they have no more investment than that occasioned by a flip of a coin. Rationalization is made an understandable process, and the stage is set for a subsequent discussion of other "coins" which influence commitments, and how these become rationalized.[5]

Role playing is the most frequently used special type of demonstration. With a well-defined social role, somewhat unlike their own, and a well-defined situation, students generally feel safe and free enough to allow themselves to participate genuinely and fully. Role playing is, of course, artificial, cannot contain all the dimensions and stimuli of "normal" life and therefore cannot elicit the full range of personal reactions. But the role playing includes a degree of reality such that when persons stop to analyze their performance afterward, they are often amazed to realize how closely their behavior followed certain predictable patterns, according to principles of behavior which they had previously known only with objective and cognitive remoteness.

Personal counseling is perhaps the most frequently used type of situation for role playing. It provides a relatively familiar well-structured situation which students find it safe and easy to slip into and out of. Much of benefit can be learned from such role-played counseling. Students are frequently surprised to find how vast a difference it makes, for example, in their own behavior as "counselees" to confront one time a manipulative kind of counselor who wants to keep the interview under his constant control and to encounter a relaxed, truly nondirective counselor another time. Acceptance and nondirectiveness come to mean something more than mere words. When we use counseling, I hope we recognize that generally we do so because of its expedience in providing a structurable, safe but also entirely pertinent kind of situation for role-playing interpersonal relations. But we should not overlook other potentially valuable kinds of situations. Parent-child, husband-wife, teacher-student, minister-secretary, minister and worshiper-at-door-after-church—all provide important dyadic relations in which much insight could be gained. Groups can also be role-played, and in principle a single person can try to imagine thoughts and feelings he would have in a particular role, though this is more difficult without the stimulating cues of others' behavior. There is no need to restrict roles to church-related activities, and perhaps much merit in letting students try to feel themselves in very different human situations. (This is one of the benefits of distinguishing teaching of psychology from the teaching of the pastoral arts. The latter requires particular vocational roles.)

Role playing is most beneficial when the roles are very carefully assigned and a well-defined situation set up in advance. This enables the instructor to provide some guarantees that particular experiences will be evoked. There is an advantage for subsequent discussion if members of an entire class share the same experience. A class, no matter how large, can be paired off and roles assigned to be done outside of class, every pair going through the same situation.

One other device which some instructors use is to provide a kind of comparative role playing. A skillful role player, perhaps the instructor, repeats the same role with a series of partners before the class (each of these successive partners being out of the room during the earlier role playing).

Actual personal experience of students is most available to the classroom when it can be impersonalized. Perhaps this can be most easily done by dealing in a general way with experiences which are likely to be common to all students. One can probably assume a good many profound experiences held in common by students. In fact, one may wonder why anyone thinks it necessary to go out to a hospital to find persons in stress. Personal struggles, such as the struggle to resolve competing conceptions of the role and function of a minister, are unique for each person but they also have some very general characteristics.

How can such resources of experience be most effectively utilized in a classroom? It should be recalled that our goal is to link experience and intellectual understanding. Intellectual, conceptual mastery of psychological principles is relatively useless to a person without some experience of the affective components of the principles. Almost any use of the psychological principles will require the student to recognize and deal with nonverbal and affective components. This includes any attempt to integrate his psychological understanding with his theological perspectives; such integration, we have pointed out, is more likely to come in terms of personal experience than through systematic intellectual mastery. On the other hand, experience by itself is useless without an intellectual handle by which it can be picked up and looked at and comprehended and used to supply illumination of other experiences. We are not, therefore, simply encouraging just any experience for its own sake but are trying to provide instructive occasions in which experience and label can become linked.

In dealing with an individual with the leisure of a personal psychoanalysis, we would need no management nor controls. We could simply let the student travel his own way and provide interpretations whenever we thought these would be useful to him. But with groups, some control is necessary to guarantee a relatively common experience—always with provision, of course, for supplementary individual consultation for those persons in whom a situation produces unique individual reactions. A film, case history, role playing, even freer clinical material, all need to be brought to clear, sharp focus. Students need to be as clear as possible as to just what is happening affectively and what theoretical interpretations are and are not appropriate to the different phases of the experience. This means structuring role playing, interviews, and such situations in advance, the instructor using whatever psychological insight he personally has so as best to produce predictable experiences. This means sharp pointed questions and clear concise interpretations after the fact. In using films, for example, I have found that even when the plot and narration of the film appear to give a satisfying sense of coherence and understanding, the simplest questions about the most essential features of the case leave the student helpless until he is forced to recount the specific relevant experiences, which he glided through quite passively during the film, and apply to them precise theoretical reformulations.

It should be pointed out that whether the learning experiences are exclusively in groups or include some individual consultation, one thing which is not absolutely prerequisite for this activity is a complete therapeuticlike openness and permissiveness and warmth. Desirable as these characteristics may generally be in interpersonal relations and as essential as they absolutely are in the teaching of pastoral arts, to be discussed shortly, they cannot be regarded as indispensable for this type of learning experience. Presumably, discovery and learning can be maximized if usual academic pressures are relaxed enough to permit students some freedom of exploration without the anxiety of having to come up with brilliant correct answers. But we do not have to feel that the teaching is in vain if the group fails to exude maximum warmth and acceptance.

Personalizing the Faith

We come now to the main task of making the minister and his ministry relevant and consistent with the ultimate realities of life which he recognizes. This is the proper focus and climax of all theological education, whether it is made part of all courses in the curriculum or whether it is assigned as primarily the responsibility of special courses in the ministerial arts, field work, internships, and clinical training. This is not a unique responsibility of psychology in the curriculum, although the psychologist may feel that he has some understanding to offer of how the processes of making relevant take place.

At least two distinct processes are critical ones in this personalizing part of the theological education. One of these is the *integration* within the personal functioning of the minister of the many strands of insight and commitment which constitute his theological education. The other process is concerned with *freeing* the minister from various restrictions and handicaps which prevent his fully effective functioning. These two processes deal respectively with skills and with motives, insofar as these can be distinguished.

The task of personal integration is directed toward the goal of making it possible for the minister to represent in each of many different types of acts all of many different orientations and commitments. The task can be schematized as follows (the labels are meant to be suggestive not exhaustive):

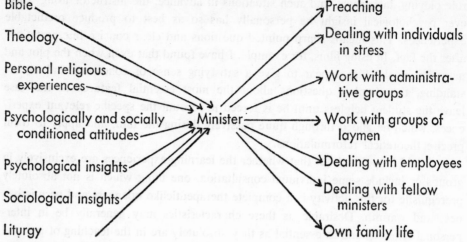

Bible

Theology

Personal religious experiences

Psychologically and socially conditioned attitudes

Minister

Psychological insights

Sociological insights

Liturgy

Preaching

Dealing with individuals in stress

Work with administrative groups

Work with groups of laymen

Dealing with employees

Dealing with fellow ministers

Own family life

The minister's situation seems very much like that of a modern parent who holds many different obligations and commitments concerning child rearing and who finds himself trying to carry these out in a great variety of interactions with the child. A parent has certain medical insight and sense of obligation as to what is best for the physical health of the child. A parent feels some convictions concerning what is best for the psychological well-being of the child, including probably some sense that the child needs a degree of permissiveness and opportunity to discover and learn for himself. A parent is aware of certain social expectations, particular standards and norms of behavior to which the child must conform if he is to live in a social group. A parent undoubtedly has convictions as to what is desirable for the intellectual development of his child; for instance, some reading is preferable to others. And, above all, the parent has had built in through his own experience as a child being raised, particular standards and norms, independent of any of these other systems. Such a list of loyalties and subloyalties (for there is probably no one consistent, integrated pattern held by any parent concerning the medical or psychological or intellectual or social well-being of his child) provides a central orientation and guide for the parent's relation with his child. The parent hopes that any single act, whether it be feeding, playing, disciplining, or whatever, will be consistent with and reflect at the same time each of these loyalties. A parent is not necessarily self-conscious and deliberate about these loyalties at the time of making each act—or he would go mad. But this is, nevertheless, his hope. Such a hope is not necessarily futile. Although many of the loyalties at particular times appear to be in conflict, there always remains the possibility, frequently realized, of finding still an additional form of word and deed which will in fact satisfy all the loyalties at once. Perhaps parenthood is best described as the attempt to enlarge the repertory of one's behavior so as to include acts which are more inclusive of the parent's loyalties. This would be making parenthood relevant.

Notice that the focus is on the *loyalties*. One does not make parenthood relevant by trying to prescribe in advance appropriate *responses* for every conceivable circumstance. With respect to the single act of eating, for example, we would not be concerned to prepare the parent for feeding a child with a high chair and without a high chair, for feeding a child allergic to beans but excessively fond of beets, or vice versa; for feeding the child cold cereal or hot, for feeding the child who resists food by spitting and one who resists by batting the spoon. A parent is prepared to meet these and the million other possible exigencies not by anticipatory drill in procedures but by more careful and explicit attention to the principles and loyalties from which his acts will issue.

The minister is in a similar situation, searching for ways of expressing in his many different activities all the potentially related but frequently conflicting loyalties he feels. The loyalties may be present for the minister in many different psychological forms. Perhaps the word "role" is appropriate for many of them, meaning a pattern of behavior consistent with others' expectations. Perhaps the term "response potential" is suggestive for others. Perhaps, for some ministers, for some loyalties, they experience it largely as a professor looking over their shoulder, and unconsciously the task is one of satisfying the many different professors in the seminary all at once. (However, if we personalize it this way, we have to add to the professors, parents, home ministers, and others.)

As one concrete example, let us take a situation in which a minister deals with a bereaved family. He has learned a good deal in the seminary relevant to the plight of grief. Most ministers rely on one or two of these orientations. Perhaps they quote Scripture. Perhaps they in effect deliver a sermon announcing their theological and philosophical understanding of death. Perhaps they pursue counseling procedures calculated to maximize the psychological effectiveness of the family's "grief work." Perhaps they rely largely on liturgics and spend most of their time with the family preparing for the funeral service. Perhaps, though this is highly unlikely these days, the minister is so concerned with the social and ethical problem involved with contemporary funerals that he uses this largely as an occasion for protest and instruction of church and community in proper Christian funerals. Perhaps his behavior is controlled by none of these but rather by his own personal feelings and experiences with death, so that he seeks, for example, to offer (himself) a heavy dose of reassurance. Whatever he does, the chances are—until such sensitivity becomes numbed—he feels some regrets over neglect of the others. There remains the possibility of finding ways of responding to grief which will in fact express at the same time all these loyalties. This cannot be easily prescribed, even by one who feels in his own life that he may have found some such solution. For the reactions must, above all, be consistent with and issue out of the more general personal orientation and loyalties which constitute the personality of the man long before he becomes a minister. What is true for this example of dealing with grief is no less true when the minister preaches or undertakes any other ministerial activity.

The process of developing this kind of personal integration can perhaps be appropriately regarded as a trial and error search for response patterns. Such training requires two main ingredients: opportunity for making the trials, and opportunity for critical judgment and reflection. The opportunity for practical experience abounds in theological education and after it. What is much less available is that set of conditions which permits and encourages the student to reflect on his experience, to judge where and in what respects his reactions have been deficient in terms of his own ideals and loyalties. What went wrong and why? Why, for example, did he happen to deliver a theological discourse on love and faith while the very manner of doing so tended to deny his words? Did he feel some-need at that particular point to prove his theological competence? What was really happening within him? No other person can make these judgments for the student, because no other person knows his loyalties and feels his experiences as he does. But probably neither can he do it by himself. He needs the model of others to set a "tradition" in which such procedure seems easy and natural. He needs an open permissiveness which removes most of the punishments one usually feels for making self-criticism and judgments. These can be provided by a trusted counselor or by membership in a trusted group. We shall return to further consideration of these conditions after we see that they also seem to be the conditions necessary for fostering the second general process of relevance and personalization: the freeing of a minister to do his best.

As students undertake to try out various kinds of responses to various kinds of situations, they soon discover that they are not entirely free agents. They sometimes find themselves compulsively doing that which they wish not, and conversely sometimes seem able to specify an appropriate response but are unable to perform it. A repertory of skills is not sufficient unto itself but in turn is governed and moved by motives within the person. A student, for example, may find himself, despite conscious determination to the contrary, continually dominating and controlling interviews with other persons and official board meetings. The minister finds himself perhaps relying exclusively on one or another of his loyalties or repeatedly performing what has here been called a self-justifying kind of ministry of good works, when he wishes desperately to do otherwise. A man finds that he gets in his own way sometimes. Particular response patterns in his ministry tend to satisfy urgent needs or to quiet persistent fears and anxieties within himself. This is to be expected and is no more cause for shame or alarm than when personal fears and wants happen to drive a man to response patterns which prove to be extremely effective forms of a ministry. But one may still hope for change.

Change is most likely when one or both of two things can happen. Perhaps his persistent fears and needs can be satisfied in some alternative form, or perhaps they prove to be ephemeral and accidental and can be dissipated by exposure to clear analysis. We may not minimize the opportunities in several aspects of the theological curriculum to accomplish either of these objectives. The acquisition of theological or psychological insights, even in academic guise, may help a person to feel more adequate and more at home in his world and may quell anxieties.

But probably the main task is a personal one and can be accomplished best with the help of the two conditions already mentioned: opportunities for practical experience, and for open reflection upon these. Experience itself can foster confidence and can provide a person with opportunity for developing various adjustive processes to cope with his inner unrest. If this is accompanied by opportunity for reflection on this experience with a trusted counselor, there is more assurance that one can better understand what is going on and better control it.

In the reflection on his experience the student may recognize that some of his adjustive processes are jeopardizing one or more of his loyalties, and he may experience the security to abandon this pattern and, temporarily unarmed, continue his trial-and-error search for more fitting patterns. The attitude toward the ministry which has been characterized earlier as one of self-justifying good works and epitomized by personal counseling as commonly practiced, is an instance of a reaction-pattern that disrupts some loyalties. This pattern is itself, of course, motivated. It is motivated by the person's anxious concern to find clear goals and positive achievements. But these anxious concerns themselves are motivated by the fact that the person has learned to depend on clear goals and achievements for self-assurance. So long as "good works" continue to serve this function effectively, as they do, this pattern will not be easily abandoned, even if a student recognizes that it is not fully faithful to all his loyalties. For this would be to abandon an important source of self-assurance. This can happen only when the student feels assurance possible from other sources—such as from the relation with his counselor, from the potentially more satisfying ministerial role which he sees ahead of him, from other evidences of assurance which constitute his faith.

The model here is, of course, that of psychotherapy and personal counseling. But it seems valid and valuable to make a distinction between therapy which would concern itself with the whole range of a student's personality and that which is concerned exclusively with his vocational functioning. It is conceivable, in principle at least, that neurotic symptoms or other signs of unrest could appear at some point in a person's functioning but not in any of his ministerial activities. Perhaps this is never true in practice but it would seem appropriate for counselors to begin with the restricted vocational objective. If everything finally comes in, then so be it.

The opportunities for mixing these ingredients—practical experience and open reflection upon it—are, of course, common parts of most clinical training programs, and theological education must learn of the indispensable and essential aspects of these programs. But we have said nothing about hospitals or about pastoral counseling. Let us try to abstract the critical and essential contributions of clinical training out of the particular and limited situation in which they have been found and to see how these might apply to a broader range of theological training in the ministerial arts. Can these essentials be adapted to field work, internships, externships, practicums, and courses in the pastoral arts, which are now primarily assigned the responsibility for this personalization of the education? Can these essentials be adapted to activities of the minister other than personal counseling and pastoral care?

Perhaps what is needed is something like a return to the early apprentice-type training for the ministry which prevailed before the establishment of theological seminaries. A student might be invited by a mininster of a nearby church to try his hand at one of a number of activities or functions in the church. A student is not hired by the church to produce and perform but is invited by the church to come in and learn. Perhaps there is some desire in the church for a men's group or for a political study and action group, and the minister finds it impossible to spare time for such a project. The student might be invited to lend a hand with this particular project. This would involve him with individuals, small groups, and large groups. It would most likely involve pastoral work, administrative work, and perhaps something like preaching. With the pressures off to produce, this could be a valuable experience for the student to discover something about his own loyalties and how he can and wishes to express them.

Perhaps the minister himself is able to serve the role of a trusted confidant. Perhaps the student finds this role is better served by a group of peers, or perhaps by a member of the seminary faculty. Without some exploration we can't say which combination is best. It does seem likely that an experience of this kind—perhaps for a semester, perhaps for a year, representing perhaps one fourth of the student's curricular load—would go farther toward personalizing and making a man's ministry relevant than most existing courses in pastoral care or pastoral psychology. Such an experience would seem naturally to come in a student's senior year. However, something like it might also come in the first year to set the stage for theological education. Existing internships and field work arrangements do so little for the student as compared with the possibilities of what could happen if there were added to them the second ingredient: opportunity for reflection.

The theological seminary itself is presumptuous and self-justifying if it is unable to recognize its own limitations of ability and responsibility. It is neither called upon nor able to equip all its students with an ability to confront every eventuality successfully. The task of the seminary is essentially one of nourishing the students in the faith—though it does not bear primary responsibility even for this. Its task is not to load them down with an unwieldy armament of tricks and gimmicks. Thus nourished, the minister is entrusted to live and express that faith as faithfully as he can, confident that the faith is made supremely relevant to the plights of men, but not by him.

REFERENCES

1. The views developed in this chapter are largely based upon an opportunity, provided by a faculty fellowship of the American Association of Theological Schools in 1957-1958, to visit several seminaries and to engage in extended conversations with many thoughtful and cordial persons from all of whom I learned much. They include Professors William Douglas, Seward Hiltner, Hans Hofmann, Paul E. John-

son, Perry LeFevre, Ross Snyder, Carroll Wise, and especially Homer Jernigan. I have also profited much from participation in the discussions of the Committee on the Pastoral Ministry of the Yale Divinity School, a distinguished group of laymen and clergymen meeting periodically during the year of 1959. Some of the views discussed in the final section of this chapter originated in discussion with other members of the Executive Committee of this Committee, Professors Browne Barr, H. Richard Niebuhr, Paul H. Vieth, and Dean Liston Pope. However, as presented here, these are clearly personal views and do not adequately reflect the opinions of these other persons or the policy of the school.

2. *The Presbyterian Pastor's Ministry to Families,* Office of Family Education Research, Board of Education, United Presbyterian Church in the U.S.A., Philadelphia, 1958.

3. Mark May, *Education of American Ministers* (New York: Institute of Social and Religious Research, 1934).

4. The best and most engrossing single case history is undoubtedly *One Little Boy* by Dorothy Baruch (New York: Julian Press, Inc., 1958). Jean Evans' *Three Men* (New York: Alfred A. Knopf, Inc., 1954) may also be useful, though her cases emphasize the abnormal and bizarre. Robert W. White in *Lives in Progress* (New York: Dryden Press, 1952) presents with less dramatic impact several normal lives. The best single source of films is the Psychological Cinema Register, the Pennsylvania State University, University Park, Pennsylvania. One outstanding series of half-hour films has been produced by the National Film Board of Canada and includes "Feeling of Hostility," "Feeling of Rejection," "Feelings of Depression." These are dramatized presentations. Some actual film case histories are also available, such as "This is Robert: a Study of Personality Growth in a Preschool Child," a seventy-five minute compilation of actual events in a boy's life from the ages of 2 to 7.

5. Daniel I. Malamud has reported many ingenious procedures for arranging and using actual classroom behavior for teaching purposes. See his booklet, *A Participant-Observer Approach to the Teaching of Human Relations* (Chicago, 940 E. 58th St.: Center for the Study of Liberal Education for Adults, 1955). Also "Educating Adults in Self-Understanding," *Mental Hygiene,* XLIV, 1 (Jan., 1960), 115-124.

GRANGER E. WESTBERG ॐ

The place and function of the hospital chaplain is often enough ill-defined and creates difficulties for him and mild suspicion on the part of the hospital staff. An encouraging exception to this rule is the position and work of Granger Westberg. Through his chaplaincy he has so fully gained the respect of the Federated Faculty of Theology at the University of Chicago and of the faculty of the Medical School at the same University that they jointly appointed him to teach medical students about the relevance of Christian faith to healing and to teach theological students about the experience which can be drawn for the ministry from close contact with the hospital community.

His close co-operation with the medical faculty has obviously given him a deep impression of the solidity and efficiency of medical education. He is willing to draw the comparisons and consequences in a critical review of theological education and its results. At the outset the editor wishes to express his full sympathy with Westberg's suggestions and recommend them highly to other theological schools for serious consideration. The main impression Westberg gains from medical education is not so much that prospective physicians are more thoroughly trained than ministerial candidates, but that they are more mature after they have gone through their four years of formal studies and additional residencies. He asks whether a theological education of three years may not be all too short and hence not allow the student to really digest all that he learns and thereby grow to be a more dependable pastor. Why should theological students be treated like college undergraduates and spend merely three short academic years in their theological school with the long summer months in between giving ample opportunity to forget everything they had learned before and fall out of the rhythm of theological learning before they enter the school again in the fall? He discusses the innovation which Augustana Theological Seminary has introduced. After two years of formal training at the school, the student is sent out for one full year of field work in a pastorate before he returns with new impetus and questions to finish the third academic year.

Although such a required full intern year between the second and third academic years is certainly an innovation, Westberg would still go one step further. He proposes a plan which involves 44 months of studies, which means four years at eleven months each. During this time the student would spend half of the day at school for his courses and half of the day in a parish situation. The hope is that the formal academic training will sharpen the student's readiness to deal creatively with pastoral problems and that the actual parish experience will renew his interest in theological learning.

It is quite evident that the relation between theoretical and practical learning in theological education today is far from satisfactorily resolved. Westberg's plan may sound revolutionary, but it is certainly promising enough to be tried out. Anything that may improve the professional confidence and skill of the minister merits the fullest attention of all those responsible for theological education.

The Need for Radical Changes in Theological Education: A Proposed 44-Month Plan

৬১ GRANGER E. WESTBERG

In this paper theological education will be discussed from my personal viewpoint as a member of the Board of Directors of a seminary which is presently evaluating its "internship" year begun some twenty-five years ago. First I shall describe the intern year and how it has operated for these twenty-five years, then make some comments on recent modifications of the plan, and finally describe several radical changes which I think would help to bring about the necessary integration of the theoretical and clinical dimensions of the theological curriculum.

In an article in the *Augustana Seminary Review*, June, 1959,[1] Dr. Theodore Conrad, Dean of Students at Augustana Seminary says that it was in the depth of the depression of the thirties that the parish year of service was inaugurated at Augustana Theological Seminary, a Lutheran school in Rock Island, Illinois. The decision had the double effect of alleviating somewhat the tense situation arising from a temporary oversupply of potential pastors. Arrangements were made for those students who had finished their second year to spend a year out in a parish before returning to the seminary for their fourth or senior year. The faculty felt that this year out would help to prepare the student for the shock of being thrown out into the world after spending nineteen years in the classroom.

In evaluating the intern year, Dean Conrad tells how from the very beginning the assignment of interns has always been made by a committee of the church— its president, together with the theological faculty. Great variety has characterized the types of parishes in which interns have been trained. Sometimes they are placed in established, "going churches," sometimes in run-down, desperate parishes, and sometimes in new missions. Likewise, the quality and maturity of the intern's supervisor, if indeed he always has one, ranges from a parish pastor to a conference

167

president or a regional director. Dean Conrad believes that experience has demonstrated the wisdom of assigning men to fairly typical parishes, not necessarily the larger, and to fairly typical pastors, not necessarily the more spectacularly "successful" ones. Over the years, Augustana has resisted steadfastly all requests, either student initiated or agency initiated, for specialized internships—whether in student work, clinical hospital training, social agencies, youth work, ministries of music, or other fields—being convinced that a broad background of parish experience is the best possible basic preparation for later specialized ministries.

The Augustana Lutheran Church continues to be strongly favorable to this type of program. Somewhat more than 60 per cent of Augustana's 1300 pastors have gained experience through internships. The congregations which receive interns finance the program out of their own budgets. They are anxious to receive help for their parish programs, but they know that it is rather inexperienced help and that it is not exactly cheap help, costing roughly $3,000 or more per year for participating congregations. They also know that from 10 per cent to 20 per cent of all internships involve some real problems of adjustment and application in the course of the intern's training. Nevertheless, they support the program loyally, as evidenced by the fact that there are always more calls for interns than men to be assigned. Through such parish-oriented internships theological students are fairly well assured of a rich and broad experience. They observe pastors in their normal range of routine and responsibility, and they learn by observation and by sharing in the work.

Dean Conrad states: "*Rapport* is the watchword of a successful internship—rapport between the principals. How the intern is received by his supervisor and how that relationship continues makes or breaks for the greater values in internship."

Recent Modifications of the Year of Internship

In 1954 the office of Dean of Students was established, and one of its several responsibilities was attention to the internship program. The mere fact that someone has had more time and interest to devote to the program has had some desirable effects. It means a good deal to interns, and to supervisors, to know that someone at the seminary is aware of what is happening in all the assignments and is available for assistance when the "growing pains" of this type of maturing in interpersonal relationships get too severe.

The intern-year plan has received constructive criticism from many angles. Partly in an effort to appraise the worth of these criticisms and partly to make the program responsive to calculable suggestions, two projects have been carried out in the past two years at the request of the seminary Board of Directors. (1) Four internship evaluation workshops have been held in various parts of the country so that interns and supervisors of the area, together with former interns and former supervisors, have devoted a day in workshop fashion to evaluation of the program. Concrete suggestions have been brought back to the Intern Committee from these workshops. (2) Four experimental Intern Study Groups have been set up in areas where several internship training centers are in fairly close proximity (Chicago, Rockford, Minneapolis-St. Paul, and Los Angeles). In such study groups, which vary considerably in format and programs, interns and supervisors get together from twelve to fifteen times during the course of a year to devote a morning to discussion and study in a clinical fashion of some of the living concerns of their immediate parishes. Interns are uniformly enthusiastic about these enrichments of their normal internships. But Dean Conrad is not certain that these values, which would seemingly call for all interns to be assigned to a limited number of areas, outweigh the values of a broad distribution of interns to suitable parishes, even at somewhat isolated points.

Whenever a group of Augustana Seminary graduates get together there is always discussion centering around the intern year. They never talk about abandoning it, but they all have the feeling that there must be ways to make it more valuable to congregations and students. Congregations, generally, regard it a privilege to have a theological student spend his year of internship with them. To offer itself as a laboratory, and its pastor as the intern supervisor, is regarded as a service to the whole church and its future ministry. Each congregation could write a fascinating chapter on its intern experience. Pastors, who have served as interns, are now supervisors of interns. The program has drawn congregations closer to the needs of the seminary. Congregations have become acquainted with professors and curricula through these students, and a wholesome working relationship between the parish and the classroom has been developed. The program has also been of value to the supervising pastor, for the presence of a student who is constantly asking questions challenges him to think through his own ministry and to consider whether or not this is good for a young man to learn and to follow. Actually, a pastor gets a "second chance" as he views his own work through the eyes of a young man who has visions and enthusiasm. The idea of clinical opportunities for theological students seems to be here to stay. Now the question is how we can learn from what has been going on for the last twenty-five years, so that we may develop a program of education that is even better than what we have.

Some of the Problems Involved in Clinical Theological Education

Before I can make suggestions for improving theological education in general, I must first point out some of the difficulties arising in the particular plan used by Augustana Seminary.

- Under the present pattern, it is not possible to establish a uniformly high standard of experience for each intern. Almost everything depends upon the quality of the supervising pastor; and because each student has only one try at it, he may be placed under the "wrong" supervisor, and so the entire twelve-month period is of less value to him.
- Twelve months in one church may be longer than it need be, particularly if the parish does not offer a good teaching experience. Many students have

said that the types of duties assigned them cease to be educationally stimulating after a few months.

- The student is limited to seeing how only one church carries on its ministry.
- Experience has demonstrated that the busy pastor does not have sufficient time to devote to the student. This is true even in cases where the pastor is an excellent teacher.
- The intern year does not provide the advantages of the group learning situation. Tutorial-type teaching needs to be augmented by the sharing of ideas and feelings with fellow students.
- In twenty-five years the intern plan has not developed a teaching pattern or structure which lends itself to any kind of examination of students. This absence of testing makes it impossible for the student or faculty to know in which areas the student needs help.
- The intern year resembles unsupervised field work much more than clinical theological education. The student is very much on his own and the insights he gains occur almost accidentally. The naturally insightful student profits much, but the plodding student who must have daily assistance in the learning process gets into ruts from which he may never emerge.
- One of the chief criticisms of the intern year away from the seminary is that the theological faculty has almost no opportunity to involve itself in the clinical experiences of these students who are now on the front lines. The fact that the students are *away* from the seminary points out the gulf fixed between theory and practice.

My conclusion is, then, that the intern year has been helpful to hundreds of theological students and supervising pastors and to the congregations they serve, but I think that constant experimentation ought to be going on to discover better ways to develop a more effective integration between theory and practice. As I have tried to discover new ways to bring about such integration I am reminded of my impressions, as a hospital chaplain, of the difference I noted between senior medical students and senior theological students. For some reason the senior medical students always seemed to be more mature. I believe that this maturity was undoubtedly hastened by the many clinical opportunities which are provided for the medical student so that he can "act like a doctor" in literally scores of situations. By the time he is ready to graduate from medical school he has been called "doctor" by hundreds of patients who have confided in him. Perhaps it was because these patients looked to him for help, as if he were a doctor, that he stood a little straighter and took his responsibilities a little more seriously than the theological student who is called Pete or Joe by everyone and not taken too seriously by anyone. As a result, the theological student does not seem to feel it necessary to take himself too seriously, for there will be plenty of time to do that—after ordination.

One of the problems of theological education is that it continues the college pattern of classroom lectures, note taking, examination passing, and fraternity-like life without expecting the student to assume more responsibilities than he had in college. It is primarily a lecture and library centered course. The school itself could be high on a hill, far outside the city walls, and it would make little difference to the basic course of study. We have taken over, without too much criticism, the European pattern of theological education. In those countries, the student who is going on to be a clergyman simply remains on the university campus for his academic studies in theology. If, after completing these studies, he still wishes to become a pastor, then he takes a brief practical course of only a few months in length. Often these courses are really not very practical at all. One European professor of practical theology explained to his American visitor that he taught "the history of the *theory* of practical theology." The European pattern of theological education which we have inherited is pointed toward preparing a man to preach or to teach theology in a classroom setting. A theological student needs to be prepared for the teaching and preaching aspects of his ministry, but he also needs an equal amount of time in order to learn to deal with the demanding duties of shepherding his people or interpreting the faith to the man in the street who never comes to hear his carefully prepared and documented sermons.

As we in America have adopted the traditional European manner of teaching we find that the academic emphasis often becomes so involved with the intricacies of semantics that it has not dealt so effectively as it might with the real theological questions encountered by the practicing minister. It is not that we want to water down our theology or to make it overly practical, but rather that we want the student to be constantly aware of the necessary interaction between theory and practice.

The majority of American parish ministers have taken their theoretical medicine dutifully while in the seminary. However, one of their real joys upon graduating is that from then on they are free from dry scholasticism and can now really participate in the life around them and apply the Gospel in a way that makes it relevant.

What I see as necessary in our present dilemma is a way to make clear to the beginning theological student the absolute necessity for a mutual and constant interchange between theory and practice so that each informs the other and both come alive because of their mutual dependence.

It is at this point that I am indebted to what I have seen in medical education. I have been impressed by the flexibility of the medical curriculum and of the professors and students who work within it. They have the unusual facility of being able to go back and forth daily between classroom and clinic, theory and practice. It has been inspiring to watch a medical professor, who is both an outstanding scholar *and* clinician, as he finishes his lecture of a highly theoretical subject and then invites his students to make rounds with him to demonstrate immediately the clinical implications of his theory. However, it is difficult for a clergyman to visualize his former professor of systematic theology finishing a lecture and then going out into the clinic, a nearby church, to demonstrate the clinical implications of the doctrines he has been expounding. Such a thought is almost ludicrous. A professor of theology is typically characterized as a man who has not been near a church, as a practicing pastor, for many years. He is a professor, not a pastor. And yet, the picture of the medical professor more nearly resembles the figure of Christ, walking among men, binding their wounds while he teaches them.

The medical profession seems to be saying that a man can be even a better teacher if he is an active clinician in daily contact with the problems of today, not those current twenty years ago when he *was* in practice. A growing number of thoughtful parish pastors are wondering why theological schools have resisted such a pattern for so long. It is true, there have been seminaries which have worked hard to emphasize practical, "how to do it" courses, and we appreciate the results of their experiments. But I am not suggesting merely that more attention be given to the practical department of the seminary. This only succeeds in dividing the theological faculty into two camps. I would like to see a few seminaries experiment with a *completely* revised approach to theological education in which the practical and the theoretical would be so inextricably bound together that at almost no point in the seminary curriculum would they be separated. Eventually I hope that every professor will also spend a portion of his time as a clinical instructor with students who "make rounds with him" in whatever form this might take. At the moment I shall not attempt to spell out this part of my proposal because the form such clinical relationships take will be wholly dependent upon the ingenuity of the new kind of professor of Systematic Theology, or Bible, or Church History. It is assumed that the younger professors called to seminary posts will have had clinical training and therefore will be able to apply the basic principles of the clinical educational approach to their own disciplines.

A Tentative Outline of a 44-Month Program for Theological Education

I. I believe that the course of theological education ought to be lengthened to 44 months in order to provide students with a wider variety of clinical experiences which demonstrate the integration of theory and practice.

Whatever I suggest here is meant to be only provocative, surely not definitive. I can only hint at ways which might be appropriate for experimentation in a particular school. No two schools will approach the problem in the same way. Therefore, I cannot go into any of the specific details and must be satisfied to discuss general principles underlying such an educational program.

The 44 months would be divided into four years of eleven months each. The student would have a one-month vacation each year. The other eleven months he would be under the seminary's jurisdiction. To be sure, the student would have more hours of classroom work, but the essential purpose of adding twenty months to the traditional twenty-four months or three-year program of seminaries would be to provide a wide variety and depth of clinical opportunities so that the student could immediately put into practice what he was learning in the classroom. It would also provide supervised guidance in "pastoral practice" during the early years of his training when he would be most amenable to direction.

I believe that the teaching pattern employed so successfully in hospital clinical training centers would work equally well in other situations. I am especially convinced that the parish, as well as certain social agencies, would lend itself well to supervised clinical instruction carried on concurrently with classroom teaching in the seminary. Such clinical centers would be located in parishes situated near enough to the seminary so that students could drive to their "clinical classroom" without too much difficulty. The faculty would also want the students to have experiences in certain special centers which might be a thousand miles away. The students would be assigned to these places either during the summer quarters or during other specially designated blocks of time during the four-year course. At each center six students would be under the direct supervision of an instructor of clinical theology who would be jointly appointed by the seminary faculty and by the particular center in which he would be teaching. Students attending the nearby centers would have their regular lectures in the seminary during the morning and then go into the clinics in the afternoon or at another time convenient to the faculty and the center.

Some advantages of the 44-month plan would be the following:

- The plan gives the faculty twenty additional months in which to include new courses in Bible, Theology, Church History, and so on, which cannot be crammed into the present three-year program, typical of most seminaries in the country.
- Students will have a better opportunity to decide whether the ministry is their true vocation. By the end of the longer four-year period, the students will have seen almost every phase of pastoral work in the several clinical situations which would be a regular part of the program of every student.
- The faculty will be in a better position to judge the fitness of the candidate for the ministry. Under the three-year plan the faculty sees the students almost exclusively in a classroom setting which gives little opportunity for true evaluation.
- When the student enters the 44-month program he gets the feel of the full 11-month year typical of the parish pastor. He should be introduced early to the rigors of pastoral work so that he will develop good work habits. His college classmates, who graduate with him and who go into the business world, must begin immediately to work fifty weeks out of the year, and so it is not asking too much of the seminary student that he follow a similar pattern. Why should he continue to be treated like a college boy for another four years? Such an attitude only retards the process of maturation.

II. Theological education ought to relate itself more closely to the life of the churches.

By using the analogy of medicine it is possible to see a relationship between the medical school and the nearby hospitals which is somewhat similar to the relationship which might be established between the theological school and the nearby parish churches.

The fact that hospitals have for many years made a significant contribution to medical education is often overlooked. Medical schools would be hopelessly lost if suddenly all hospitals refused to allow medical students to use them as workshops or laboratories. The parish church has not played a similar role in theological education. In many seminaries there is some tie between local congregations and the school through field work assignments. But field work does not imply a truly integrated relationship between instruction and the clinical teaching potential to be found in the average congregation.

The outstanding hospitals in any community have as their threefold purpose: patient care, teaching, and research. Hospitals which have little interest in teaching and research claim that this gives them more time to give superior patient care. This sounds good, except that in the long run, such hospitals inevitably have to turn to the teaching and research hospitals to learn new ways to improve patient care. Hospitals which de-emphasize the importance of teaching and research also find it extremely difficult to attract interns and residents. Some of these hospitals are now admitting that teaching, research, *and* patient care go hand in hand. As these hospitals add good teaching programs all the departments seem to come alive. When a large portion of their hospital family regularly take time to reflect on the nature of their tasks, in the presence of alert and inquisitive young interns and residents, it becomes clear that teaching and research actually contribute to the improvement of the hospitals' main task—patient care.

If hospitals improve their service to patients because of their teaching programs, then might it not follow that parish churches could improve their care of parishioners by instituting a teaching program for theological students? Such a program should not be patterned after the present form of field work, where the student is usually alone and does his work under little or no supervision. What I am describing is a pattern which is entirely new to the parish but which has been exceedingly effective in clinical training programs in hospitals. I see no reason why this pattern cannot be taken over and used in the parish. It would work somewhat like this:

- The seminary faculty, together with the board of elders or deacons of a particular congregation, would agree to try a clinical pattern similar to that used in medical settings. A faculty member would be called jointly by the seminary and the local congregation to function as an instructor in "clinical theology." He would participate fully in the life of the seminary as a member of its faculty, but his teaching would be done primarily in that particular church. The local parish becomes the classroom where this instructor meets his students. The man who is chosen for this unusual position would probably be an able parish pastor who has shown ability in relating theology and pastoral care and who has some serious academic interests. If he is called as a half-time instructor in clinical theology, then he may, at the same time that he is teaching, pursue work toward his doctorate. Though he must, of course, have had specialized clinical training himself, it would be better for the integration of all aspects of theology if these clinical instructors would represent a wide variety of theological interests.

- The new faculty member would serve as one of the pastors on the staff of this church. His salary would be paid in whole or in part by the local congregation as a demonstration of their participation in preparing men for pulpits like their own. (It costs hospitals something too if they want to be clinical training centers.) This instructor's service to the church would be chiefly as a teacher of the students who would, under careful supervision, in turn serve the members of this congregation. He would be in regular contact with the theological faculty. If possible, he would be on the campus a part of every day, teach an occasional joint seminar with other faculty members and participate in all discussions of policy and curriculum.

- Approximately six students would be assigned to each instructor. They would take this course in clinical theology just as they take any other course. It would not be thought of as being like an outside job, which is so often the case with field work. Clinical courses could be taken either concurrently, say three afternoons a week, or during other selected periods of the week, or in larger blocks of time when the students would spend their full time in a particular parish center. This might be anywhere from one to three months.

- Assignments in the clinical course in the parish (or other type center) would always be given with both the student and the educational process in mind. The meat of the clinical courses would be concerned essentially with the implications of Christian theology in human experience. The course proceeds on the premise that a student can learn how to give pastoral care only as he sees how it is related to everything else he is learning in the seminary. This implies that the instruction in the parish setting will always of necessity presuppose doctrinal and theological content with opportunity for analysis and reflection upon the quality and purpose of the pastoral work being done in that parish.

- The six theological students assigned to a particular church would rotate among the many kinds of services offered in the life of that congregation. This would be much like medical students who spend so many weeks in surgery, so many in obstetrics, and so on. For the theological students these services would include working with the youth of the church, teaching in the educational program, ministering to the sick, working with the aging, dealing with problems of church administration, and learning how to work with social agencies, family counseling centers and the courts. The student would also be given opportunity to lead the worship, to preach, and to observe the pastor in his daily rounds.

- The teaching emphasis in the clinical center at the church would relate itself significantly to the purpose and meaning of the minister's task. There would always be enough students available to perform real services for this congregation, but no student would be given more responsibilities than he could assimilate into his growing understanding of himself as a pastor. When, for example, he is assigned to talk with a high school student about vocational plans, the interview may be recorded. Before he sees this parishioner again he will spend a period of time with his instructor analyzing the theological and psychological implications of the conversation. Or when he speaks at a midweek service, his instructor would actually be there, and the student would be speaking to a live congregation. This service could be recorded for later study. In this way teaching would be intimately related to clinical experience.

- The instruction would proceed along the lines developed during the past twenty-five years in clinical theological training in mental and general hospitals. The instructor would often go with the student on his assignments. Each student would have a weekly personal interview with the instructor. The group of six students would meet together in twice-weekly seminars. The pastor of the church would be invited to be a regular participant in these seminars, which would employ the case study approach, the role-playing approach, and other proved techniques. From time to time other faculty members would sit in on these discussions in an attempt to bring theologians and parish pastors into a closer relationship.

- If this program or various modifications of it would prove to be educationally sound, it would be possible to add more churches and instructors to the experiment. Though it would seem best for the churches to be in the general vicinity of the seminary, this would not always be necessary, particularly when the students under an instructor would spend full time (three months) in one parish. It is not at all unlikely that an average seminary could have clinical centers in five or more churches, depending upon the number of students they wish to have involved in clinical training at a given time.

- "Clinical classrooms" need not be limited to the parish situation. I have stressed the parish because I think it has been overlooked as an educational institution. There is every reason to believe that dozens of other kinds of institutions would provide excellent clinical classrooms if conducted in a similar manner. Such clinical centers could be arranged on college campuses, in nearby social agencies, settlement houses, homes for the aged, industrial plants, hospitals, juvenile homes, police stations, and prisons, with a clinical instructor in charge of each center.

It is my belief that such an integrated program of clinical instruction in the parish and a variety of other centers would be beneficial to the seminary, the parish church, the instructor, and the student in the following ways:

- For the seminary it would put clinical training in its proper setting as an integral part of the theological enterprise, not disconnected from it.

- The parish church in this program would make a real contribution to the education of ministers and at the same time, like the teaching hospital, they would find that every department of the church's work would be enriched by having students and instructors raising the kinds of questions that need to be asked if the church is to speak relevantly to today's world.

- The instructor in clinical theology would have an exceptional opportunity to grow both as a scholar and as a pastor because his unique joint appointment would encourage an unusual relationship with theological professors, parish pastors, theological students, and parishioners. It would be hoped that this new kind of instructor would soon make some significant contributions to theological research as he keeps in tension the theoretical and practical aspects of the Christian message.

● The student would be fortunate in that he would be placed in situations geared to his own development. As he goes through the normal crisis experiences connected with understanding himself and the Christian faith, he would have four resources for help: his clinical instructor, his group of classmates, the parish pastor, and the theological professors who normally are not available to the young man starting out in pastoral work. Further, he could enjoy the exhilarating experience of seeing the mutual significance of theological study and the church's task because he is not being unnecessarily weighted down by either one of them.

III. Theological education of the quality, intensity, and length I have described should then offer the graduate a doctoral degree.

This degree may be a Th.D., an S.T.D. or a D.D. Those students who have not reached a certain level of scholastic attainment could receive a Th.M. or S.T.M. degree. I need not labor the point that it is rather ridiculous to offer a theological candidate another bachelor's degree after four years of additional work. Medical schools which require only three years of college work offer a doctoral degree after four years of postgraduate work. A number of schools of law offer a doctoral degree in jurisprudence after only *three* years of postgraduate work.

The program above naturally provokes many valid questions. I shall now attempt to speak to several of these questions.

● When during the formal training should the student learn any given aspect of clinical theology?

Much depends upon one's convictions regarding the learning process. I believe that a person has real difficulty assimilating new ideas unless these ideas are seen to be clearly relevant to what he is doing. In theological education we have for the most part employed the delayed reaction method of teaching. Here the student is given many ideas which for him will have little importance until years later, and so they are stored away in a notebook which may never be opened again. Even when this same student is assigned to field work he is often kept so busy doing the particular task assigned him that he never has time to reflect upon the religious meaning of this particular task. Teaching is always of more value when integration takes place where theory and practice meet. That they do meet has been attested to by experiments which have been taking place in many other areas of education.

The task of theological education is to give the student a background of knowledge concerning the essentials of the Christian faith and how these essentials have relevance for today's world. To make meaningful for the student the relevance of the Christian faith, theology must always be seen in its clinical dimensions. And the learning process is still further enhanced if the student has reason to use these ideas immediately in a pastoral care situation. With this in mind it would be well to introduce the student to the normal experiences of the parish ministry before and during the *first* year of seminary. It will not always be possible to give the student graded experiences, yet the instructor in the clinical center would be in a fairly good position to decide which kinds of experience a particular student is ready for. Such experiences might include visiting the aged and the shut-ins, making prospective membership calls, teaching a class in the church school, vocational counseling with high school and college students, and working with small groups and committees in the church on plans for organizational life. These and many more types of experiences could profitably be entered into and later discussed with the instructor. The discussion could be kept on the introductory level, but always with the question in mind, "How does what you are doing relate to both theological context and to the responsibilities of a young pastor?" During his first year, the student ought also to have a course in the dynamics of human personality so that with the help of his clinical instructor and his discussions with his fellow students he can begin to understand what is going on inside himself and the people around him. Clinical courses tend to force growth faster than straight field work assignment because more time is given to reflection upon the nature of the work, but care must be taken lest the student be pushed too fast in self-understanding, for too much of this material too soon is threatening to one's self-concept.

- Should the theoretical knowledge of some psychology of personality, abnormal psychology, psychotherapy as well as psychopathology, precede or follow the student's clinical situation?

By all means, the student should have a good deal of theoretical knowledge of the various types of psychology before he goes into even a general hospital clinical training center. And more than that, this knowledge should have been given him in a theological setting so that he already understands the psychological implications of religious experience. He ought to be quite well informed in these areas when he enters the hospital clinical center or he will be easily overawed by the sophistication of some of the other professional people with whom he will be working.

I think the student should have his first hospital experience in the general hospital where the patients are more like the people he has met in the parish. I would also prefer that the student have both parish and general hospital experience before he goes into the mental hospital. In the general hospital the student is not so much tempted to act like a physician or surgeon as he is tempted in the mental hospital to act like a psychiatrist. Because the minister and the psychiatrist both use conversation in their care of people immature students are led to feel that they will be most effective if they copy the philosophy and technique of the psychiatrist. For this reason he should have had sufficient opportunities in other settings to clarify in his own mind the specific role of the minister in relation to those who are ill.

- How much time should the student spend in hospital clinical centers?

If this clinical curriculum is to include *all* theological students, then each student cannot be expected to spend more than about 6 weeks, full time, in each of two kinds of hospitals. The student who has more than average interest in hospital work may stay on for an additional period. The plan should be sufficiently flexible to allow students to follow through on particular projects of a research nature. I would hesitate to invite a theological student to come into the hospital if he has had no parish experience. Most students who have done this spend too much of their time trying to understand their own professional role in the midst of other professionals simply because they have not had sufficient opportunity to identify themselves with pastoral figures.

- How should the student be supervised and stimulated to see his own personal potentials as well as his professional role?

It would be hard to picture a student, under a competent supervisor, who would not be stimulated to take a deeper look at his own personal potentials and particularly as these relate to his professional role. I would hope that such self-analysis would go on in all clinical centers, whether in churches, social agencies, industry, or hospitals. On the other hand, I react negatively to the kind of supervision which insists that nothing less than a complete psychoanalysis is necessary for every theological student. I have seen harmful results where students have been forced into analysis under a therapist who has not worked through his own religious problems. And if the analyst says that he will stay away from religious issues, then the analysis will not really wrestle with the student's basic problems. Each seminary will have to work out this problem in its own way.

- Does the student, as a result of this clinical experience, become more interested in the traditional disciplines of theological education?

This will depend both upon the extent of the theological undergirding of the clinical instructor and upon the ability of faculty members of the traditional disciplines to make their subjects live. It is true that the clinical training movement in its early years was led by supervisors who were in revolt against traditional theology, and so their students were subtly influenced against it. In fact, some centers were so psychologically oriented that students could go along for weeks in clinical class sessions without the name of God being mentioned. A theological revival has taken place within the clinical training movement which has caused it to bring the Bible, theology, and pastoral care into the center of focus.

This question raises the further question of how long our seminaries are going to be content to have their students supervised by instructors who have not been specifically called by the seminary. The leaders of the clinical training movement have always said that it was their purpose to demonstrate the importance of such training so that seminary faculties would incorporate such clinical courses into their own curricula and then the outside agency could go out of business. But the seminaries have not yet taken over the function of these clinical groups.

Seminary faculties seem perfectly willing to let the outside groups continue to carry on this part of the instruction. Nor have faculties appropriated many of the new clinical insights in the teaching of their own courses. The two groups operate quite apart from each other.

Such separation of clinic and classroom is not healthy. It indicates to the student that faculty people are not yet convinced that clinical instruction can really qualify as a necessary part of the seminary education. Clinical instruction is still only a "frill" or a "tack on," and theological professors are not yet giving it the status it must have if all theological students are to be given the advantages it offers. As a result, at the present time, the students who need it most are not availing themselves of it. In order to be sure that what is taught in the clinical centers is thoroughly related to the traditional disciplines of theological education, it will be necessary that all clinical instructors be selected in the same manner as are other members of the seminary faculty.

- How are the dangers counteracted that the student wants to imitate hospital staff officers, rather than be a minister?

This question is related to the matter of when a student should be assigned to a hospital clinical center. It is also related to the quality of the pastoral role which the instructor typifies. The student should not take his hospital training before he has had opportunity to work in the parish setting under strong pastoral figures. Otherwise, if he has not worked under a pastor who is worth emulating, his natural inclination will be to copy other professional people. And if his clinical instructor is a weak person who commands no respect as a pastor, then it would be most unusual if the student did not try to imitate hospital staff personnel. This question points to a valid criticism of the clinical training movement, but the fact cannot be avoided that any student tends to imitate people he admires. This is all the more reason why the office of pastor should be given more attention in the training of future ministers.

Because the clinical instructor will always be compared by his students with the other professional people in the medical center, this instructor will have to be selected with the greatest care, even being a notch above the average run of pastors or theological professors. One way to get at this problem is to select only those pastors who have been very effective in the parish because of an unusual sense of pastoral responsibility. These men should also be gifted as teachers and should be given a period of time to work on advanced degrees before they are called to a joint appointment on the theological faculty and the particular clinical center to which they are assigned. Their first responsibility is to symbolize for the student what it means to be an effective pastor in a wide variety of situations.

- What differences in the training program should be envisioned between those who want to go into the specialized ministry of the chaplaincy, or a teaching career or those who want to enter the parish ministry?

A Possible Pattern of the 44-Month Plan

1st Year

Summer Quarter	Students to be introduced to parish life in a clinical center located in a church
Fall Quarter	Academic studies only
Winter Quarter	Academic studies only
Spring Quarter	Academic studies and 10 hours weekly in concurrent clinical assignment (possibly in a social agency or a parish church)

2nd Year

Summer Quarter	Clinical center assignment (I suggest an inner city or rural parish, a summer camp, or a religion-in-industry project)
Fall Quarter	Academic studies
Winter Quarter	Academic studies
Spring Quarter	Academic studies and 10 hours weekly in concurrent clinical assignment (possibly in a child guidance clinic, family agency, juvenile work)

3rd Year

Summer Quarter	Clinical center assignment (general hospital, religion-in-government center, Greenwich Village type center, or parish)
Fall Quarter	Academic studies and 10 hours weekly in a parish center not previously assigned to
Winter Quarter	Academic studies and 10 hours clinical instruction in a pastoral counseling center or nearby hospital
Spring Quarter	Academic studies and 10 hours weekly on nearby college campus or in hospital, social agency, or parish

4th Year

Summer Quarter	Clinical center assignment (choice of assignment)
Fall Quarter	Academic studies and 10 hours clinical instruction (pastoral counseling center or parish)
Winter Quarter	Academic studies (no clinical work)
Spring Quarter	Intensive one-to-three-week workshops and seminars on a variety of subjects

I think there should not be too much specialization during the four basic years of theological education. If the pattern which I have been describing were to be followed, it would insure every theological student of several kinds of clinical opportunities. It would certainly not be wasted effort for a man going into student work on campus, for example, to have the experience of working with all kinds of people in the setting of a congregation, a social agency, an industrial plant, a juvenile home, a hospital, as well as the clinical center on a college campus. In his later work with students he would always appreciate the insights gained in all these centers as they applied to the varied problems brought by students. Under the 44-month plan there would be sufficient freedom and flexibility to permit the student to elect to major in a particular kind of clinical center provided this was balanced by sufficient experience in other types of centers. It would be hoped that most students would complete the basic four-year course, with its well-rounded variety of clinical experiences, before specializing. Specialization takes place best at the Ph.D. level just as physicians, after completing the four-year basic course leading to the M.D. degree begin to specialize only after their internship.

• How do you propose to finance the additional costs of the 44-month program?

The 44-month program would make it practically impossible for the student to be engaged in any remunerative employment during these four years, yet he would be giving many months of work to the churches or institutions in which the clinical training centers were located. But the money which might be available for student help will have to be applied on the salary of the clinical instructor. This means that the church will have to find other ways of supporting these students during seminary years. It happens that recently a number of congregations, when they learned that many students hurt their educational program by employment at jobs having no vocational value, offered to support a theological student as their particular contribution to enriching the quality of the church's educational program. I believe that as it becomes known that students for the ministry must spend full time in classroom and clinic, with no opportunity to make money, there will be many churches which will want to provide scholarships. In the long run these churches will greatly benefit by having their pastors given a more thorough education. In some communities several churches will want to go together to support a student. The cost of an 11-month scholarship which includes tuition, board, and room should be approximately $2,000.

REFERENCES

1. It has been suggested that Dr. Westberg's selected quotations from the articles in the June, 1959, issue of the *Augustana Seminary Review* convey an impression relative to Augustana's experience with internship which is not held by many who are close to the program, and that persons interested are invited to gain firsthand impressions by referring to the aforementioned articles.

EARL A. LOOMIS ॐ

Union Theological Seminary in New York City has been undertaking a very bold attempt to study the relationships between religion and psychiatry. Its leadership is not satisfied either with having a theologian speak about psychiatry or with merely calling a psychiatrist in from time to time to enliven academic sessions on such subjects as pastoral counseling. In calling Dr. Loomis, who after one year of theological studies at Princeton Theological Seminary decided to go into medicine and subsequently into psychiatry and has specialized in child psychiatry, Union brought into its faculty a man with a genuine interest in the significance of religion for human development. In studying children one is able to observe the primary and fundamental impact of religious symbols and imagery on the growing personality. The disciplines of child psychology and child psychiatry both enable their students to differentiate between constructive religious influence and idolatrous narrow-mindedness. In both cases the growing child eventually reaches a crisis in which he either has to throw away his faith in order to be realistic in his world or withdraw from some aspects of his adult life in order to maintain his immature piety. Dr. Loomis is an excellent clinician and director of research in child psychiatry. Being actively connected with child psychiatry at New York hospitals he is able to take his students with him and allow them to struggle actively and directly with the possibilities and difficulties of research in that area. Although Dr. Loomis does not claim to be either a theologian or a philosopher, he is very eager to gain an understanding of the vital issues of man's faith and philosophical outlook on life. For this reason he is able to ask his students very challenging questions. This helps the student to realize how much more seriously he has to grapple with his own studies in theology and philosophy in order to be conversant with representatives of psychiatry and social sciences.

Moreover, Union Seminary has Professor Charles Stinnette, a theological counterpart to Dr. Loomis. Professor Stinnette made a name for himself while he was at the College of Preachers in Washington, D.C. Under the challenge of modern psychotherapy Charles Stinnette is eager to see theology come into its own and reconsider seriously its own presuppositions. The combination of serious theological thought and the desire to make theology truly relevant in modern culture mark the contribution of Professor Stinnette to theological education far beyond Union Seminary.

Precisely because Dr. Loomis and Professor Stinnette have not yet produced a full-fledged systematic integration of the two fields of religion and psychiatry their students are forced to wrestle for themselves with the impact of a competent representation of theology and psychiatry. The stimulation of the Union program lies in its challenge to the student to grow in his understanding of theology and psychiatry in order to be able to find his own independent and open approach to the significance of these two respective fields. Dr. Loomis in the following chapter was modest enough not to point out the true vitality of the Union Program in so many words. Nevertheless, the intelligent reader will be able to appreciate between the lines the originality and frankness with which the Union Program on Religion and Psychiatry is working. Anyone who is interested, either for his own sake or for the sake of another theological school, in studying a program in this area while in midstream will greatly benefit from the concrete and practical way in which Dr. Loomis discusses the academic offerings at Union, their potentials, and the inevitable difficulties which arise from any such endeavor.

The Religion-Psychiatry Program at Union Theological Seminary, New York

⋅§ E A R L   A .   L O O M I S

Introduction

Since no two programs for the enhancement of the ministry can be identical, it may be profitable to review the rationale behind the unique pattern of our staff and its program.

A few thousand years ago, the priest and healer were twin identities of one man who was both. Over the centuries, bit by bit, there came to be a differentiation of various functions until the profession of medicine established its own autonomy as a separate discipline. Even as this was happening and for some time to come, the overlap in roles was considerable, particularly in the area of mental illness, in care of which the church continued to play an active part. However, with the rise of scientific medicine and with the decline in the church's hold on either man's body or his mind, psychiatry became the exclusive property of medicine, and religion somewhat reluctantly abrogated its claim on the human mind, all the while finding it harder and harder to barricade the boundaries of the soul against the persistent incursions of the rambunctious new sciences of the mind. Happily, this state of warfare, which marked the end of the nineteenth and the beginning of the twentieth century, has largely ceased. Religion has seen science's legitimate role, and the sciences, including those of man, have begun to move away from the naïve atomistic mechanism and determinism, and have grown holistic, organismic, and even value-conscious. Within the medical sciences, the stepchild, psychiatry, has come to play a decisive role in regaining for medical practice the human and personal qualities that were undermined by the earlier period of scientism, which, however, constituted an admittedly necessary forerunner to medicine's coming of age.

Psychiatry has found itself, in midtwentieth century, performing many services

185

and drawing its understanding from many sources including biology, ethnology, medicine, the social sciences, history, philosophy, and even religion. Ironically, modern psychiatry, whose spiritual father is unquestionably Sigmund Freud, the atheist, is now performing a bridge function between religion and medicine without, I would contend, violating the spirit of its father. He could not have anticipated the philosophic maturation of either science or theology and the potential that this might ultimately provide for a *rapprochement* between the two fields.

Despite the possibility of an intellectual dialogue between theologians and scientific philosophers, the task of communicating at more practical levels and of applying the fruits of this communication to the care of patients and parishioners is a difficult one, and one for which few ministers are yet prepared.

This Religion-Psychiatry Program has as one of its principal objectives the furthering of conversation, both creative and critical, at all levels from the highly theoretical to the strictly practical. With the foregoing background in mind, the designers of the Program elected to pattern its staff and aims around the interrelations of psychiatry and religion. This meant bringing into the Seminary community a representative of the medical and psychiatric professions as a full-time faculty member. According to the design, the psychiatrist-director was to have as his colleague a theologian with both clinical experience and advanced philosophical training. An additional colleague was to be appointed later. Two initial objections to the present design, which is thought to be the first of its kind, include the fear that students would suffer role confusion through being taught by a nonclergyman, particularly since there is a temptation nowadays for some students and ministers receiving training in hospitals and clinics to overidentify themselves with physicians and members of other helping professions. The anticipation that the pressure of student needs for psychotherapy would crowd in on the director's time and that he would be unable to resist this formed the second objection. In other words, the very traits that might qualify him as a responsive psychiatrist might prove to be his undoing in an academic community where he would be the only one available to provide help. Despite these threats which were clear to me as real ones, I began this exploration as both experimenter and guinea pig (which, in a sense, is true of every involved researcher). Frankly, the idea of trying to develop and modify in another discipline some of the principles which had grown out of my previous teaching appealed to me.

As we enter into the fourth academic year, the scene is sufficiently different so that when we look backward it is not difficult to perceive the contrasts and pick up the threads of a number of trends, which are reflected in our courses and in our participation in the life of the seminar community.

Despite the broad perspective in time, and the comprehensive scope around which I report on our first three years, it must be stressed that I am describing them as they are seen through the eyes of a psychiatrist and of my own personality and not necessarily as reflecting the different focus of my nonpsychiatric colleagues or of other members of the Seminary community. Doubtless some of their reactions will be reflected in what I am about to relate, but my judgments about them are my own. It is impossible for one man to represent with full vividness the team approach of our Program since it would probably require a joint writing effort to portray the joint working arrangement within which we live. The latter kind of report will be reserved for a later presentation.

Perhaps one of the best ways of presenting our purposes and goals, the changes we seek in ourselves, the Seminary, and the students, is to describe somewhat discursively some of the things we actually have been doing and to tell some of the reasons why we have done them this way. After an initial resistance to giving courses, we consented to teach a few, and as can be seen, the list has grown. Here is our curriculum in the approximate sequence of its development over the past three to four years.

Religion and Human Development (P.T. 283, R.E. 263)

We began with the assumption that all students should be provided at the earliest available time in their curriculum (which with present curriculum design is the second year of the B.D. candidates, the first year in the case of M.R.E. candidates) a course on human behavior and development. This is considered to be the minimum essential foundation for any minister, and all students who have not had such a course are encouraged to take this beginning course which has been entitled variously Psychology and Religious Development, Human Development and Behavior, and Religion and Human Development. This course, or its equivalent, is prerequisite for all subsequent courses in this Program. It is an elective and has been taken by approximately one-fourth of the B.D. students. Since it or its equivalent is prerequisite for subsequent courses, this means that we have been reaching something under one-third of the B.D. population while they are undergraduates.

In this course the attempt is made to present through lectures and parallel discussion groups an exposure to basic data of human biology and psychology. These are presented developmentally in such a way as to cover the entire life span and to depict the human being as both organism in a physical-biological milieu, person in a social field, culture bearer in a society, and creature in the economy of God. During the Program's first year this course emerged as a continuation of a previous offering of the late Professor Lewis Sherrill, professor of religious education, who had developed it throughout many years of confrontation of his theological message with its psychiatric counterpart. It was my privilege to be co-lecturer with him during this first year. Out of our tandem teaching grew much of the impetus to continuing attempts at integration and parallel presentation of biblical and theological aspects of human nature along with the scientific data and principles.

Out of this first course emerged for many students a first awakening of self-knowledge and beginning insights into the roots and effects of much of their behavior. Such knowledge is always disturbing, and for a few students its emergence led to earnest consultation and eventually referral for psychotherapy. For many others, it simply added a further dimension to the ongoing inquiry into human nature which is one of the top agenda items in student bull sessions.

After the first year a required weekly seminar was added to the two-hour lecture. Students were divided into groups of about ten for these meetings which were led by colleagues other than the lecturer. Their purpose included closer contact with the students, a chance for students to "sound off" and to bring in concerns and examples from their parish experiences. Finally, one of the main functions of the seminar groups has been the valuable feedback to the professor which has included not only information about what the students have learned and failed to learn from his lectures and their reading but also the trend of their changing attitudes toward the material, the course, the professor, themselves, and theology.

Psychopathology and Religion (P.T. 384)

The class, a seminar limited to 25 or 30 students, is divided into three groups. Each member of the *first group* is asked to prepare in writing and for presentation to the class the story and description of a person in his parish or clinical situation. These may be persons suffering from mental illness or personal problems, but are necessarily persons with whom he has had firsthand contact. His presentation may include actual excerpts from hospital histories or from pastoral counseling notes. On the other hand, it may be a reconstruction from memory of earlier contacts which are particularly vivid and through which the student can present a picture of the person and his own interaction with him in a helping or pastoral situation.

Students in the *second group* are assigned the task of studying carefully one of the foregoing writeups (all of which have been prepared for use at least a week in advance of the scheduled class presentation). Second-group students then prepare a psychodynamic and psychopathologic formulation of the assigned case, each from one of the various schools of psychopathology to be covered during the semester. Thus, sequentially, each weekly two-hour seminar consists of a case presentation by a member of the first group, a case formulation by a member of the second, and a general discussion with comments, summary, and critique by the instructor, who also applies and tests the participants' familiarity with the assigned readings in the works of the founders of the various schools of psychodynamics.

Each member of a *third group* is assigned the task of preparing a written summary of one seminar's discussion and the discussion process. The latter reports are of value to the students in relating them to the importance of the process as well as the content of the discussion. They also have special value to the staff in reflecting the general level of student comprehension and participation on the part not only of the reporter, but also of the class as a whole. In addition, from these reports it is possible to develop an elementary index of the extent and kind of student participation in each topic and case and of any individual student's activity pattern and sequence. These reports can be checked against an electronic recording of each seminar which provides verification or further details where needed.

This course has a heavier assigned reading load than any other beginning course. The assignments are almost without exception the original classics and usually include two substantial books from each major school. The reading assignment has varied somewhat depending on whether the student is in group one, two or three.

Despite initial vigorous complaints about the allegedly heavy required work assignments which managed to discourage auditors and cause one or two first-week drop-outs, this course proved to be popular and most of the students did all their work and did it well. It was as if making the course difficult and "pitching" it at a substantially higher level than the first course served to recruit a selected and highly motivated group of students, most of whom were candidates for advanced degrees. However, the B.D. candidates held their own fully. It is expected that this course will become more and more accessible to B.D. candidates after the backlog of advanced students has passed through it.

Though in one sense this is a second course and academically is the immediate sequel to the course on human development and behavior, in another sense it is an advanced course presupposing clinical or at least enlightened pastoral experience, and the capacity to deal critically with competing schools of thought. It is not required of B.D. candidates in general, but it is prerequisite for many advanced courses and is mandatory for candidates for advanced degrees in our Program.

Psychodynamics of Groups (P.T. 386)

This three-point course has met weekly throughout the second semester since the beginning of the Program. The first hour is devoted to a lecture on the theory of group process and group dynamics as derived from the theories and experiments of social psychologists and the experiences of the National Training Laboratories in Bethel, Maine, and the Group Life Laboratories of the Episcopal Church. (Our associate director, Professor Stinnette, has had extensive experience in group dynamics and brings a special interest in this field and its application to the whole life of the church.)

The second period each week is a two-hour laboratory session in which groups of about fifteen students each meet with a "training-group leader." This latter period is devoted to the experimental and experiential encounters of the members with each other and of the development of the group as a whole. Herein occurs the possibility and context for the actional discovery, both of group processes and of the impact of each individual's behavior on the life of the group. Hence, considerable "self-discovery in role" inevitably takes place, through a member's own observations of others' reactions to his behavior. Emphasis is, however, placed upon interactions and transactions from the standpoint of the group as a whole which are therefore generalizable more readily to other group situations, especially those in the church.

The whole group dynamics program is designed to constitute and embody its own built-in self-evaluating principles and procedures. These include not only the ongoing verbal and nonverbal feedback of the T-groups but also observers' reports and written evaluation forms which the student fills out after each lecture and each T-group meeting ("PMR's"—postmeeting reports).

Some Reflections on Teaching Method, Sequence, and Timing

We have tended from the beginning of the Program to trifurcate our teaching efforts—that is, to divide them into communication of information about people and processes in general, into interactive communication between class and teacher in intimate discussion groups, and finally into exposure of the student to the raw experience of immediate transactions with parishioners, counselees, patients, and inmates. Out of a background information comes a certain bridge with the student's former learning processes. He is accustomed to being given an outline and some facts to hang upon it. He gets anxious too readily and too early, if at least some of this is not provided as a beginning step. It is as if consciously he has to believe that the teachers have things under control (which of course isn't true, but which may be a necessary temporary illusion) while more probably the truth, which is likely to be unconscious, is that he hopes that the teacher can keep him under control while he is exposed to the raw, disconcerting underworld of human motivation, fantasy, and conflict.

If at the beginning someone is there who will agree with him that "this, that, or the other situation" is just "a nice example of last week's psychopathology lecture," then he is less likely to imagine too early that this psychopathology is rather the reflection of his own. He may well have to face this fact sooner or later. The question is how soon, under what circumstances, under whose protection. So far we tend to favor an initial exposure to general theory cast in fairly stable outline and not over-personalized. It is clear that even as early as Course I the Program feels defensive: we don't want to be accused of creating pathology, we don't really believe that we do this or are likely to, but we know very well that there is enough pathology or near-pathology lurking just below the surface, or peeping out above it, among students, including seminary students, to make us hesitant if not unwilling to "take the rap" for precipitating excessive anxiety or disorganized behavior.

Clinical Pastoral Training

Since we viewed our Program as both more comprehensive in scope and less focused in method than most existing nonseminary clinical training programs, it was decided that although an emphasis in this area was inescapable and indispensable, a foray into the complicated terrain then occupied so ambiguously by the numerous vying groups involved in training and accreditation would be untimely. It appeared to us that a program as young as ours would be dissipating its energies either to commit itself to one or another position in an ambiguous struggle that seemed, in considerable measure, to be historical, political, and irrelevant to this Seminary's direct goals and which also showed signs of moving toward an ultimate, amicable resolution on the part of a number of the rival groups. Hence, without prejudice to any, and with recognition of the invaluable contribution of the clinical training movement to the ministry and to the seminaries, we chose to remain aloof from party strife in this area and to co-operate with all the existing groups to the extent that they shared our general goals and maintained responsible supervision and clinical experience. Hence, the faculty of our Program includes those who are members of, trainees of, and officers of both the Council for Clinical Training and the Institute of Pastoral Care. In addition, the Seminary became an Associate Member of the Council—a procedure which signifies the assistance in summer placement which is a prerogative of that class of membership.

Interest of the student body in general has been moderate, with about a quarter of the class applying for summer clinical training. Of these, an average of twenty have been accepted and completed their work each year. Enthusiasm has usually been keen by the end of the summer, and the effects of summer clinical training on subsequent performance in our Program have been quite generally observable. In a few instances we have had reason to be dissatisfied with an individual program or supervisor, but these have been the exception.

In addition to the more conventional clinical placements in hospitals and prisons, we have seen fit, in special instances, to encourage and approve the participation of certain students in supervised clinical situations which were not strictly ecclesiastical, or at least not chaplain-related, either in student duties or in supervisory personnel. For example, a therapy camp provides opportunities for supervised experiences as child counselors which are offered on an interdisciplinary basis to medical, social work, psychology, and education students as well as to ministerial students. Where opportunities such as these meet the requirements of adequate supervision and clear role definition (even if the latter is not in the role of clergyman) we have felt they offered valuable training for selected students. Similar programs in interdisciplinary settings have been advocated for internship years.

At the present time four semester points of credit are granted for a satisfactory completion of twelve weeks of full-time training, two points for six weeks. Students are expected to secure the approval of the Program at the time they seek assignment for summer training.

Introduction to Clinical Pastoral Care (P.T. 387-388)

Despite our respect for and appreciation of the indispensable summer clinical pastoral training of which many of our students avail themselves, we felt from the beginning the need for a laboratory and a clinic to go with our lecture halls and seminar rooms, and hence to round out our image of a balanced program.

It was not our desire or expectation to train specialists during the few available hours into which laboratory and clinical exercises could be squeezed during the average week of the busy seminarian. How much time could he actually spare after required hours for classes, study, and field work were subtracted? It appeared that on the average we might legitimately expect about one day or its equivalent, that is, in the case of a student who has only a light or moderate field work assignment. In no case would it seem feasible for a student with a heavy parish assignment and a full-time academic load to tackle even this much additional work. It seemed evident, therefore, that we should plan a program within the available time of the average middler or senior student, which could fit his schedule and which would accomplish our purposes.

Briefly stated, our purposes are (1) to provide an opportunity for a student to be exposed to individual weekly supervision of his work with persons in stress situations, and through this experience to come to recognize in them and in himself the human qualities, both pathological and reparative, about which he had studied in his courses on development and pathology. In other words, here was a place to experience in real life the play of human emotion and the gamut of interpersonal phenomena which every pastor ought to be expected to recognize in himself and his parishioners. Though such an exposure is potentially both frightening and elusive, the presence of the individual supervisor, who reflects with him upon the content and interactions of each interview he conducts, leads to his eventual freedom to perceive and feel hitherto unrecognized or unidentified facets of himself and others. These would include such perceptions as sensitivity to the gestures, posture, intonation, and other nonverbal indices of a parishioner's emotional state. They would also involve the student's coming to be able to recognize his own emphatic anxiety and his own responses to the claims of, or rejection by, his counselee.

(2) The second purpose is a sampling of the sort of experience available in higher intensity during full-time clinical training. Our purpose is avowedly to interest and involve more students in the more intensive program. We judge, however, that a miniature but choice sampling may well whet the student's appetite for more, and in other cases may allay anxieties which might have prevented a student from undertaking clinical training.

(3) The third goal of the course is to provide contacts with an interdisciplinary clinic team which usually includes collaborating representatives from at least three of the following disciplines: psychiatry and other medical specialties, clinical psychology, social work, nursing, penology. Learning his own role as pastor-chaplain in relation to the roles of the other professionals and under the supervision and example of his supervising chaplain, he comes to define and demarcate his own functions, those of his colleagues, and the relationships between them.

Clinical associates have been appointed in three general hospitals and in a jail, a prison, and a hospital for narcotic addicts. One of the general hospitals provided a psychiatric in-patient service and a child psychiatry clinic. We have not used all these facilities in any single year, but during each of the four years, counting this one, we have had at least four facilities available. Though schedules varied from center to center depending upon geographical location and institutional differences, the general pattern has been as follows: two to four hours spent with patients (calling on the general hospital wards, individual interviews, or group leadership in the prisons, parent interviews in the child guidance clinic, and recreational duties on the psychiatric ward), one hour of individual supervision, one to two hours of interdisciplinary staff conferences, one hour of group supervision of theological students, and until the current year one hour per week in a co-ordinating conference at Union Seminary attended by students from all the training centers. Except for the latter, all the activities have been held on the premises of the training center and under the auspices and direction of the clinical associate in charge of the unit, together with the co-operating staff members of his facility. Students generally spent one day or two half-days per week in the institution, frequently taking their meals with the staff, dressing in a prescribed manner, and assuming the roles and duties designated by the institution. They hence were exposed to the inevitable routines and rituals of institutional life and were expected to conform to them. Often this latter challenge constituted major agenda during early supervision.

Between twelve and twenty students have been enrolled each year in this course, of which half are usually candidates for advanced degrees.

It is made clear to each student both verbally and in writing at the time of his registration for introduction to Clinical Pastoral Care that this course does not constitute a parallel or equivalent to clinical pastoral training and that he should not expect to receive credit for it if he should later apply to one of the chaplain-accrediting bodies.

One of our facilities, St. Luke's Hospital, provided us during the first year with a general hospital setting and the supervision of its own chaplain, Otis Rice, an approved supervisor and a pioneer in the clinical training movement. Following his retirement, our activities in St. Luke's shifted to the in-patient psychiatric service, and we continued the special program in the Child Psychiatry Clinic which had been under way since the beginning under my own direct supervision.

The pattern of training in the Child Psychiatric Clinic was not directly pastoral. It rather constituted exposure to an interdisciplinary child guidance team approach to disturbed children and their parents, who are often disturbed themselves. Seminary students had an opportunity to learn about family stress situations, to participate in parent interviews, to learn how to take developmental histories, and to engage in parent guidance while the children received psychotherapy concurrently from another member of the clinic team.

In the Adult Psychiatry Ward every patient has a therapist who is either a private psychiatrist or a psychiatrist-in-training. The Seminary students are not expected to usurp the function of the psychotherapist, and at first there was hesitancy about having them enter directly in the role of chaplain; and so in the second year of the Program, when we first sent students to that service, they functioned initially as observers under the general guidance of the staff psychiatric nurse and received concurrently both individual and group supervision around their general functioning from members of the Seminary faculty. The purpose of the latter was to provide the general advantages of supervision and also to clarify any possible role confusion growing out of their nondescript status on the Psychiatric Ward and also the out-and-out fright which some of them experienced in their direct exposure to the patients.

As time has gone on, the Psychiatric Service and the Seminary have together progressively clarified the role assignment, until our students now are unambiguously identified as student chaplains and have clearly allotted duties of a more specifically pastoral type, in contrast with their earlier functions as observers, *ad hoc* recreational therapists and occasional confidants of certain patients. The psychiatric staff have accepted them in the pastoral role and for the past year have invited the new associate chaplain of the hospital, in charge of training, into the psychiatric staff meetings where he is becoming more and more a professional image to the students. Their supervisor is currently a Christian layman—a nurse who is an experienced psychiatric nursing educator, and double supervision has been discontinued.

Sheer distance and time problems scattered our clinical student body, making co-ordinating seminars difficult to schedule and sometimes onerously inconvenient. The wide gamut of differing roles between direct calling on patients, teaching a Bible class for homosexual prisoners (actually group therapy as well), serving as a parent counselor or functioning on a Psychiatric Ward was sometimes difficult for the seminar leaders to encompass. The latter also found that it was not always easy or possible to find topics or clinical cases of equal relevance to all concerned, and this added to the integrative task of the leader.

Despite this, it was felt that the co-ordinating conference served useful purposes through providing feedback from the clinical outposts, through having a tendency toward insuring a minimum uniformity and comparability in the experiences of all students, and permitted the occasion for exploration of theological implications which might not have emerged in any one individual clinical setting. In other words, there was a pooling of experience, of background, of interests. There was also an avowed intent to ask the theological question and to confront both the clinical sciences and theology with one another.

The groups varied from year to year in their effectiveness. We are now experimenting with a new model which replaces the previous co-ordinating seminars with a monthly lecture series to be addressed by various clinical associates, academic faculty, and guest speakers. This shift would seem to imply a dissatisfaction with the former co-ordinating seminars; and this is actually the case, although the faculty is divided in its judgment as to whether or not the co-ordinating seminars could have been or still could be successfully revivified and whether or not the present plan is an adequate substitute regardless of its own intrinsic value.

The foregoing issue reflects in part a continuing tension between two styles of teaching and administration (and more than likely their characterological correlates within the staff). It is not entirely clear that any one of us represents one style all the time, for from time to time we find ourselves on different sides of the same fence, occasionally defending the other's former position against his new one. At any rate, it has been one of the most stimulating and ultimately gratifying (as well as periodically frustrating) aspects of our Program that we have been able to work together in an uninterrupted harmonious functioning despite strong contradictory emphases. What are these emphases? They might be variously paired as spontaneity versus order, "playing by ear" versus structured planning—less affectionate terms for either polarity would be groping, bungling, fumbling, overpermissiveness, disorientation, and sheer unpreparedness on the one hand, with inflexibility, insensitiveness, rigidity, spoon feeding, narrowness on the other. Actually, everyone seems to want the Golden Mean, or the ideal combination of structure and freedom, process and content, sensitivity and discipline. But the way in which these are reflected in course design and demonstration continues to vary and differ. The fact that our students must be prepared to hold their own with graduates of other institutions in factual knowledge, personal sensitivity, and professional competence demands a minimum end-point for the training program which quite naturally we hope to exceed. Just how that goal is reached, however, is a question with which we are still struggling.

Over and above the varieties of approaches to teaching, and the important and stimulating but not incapacitating stress deriving therefrom, were the routine duties with regard to our clinical students and to our clinical associates. To some extent both the director and the associate director, but for the most part the associate director, assumed the principal responsibility for assignments and co-ordination of the whole clinical program for the first two years. It was in the plan of the Program from the beginning to introduce in the third year a third full-time faculty member. His appointment was originally envisaged to fulfill duties in the areas of research, human development, and social psychology. The interests, however, of the first two men covered these areas so fully that it seemed wise not to duplicate in these areas, but rather to introduce a colleague who could bring special abilities in three areas, among them clinical supervision (the other two were teaching supervision to field work supervisors and providing counseling and psychological referral functions). We were fortunate that through the availability and appointment of Jack Greenwalt of Pittsburgh, the needed talents were brought gratifyingly into our team.

The Relation Between Supervision and Therapy

This question must be examined in the context of the whole of a student's education. First of all, it must be recognized that there is a difference between students' learning from reading and lectures on the one hand, and learning from personal involvement in life experiences on the other. Our Program attempts to relate these two types of learning through connecting the conceptual and the concrete, the existential and the theoretical. This means providing situations in which clinical experiences bring feelings, commitments, and responsibility into prominence. Without the connecting of the theoretical and the concrete, without the student's development of understanding of others, there is likely to be no real understanding. The mere *possession* of knowledge can be precarious, can get students into trouble (even into attempting intervention in inappropriate cases). Furthermore, it can come between a man and his really knowing and being known by the object (rather, perhaps, the *subject*) of his clinical pastoral encounter. It is therefore to the end—the personal knowledge and involvement of the student in seeing his parishioners in sickness and health, in hearing them in their joy and their sorrow, in speaking to them out of his own appropriation of the truth in which both pastor and parishioner participate—it is to this end that our work is directed.

When we attempt to teach at this level, the student's personal life situation and his mental health become even more significant in the teaching and learning relationship. Because of this some have suggested that (1) only students who have received psychotherapy should undertake such training; (2) only students who do not require therapy should be accepted. These two extremes have both been rejected by our Program. Rather we have attempted to employ the supervisory situation as the occasion for most sensitively discovering (by both supervisor and student) the need for therapy. It is in the supervisory situation and relationship that the student's emotional blockings to understanding his parishioner appear. It is in the supervisory situation that exorbitant tendencies to anachronistic types of transference and countertransference behavior are disclosed. It is in the supervisory situation that the student pastor's "acting-out" toward his parishioner can be identified. When the student's blocking responds to simple confrontation and explanation of the reality situation, supervision suffices. When the transference and countertransference phenomena are simple and nonmalignant and respond to clarification and explanation, supervision may suffice. When acting-out ceases upon being pointed out by the supervisor, treatment for the student may not be indicated. But, when the foregoing fail, when the student's personal problems get in the way of his interpersonal competence, his pastoral commitment and performance, his spiritual orientation to his work, then psychotherapy may be indicated. And where better to discover this and interpret it to the student than in the supervisory setting where it appears?

In other words, the supervisor comes to be the one who confronts and clarifies. He shows the student *what* he is doing and may help him in general to understand why such things may be done. He will avoid probing for or encouraging expression of *why* the student behaves as he does. That is the work of the therapist. But the two work hand in hand, supervisor and therapist. Otherwise there is real danger that the student will, wittingly or unwittingly, play one off against the other.

A major problem in the life of most ministerial candidates, at one time or another, is the question of *vocation*. "Am I called to be a minister or priest? Am I suitable for this high calling? Can I fulfill its requirements? Isn't there another profession in which I really belong?" These nagging doubts, and many others related thereto, recur with almost predictable frequency in work with seminary students. They are often realistic questions. Students are appropriately impressed by the high calling of the ministry, by its great responsibilities and demands, by the sacrifices and rewards of the priesthood. But over and beyond the realistic appreciation of their limitations, some students have serious ambivalence expressed in ruminative doubts which rock the theological bark and trouble the waters of their training. Such men can be sent back to their families; they can be sent back to their classes; they can be sent back to their prayers. But for some of them the doubts constitute evidence of illness. If their doubts and questions significantly and continually interfere with their spiritual devotion, their academic studies, their social adaptation, and their capacity for forming object relations with others, the need for treatment is evident. This rather than remonstrating, expelling, or attempting to reassure.

Advanced Clinical Pastoral Care and Controlled Supervision (*P.T. 491-492*)

Among the requirements for all graduate degrees in our Program is the completion of an adequate period of full-time clinical pastoral training or its equivalent. In the case of the Master's degree candidates, the minimum requirement is one quarter, and in the case of doctoral candidates, it is one year. Because of the impossibility of personally evaluating clinical training done elsewhere, or the degree of personal development and competence thereby acquired, we have required all our graduate students to complete, in addition, a period of supervision under a member of our faculty or clinical associates group. In the case of students who have had more than one quarter of clinical training and who have demonstrated proficiency in their pastoral care relationships, we have encouraged, and in the case of doctoral candidates have required, the undertaking of a year of junior supervision or supervised supervision in one of our related clinical settings. Hereby it is possible for the clinical associates to assign to the junior supervisor both a parishioner-counselee and a student-counselor. The senior supervisor will supervise both the junior supervisor's work with his parishioner-counselee (which gives him a chance to learn how the man performs in a direct counseling situation), and at the same time he will supervise the man's supervision of a less advanced student and work with him around the understanding of the supervisory process and its relationship to the personalities both of the supervisee and the supervisor.

Hereby is developed an experimental demonstration of the identifications and cross-identifications which arise around the supervisory process and which, if not understood, can cause misunderstanding or blocking of success in supervision.

This year's training on a one-day-a-week basis in no sense is deemed equivalent to, or a substitute for, the supervision training and requirements established by the chaplain-accrediting bodies. It is, however, a laboratory wherein we can learn more about our advanced students as they actually function and can provide, even for less advanced students, an opportunity for learning the basic principles of supervision and of becoming comfortable in their use. This preparation is not calculated to qualify the graduate student for training chaplains or functioning as a chaplain-supervisor, but rather to prepare him to deal with the needs for supervision of members of his parish staff, lay workers, and lay leaders. This preparation is deemed valuable since the development of adequately trained and supervised laity is a responsibility of every pastor. Hence, every pastor should have had the experience both of being supervised himself and of providing supervision to others under controlled conditions. Three points per semester are granted for this course and the clinical responsibilities pertaining thereto.

Psychiatry Seminars (P.T. 395-396)

Since only a small percentage of the students have the opportunity of working with psychiatrists or hearing psychiatric cases presented, an additional opportunity was afforded through the generosity of St. Luke's Hospital, through its Director of Psychiatry, Dr. John Cotton, who issued an invitation to any qualified students to attend his seminars in psychiatry. These include weekly case presentations of both adult and child patients, sometimes actually "demonstrated" and occasional lectures on topics of current interest in psychiatry and related fields. Students are welcome to raise questions for discussion when there is time.

From the standpoint of child psychiatry, a similar experience was provided through the Child Psychiatry Clinic's weekly diagnostic staff conference. Here an interdisciplinary presentation of history, psychiatric examination and psychological tests leads to a child-and-family formulation of etiology, dynamics, prognosis, and therapy plan. Students are encouraged to participate in eliciting and elucidating the religious dimensions of the problems.

It was recognized that direct exposure to raw pathology would be threatening to unprepared students, so we have required not only the academic preparation of the first course, and where possible the second, but also concurrent clinical supervision or, in some instances, psychotherapy. The purpose of this requirement is to obviate any student's developing overidentification with or emotional reactions to the patients and their pathology and, unnoticed, to move into anxiety states which had been unwittingly precipitated by the experience. Having someone with whom he can "check out" each week's reactions to, and his feelings toward, the psychiatric staff tends to reduce anxiety and prevent the development of misconceptions about psychiatrists or patients. These precautions have been waived in the case of mature and experienced persons who have already completed therapy, supervision, and previous exposure to analogous situations. One point of credit each semester is given for attendance at either one of these seminars.

Psychology and the Pastoral Office (P.T. 483)

This was taught first as a lecture course for undergraduates. Professor Stinnette and I presented it jointly and attempted to outline the major areas of function of the pastor in psychodynamic and theological terms. We were particularly sensitive to the call of the minister; the multiple claims upon him, his roles and functions, and the psychological meaning of the life situations within which and into which he must move, his symbolic meanings in the eyes of his congregation, their expectations of him, and their possible uses and misuses of him were all considered. Psychological first aid and the use of community resources were also considered.

Theology and Psychiatry (P.T. 485)

This course grew out of the teaching experience of Daniel Day Williams, professor of Systematic Theology and currently the chairman of this Program's Faculty Advisory Committee. It was he who proposed, as early as a year before the Program got off the ground, that he and I consider offering a joint course. It was his vision that our undertaking would represent our own adaptation and development of a seminar which he had taught jointly with Seward Hiltner and, at one time, with Anton Boisen at the Federated Theological Faculties of the University of Chicago.

We chose seven to ten major themes of human existence, on each of which we attempted to focus the light of both psychiatry and theology. Running through the entire course's assignments, and representing something of the clinical, anecdotal or existential dimension was the reading, study and analysis of a novel—the protagonist of which during the first two years was a physician embroiled in an identity struggle; in the last year he was "the artist as a young man." The introduction of the biographical vector gave longitudinal perspective and developmental dimensions to the more cross-sectional and topical examinations of each of the weekly presentations—the latter included consideration of love and hate, work and play, suffering and martyrdom, freedom, faith, guilt and shame, hope and joy. There was specific attention also to methodological problems.

Guided Reading and Guided Research in Psychiatry and Religion

Seminars for groups and private sessions for individuals are arranged each semester to meet the needs for students to fill in major areas of interest or deficiency in their knowledge of the literature of the major fields in our syllabus. The latter comprises a broad spectrum of learning and lore from a variety of disciplines relevant to human behavior and mental health. Usually a theme or pair of themes runs through the seminar's assignments. For example, one semester a major emphasis was on ethnology and the relationship between the innate and the acquired, with concurrent theological reflection on the implications of the newer learning for philosophical anthropology. Another semester's concerns dealt largely with philosophy of science, the works of Einstein, Bohr, Heisenberg, and others, while attempts were made to re-evaluate issues such as freedom and creaturehood in the light of changing perspectives and methods in science. Currently one group is examining the relations of existential philosophy and existential psychotherapy, while another is following a serious train of thought in philosophical biology and systems theory.

Guided research is of course the heart of any graduate program, and though individual projects may be worked out at various levels of a student's development, the two places in which his preparation is most thoroughly focused and tested are in his individual thesis work and in his thesis seminars.

Thesis Seminars (P.T. 481-482, 497-498)

Two thesis seminars have been provided, sometimes concurrently, sometimes alternately, depending on student needs and faculty load. The first seminar is primarily for B.D. and beginning Master's candidates, especially those who have had no prior preparation in scientific method, statistics, or research design. This seminar is designed to introduce the students relatively quickly to elements of the foregoing which will aid them in either acquiring or utilizing empirically derived data in relation to hypotheses relevant to issues in psychiatry and religion. All students writing theses under the supervision of this Program are expected to demonstrate familiarity with the issues of the legitimate and illegitimate uses of data and to base at least some aspect of their thesis on empirical findings. The latter need not necessarily be limited to experimental data and certainly would rarely represent "instrumental readings." What is required is that the student has some concept of a hypothesis, a method of testing it, and a way of testing the reliability of his method and demonstrating its communicability to others.

At the Bachelor's and Master's level such undertakings must necessarily be limited in scope and parsimonious in conclusions.

The doctoral thesis seminars are limited to doctoral and advanced Master's degree candidates and deal with longer-term problems. It is as if in the first seminar one must assist the student to plan his project and collect his data, while in the second seminar he will be assisted in drawing conclusions and writing his thesis. In the case of the doctoral seminar, however, the long-term aims change the perspective; and larger issues of methodology, repeated progress reports of ongoing projects and special techniques can be considered. Students in the latter seminar have tended to deal with issues involving (1) psychosomatic medicine and the relation of the chaplain to healing, (2) relations between theological and psychological concepts, attitudes and techniques such as love and experience, psychological and personal aspects of prayer, play and grace, and images of the ministry, (3) social-psychological studies of individual responses to various rites and functions of the church and its ministry.

Extension of the Clinical Perspective Through Sharing in Field Work Responsibilities and Training

During the Program's first year its staff assumed responsibility for a supervisory seminar consisting of a seminar group of junior field work students. We also supervised them individually and visited their parish situations with them. When Professor Greenwalt arrived in the third year one of his three functions was to share in field work staff discussions and to conduct individual and group supervision of field work supervisors.

It was felt hereby that our Program could make a significant contribution to field work by introducing certain principles and practices of clinical supervision. At the same time our Program would be kept abreast of trends and developments in another area of the Seminary which constitutes a major growing edge in the study and improvement of the teaching-learning process.

Making the Ministry Relevant

In order to make the ministry more relevant it is essential to look at the man in the ministry and to become aware of the demands upon him and how these demands relate to one another.

The Christian minister feels the impact of demands from at least three sources: First, the community of need, for example, men and women to whom he and his church minister as the redemptive community or the nucleus thereof. Second, the spiritual calling and its traditional and ecclesiastical representations, for instance, the Gospel that must be preached, the faith to be delivered, the calling and command to preach, to minister, to serve and to teach. Finally, his own inner needs for self-fulfillment and expressing himself in his vocation, such as the sublimation and gratification of his drives, the integration of his defenses, and the clarification of his goals.

Historically, the ministry may be viewed as always related in some way or another to each of these three sets of demands. There have been times when one or another of the demands has been accentuated. There have been times when one or more of the demands have been ignored. But it is in the nature of things that demands go right on making their claims regardless of our ability or willingness to allow them conscious recognition or overt expression. Hence it is not surprising that even in an age relatively oblivious to the historical message and the spiritual dimensions of religion, there have continued to be "break-throughs" of a prophetic nature. In fact, the scriptural record suggests that this is the pattern. Could it not be that an analogous situation also exists for the other two sets of demands?

For example, is it not likely that if the needs of parishioners and the outer community to whom the church and the clergyman minister are not met, these will in some way seek their expression and fulfillment through a dramatic explosion which constitutes a claim upon a church or a judgment upon its failure? In America it has become almost commonplace to recognize in each of the newly emerging cults and sects (for instance, Christian Science, Pentecostalism, Jehovah's Witnesses, Seventh Day Adventism, Spiritualism), the eruption of a popular claim that cannot be ignored, the demonstration of a human need whether expressed directly or in disguise. Finally, could it not be that if the deep inner needs of each minister to find himself, to fulfill himself, and to express himself in his vocation are not distinctly met and recognized, there will occur an eruption or substitute formation which signals an unfed hunger?

Historically speaking it is likely that the central core of the spiritual demand, that is, that of God, the Gospel, and the historical church, will change least of all, although it may undergo modifications of expression even as scripturally we see the prophets proclaiming doom and judgment sometimes, other times uttering words of promise and comfort. Likewise, the basic inner needs of men will probably remain fairly constant within the species and their expression will remain *relatively* constant within the culture. It is, however, at this latter point that advances in ego psychology, particularly in the area of identity formation have made a difference. The approach of Erik Erikson to "ego-identity" brings into the open the fact that the human self in action and life is a bridge between biologic individuality and the larger body of the community. It is in the area of the latter's needs and demands, both as they exist in themselves and as they make their explicit and implicit claims upon the minister and the ministering community, that the possibility of an ever-changing spectrum of need-and-demand representations is likely. In other words, "new occasions do teach new duties." The question is, How are we to *use* the occasions so that we will *learn* the duties?

How can we best come to know about all three sets of demands, particularly as these converge upon the pastor in action or in receptive potential responsiveness? This it seems is one of the goals of the ministry: namely, the co-ordination of the three sets of demands, in the paradox of claim, call, and freedom. Creature of paradox—as he must be to minister to other creatures of paradox—how can he best know the truth, purify his intentions, and feed his sheep? I confess that we do not have the answers to these questions worked out on the basis of syllogistic demonstration, empirical evidence, or experiential conviction. The faith that these ideas are part of the answers which we seek, that these are seekable and potentially findable—or at least that the seeking itself has value—these have been the beliefs of our group as we have tackled the shaping of this Program and the working within it, within the life of the community of the Seminary, and in relationship to the philosophic and scientific disciplines also relevant to the interests of the Program.

If Bultmann is correct in his judgment that the presuppositions that are in our minds when we ask the theological questions make the difference as to the kinds of answers to which we can be open and responsive or the way in which we are able to ask the questions—then the sorts of emotional openness and interpersonal insight a student might gain in pastoral training in programs such as ours may make a decisive difference in his capacity for "affinity" or resonance with those who have written what he reads—then he may bring a whole new side of himself to his hermeneutics. Another way to put this is in terms of the recollection-surprise paradox. There is a sense in which we learn nothing new, but rather that we always discover what we already knew but didn't recognize as known—Plato's doctrine of recollection and Bultmann's thesis each point to this phenomenon in their own way. But on the other side of the paradox is that *surprise* seems to be an indispensable or at least common characteristic of the emergence of significant insights or of moments of illumination or revelation. Professor Muilenberg stresses the fact that as well as they seem to have known him, Jahweh is always coming to the prophets as a great surprise. This fits in too, with the psychoanalytic theory of surprise as the abrupt crossing of a barrier by an idea, an image, an affect, or a "unit of psychic energy."

Bringing future theologians both to recognize the overlooked commonplace and to be open to surprise thus may constitute a twofold contribution by our programs to the science of theology. There may be many ways of bringing this about. Only the continuing comparison and contrasting of them can lead us to the beginnings of necessary evaluation of the preferable patterns.

Mental Health Instruction in
Theological Schools

I

The National Institute of Mental Health, when it initiated through a grant the Harvard University Project on Religion and Mental Health, had a threefold goal in mind. First, a program would be set up which would allow the Harvard Divinity School to take full advantage of the resources available in the whole University, experiment with different methods of instruction, and exchange its findings with other theological schools in the country. Second, guides, textbooks, and other useful material would grow out of the experience of teaching and serve later in the classwork of the other seminaries and divinity schools. Third, prospective teachers in the field of religion and mental health would be trained at Harvard in order to work in this branch of theological education.

At this point, the Harvard Project has just passed the halfway mark in its assigned duration. A guide to religion and mental health, comprising prepared case material for discussions and a syllabus on books in the area, is ready for publication together with two symposia which deal with the significance of such teaching in theological schools for the church and its ministry and with the practical experience which some have had in trying it out. Twelve doctoral students in a joint program of the Graduate School of Arts and Sciences and the Divinity School are preparing themselves for their teaching careers. Their dissertations promise to add substantially to the publications of the Project.

Two books will appear toward the end of the Project. One is expected to outline the role of religion in the growth of the personality. The other will offer, as a textbook, a short introduction to the field of psychology of personality, abnormal psychology, psychopathology and psychotherapy designed for ministers and others who do not plan to make clinical psychology their career.

The pages of this chapter contain a preliminary account of the teaching experience in the field of religion and mental health at the Harvard Divinity School. The aim is to submit them, with their suggestions to other interested people and institutions in order to arouse as broad and vigorous a discussion as possible. Such a conversation and sharing of different viewpoints and approaches is needed to give birth to a final plan of instruction which can benefit from all of them and be applicable to most of the theological curricula in operation in schools throughout the country.

The mutual exchange of diverse ways of teaching is particularly in order within Protestantism inasmuch as there the attention to the problem of religion and mental health has already produced a variety of programs. They stem from responses to specific needs and bear the mark of any given theological bias and practical intention. To co-ordinate them does not mean to rob them of their unique characteristics or function. But they can stimulate and enrich each other and drive for still deeper penetration into the relation between religion and mental health. Even the most elaborate teaching methods are but a very elementary probe into a field which can yet provide the stimulus for a veritable reformation of the church and its ministry.

Two basic problems make a radical reconsideration of the training of prospective ministers in the field of mental health mandatory. The first is that the present-day pastor no longer has a clear-cut and generally accepted understanding of his communal role. His professional preparation at school, therefore, is apt to focus on academic subjects which have no immediate bearing on his pastoral duties as he finds them cut out for him by the wish of the congregation he wants to serve. He feels highly incompetent to meet these demands because they were hardly mentioned by professors interested primarily in the scholarly pursuit of their own speciality.

The second problem lies in the divergency of approach between the clergyman who feels himself called to further the divine cause by proclaiming revealed truth to man who without God's grace is a sinner, and the social scientist or psychotherapist who scrutinizes the human predicament empirically and seeks to help people on the basis of their concrete needs.

To merge these two diametrically opposed points of departure into a happy union can be done only at the price of dishonesty, growing mutual disrespect, and misunderstanding which must lead eventually to antagonism and alienation, or at least to a loss of efficiency on both sides.

To introduce subjects which have their proper origin in the empirical, pragmatic concern of the social and medical sciences into the theological curriculum is equivalent to planting a hostile virus into an organism. Either the organism produces enough antibodies to isolate and finally expel the virus and thus defend its own nature or it succumbs to the assault and is transformed by its impact. A third way is not given.

It is indeed futile to subsume secular knowledge about the human personality safely under the traditional teaching of the Christian doctrine of man. It is equally useless to add to the practical domain of pastoral training a theoretical exposition on how psychotherapists deal with people. All that the social sciences have to say about human behavior makes it impossible to integrate it successfully into the scheme which theology uses to expound the relation between the creator, God, and his human creature. Either the secular knowledge about man will render the theological presuppositions mere metaphysical hypotheses without any direct relevance to the secular understanding, or theology will carefully dissect the total thrust of the social sciences and divert their insights into serving solely as marginal illustrations to selected details of theological doctrines.

Psychiatry as a medical science is based on the biological and biochemical structure of the human organism, just as is any other medical discipline. When it transcends the orbit of the natural sciences to take into account the environmental influences on man and his reactions to them, then it is for the sole purpose of becoming better equipped to deal with his psychopathological problems in therapy. Psychiatry has no innate interest in any theological or philosophical speculations about man per se. They become significant merely as possibly telling symptoms of a neurotic or psychotic escape mechanism designed by the organism to avoid facing up to an intolerable challenge.

If psychiatric assumptions or clinical evidences are forced to support a method of pastoral counseling, they, by necessity, are taken out of their clinical context as therapeutic tools of the doctor with a sick patient and used for an alien purpose, namely to define the relation between two independent, responsible human beings.

Granted, the dividing line between theology, on the one hand, and the social sciences and psychiatry, on the other, cannot always be drawn so easily and sharply. Nonetheless, their distinctive characteristics and hence their natural incompatibility have to be kept in mind. In terms of the administrative organization of a theological school, the result is that the division which studies and teaches the relation between religion and mental health has to be set up as a separate unit, independent from all other branches of theological education.

The function of such a division is to present, clearly and objectively, those evidences from the social sciences and psychiatry which are pertinent to a better understanding of the personality and its environmental involvement. They should not be screened according to their possible congruence with the theological outlook and not evaluated from this point of view. The full challenge which such an un- biased presentation offers is the only chance that a fruitful conversation can take place. Ideally, the respective social scientist, regardless of his personal religious leanings, should be asked to expound the method and findings of his specific field. No special reference to religion or apologetic attempts to justify or mitigate a given point of view are in order. The meeting ground is not the apparent similarities between theology and the social sciences but the understanding of human beings and their situations.

The psychiatrist can make his real contribution in explaining his profession to theological students only if he does it within the natural confines of his own activity

—the hospital. He, and not the chaplain, is to select the patients and circumstances or the staff meetings and private discussions through which the student will gain an introduction to the various aspects of psychiatry.

The hope that the theological student may have undertaken such studies already in college remains an unrealistic wish. Usually the applicant for theological education has gone through the grade mill of introductory courses but not gained any appreciation of the field as a source of solid and vital knowledge. Only in the rarest case does a college student form his own judgment as to the implication of course offerings for an integrated understanding of the personality which firmly stands up to the challenge of another discipline.

The advantage of having such courses as an integral part of theological education is that a confrontation with the intrinsically theological subjects then becomes possible. The student himself rather than a remote academic concept becomes the battleground between the diverging views. The theological teacher who will participate in the confrontation with the secular disciplines presents the tradition of the Christian faith in correlation with the topics discussed by the secularist. But he avoids running a merely competitive course in order to outdo his teaching partner.

One asks far too much of a student when one expects that he will be able to interrelate two courses which do not run parallel and in clear connection with each other. This is not solely a matter of scheduling but more so of joint preparation by the instructors who beforehand have to see to it that they speak a mutual and thus for the student understandable language. This added burden for the teacher is by no means a luxury but the indispensable precondition for the success of the total endeavor.

Certainly, the absence of a ready-made synthesis between and integration of secular and theological components by one and the same theological teacher requires much of the student. He has to bring with him the maturity, objectivity, and judgment to face and digest such a confrontation without escaping it by identifying prematurely with one or the other side. If he is not able to take this, he disqualifies himself for the parish situation where such a predicament will surely arise, provided that pastor and parishioners choose to be honest with each other.

The personal qualification of the entering student is probably the most crucial problem of theological education. The faculty has to decide whether it wants to train people or merely to teach them subject matter. This decision will have definite implications for the quality of future ministers.

According to psychological inquiries it is far from true that the most mature, most intelligent, and most open-minded college graduates decide to study for the ministry. On the contrary, more often than not, neurotic difficulties and a general unwillingness to face the competitive selection in other professions drive the more timid and still quite dependent boys into applying to theological schools. This trend is not necessarily detrimental to the recruitment for the ministry. To accept this risk, however, demands that specific steps be taken to insure personality growth.

Psychological testing screens out those applicants who are in need of such extensive psychotherapy that it will interfere unduly with the adequate pursuit of their studies. On the other hand, previous psychiatric treatment should not automatically bar an applicant if an interview by or the recommendation of a qualified professional reveals that sufficient improvement has been achieved.

Not even the most ideal screening of entering students could or should ever relieve the school of the responsibility for providing ample opportunity for psychological and, if need be, for psychiatric attention to the student. Pastoral care and academic advice are indeed just as needed but are never a substitute for help in personal growth and its possible complications.

The contrast between the stipulations which a church puts forward in seeking a new pastor and the requirements which a faculty imposes on its student is so striking that the cleavage between the theologians and the actual church situation needs no further proof. Members of the congregation look for a man who is able to understand them and cope with their personal as well as religious problems in terms which they can understand in the light of their personal experiences.

The seminaries want to graduate a young man who has satisfactorily demonstrated his ability to deal intellectually with the tradition of the Christian faith to be preached and taught. He is also trained to function properly in regard to the liturgical, administrative, and interpersonal duties of his office.

The parish wants a human being who incorporates in his personality all the qualities which mark the religious leader. The seminaries prepare a professional representative of a specific ecclesiastic orientation. Small wonder that the faithful and their newly ordained pastor both have great difficulties in seeing each other for what they are, before they gradually work out a modus vivendi which hopefully is mutually agreeable. In reality, though, such an open or hidden gentleman's agreement leans heavily toward the side of the congregation which, after all, pays its minister and effectively controls his social acceptance in the community.

In any case, the actual job analysis of the parish minister has little to do with his intellectual training in school and leaves him next to no time to keep up with the rather ambitious study habits which his teachers have tried to acquaint him with. Looking back on his studies, the minister either nostalgically misses or still abhors the hours given then to theoretical speculations which had one single result. They furnished him with the certificate which allowed him to become ordained and allows him now to execute his performances and make his living.

All professional schools in the academic world, as, for instance, medicine, had to face the painful realization that the promotion of scholarly activities is not readily reconcilable with the demands of professional proficiency which are dictated by the brutal facts of actual needs and not by the desires of the scholars.

That theological education is so tardy in following suit stems from the allowance which the world makes for the representative of the other-worldly. A physician who is not up to the professional measure is coldly bypassed. A minister has not enough direct and dire influence on the welfare of people to elicit an equally severe professional evaluation. Therefore, he is given a blank check to work in matters so ethereal as not to be immediately understood by anyone but himself. If he is only a good man who stands for what his people believe in, his precise theological training or orientation is quite secondary.

The second reason for the unwillingness of theological education to bridge from its side the chasm between theory and practice in the ministry has to do directly with the possibility of bringing instruction in religion and mental health into the divinity curriculum. The only basis on which the problem of the psychological and socio-logical understanding of personality and the concepts of mental health and illness may be dealt with is experience and its understanding through observation. It is for this reason that one always speaks of religion and mental health but never about theology and mental health.

Religion and religious experience, however, have come into special disrepute with contemporary theology. Religion consists in the personal experience of an intimate understanding of one's own origin, meaning, and fulfillment in this world, and the expression of that meaning. Religion is anthropocentric and can hence be studied in broad human and cultural terms within the context of other cultural and time-bound undertakings.

Theology has today a quite different understanding of its own subject matter. God, not man, is the prime factor of its consideration. His self-revelation in history, leading to and from its culmination in the God-man Jesus Christ, is the foundation and sole reason for the existence of theology. The Bible, as the record of divine initiative, contains all basic knowledge needed and constitutes the measure by which theology professes to view man and the world.

The possibility that man could know God through his own effort is as much ruled out as the gradual diminution of the cleavage between the sovereign God and sinful man. Only once and in one person did God in the past overcome the total separation. In Jesus Christ, the real and true man, as God wants him to be and toward whom He wants to transform all men, the prototype of the theological understanding of man is established. Theology is not trying to find out what man is or could be according to his innate potentials. Theology knows already, on the basis of absolute, revealed truth; it tries to tell people what they are and are not, but especially what they should and could become through the divine, redemptive grace.

The theologians are well aware of the irreconcilable distinction between such knowledge of man and all other empirically established indications concerning human nature. They insist that the two competitive approaches have to be dis-tinguished as man's attempt to understand himself by himself and to build a dependable knowledge of the world and finally God upon it, contrasted with the proclamation of God's intent to build his kingdom on earth and renew man by bringing him into this historical enterprise.

Only the church, as the communion of the believers and all those who through total commitment join with it, can be convinced of the absolute accuracy and relevance of theological thinking. Outside of the church not only is there no salvation but also no theological understanding. No empirical verification of this absolute truth by secular methods is either possible or needed.

Not always and everywhere will the church- and Christ-centered theology state its position in such brusque words. Ideological thinking never has entirely captured the American mind. Still, the hesitation of theological education to yield its approach to the needs of the parish situation and start its consideration from there must be explained on this ideological ground. For the same reason, the instruction in the field of religion and mental health is either unwarranted within the framework of a strict theological orientation or must be set up as a radical challenge to it. At the present, the latter possibility is certainly most workable.

Since it is to be hoped that the study of the interplay between religion and mental health will reform the theological outlook, these new inquiries must be as diligent as possible. Half-truths, undue generalizations, and premature syntheses have already confused the picture all too much. They lead only to further hiding from the real issues.

It should therefore not surprise the reader if the following course suggestions are intensive and extensive at once. Their goal is to outline a study program which brings the student to grapple first with those findings from the social sciences and psychiatry which alert him to man and his present predicament as they really are. From such a sensitizing of his curiosity as to how in this world theology, the church, and its ministry can have real impact he will begin to ask questions.

An immense handicap in theological education heretofore has been the failure to meet the student in the center of his active interest. With the charming, though blindfolded, zeal of the neophyte he is usually overeager to jump right into the parish activity while, or certainly not long after, he has gathered some few "know-hows." The formal teaching of biblical scholarship, church history, doctrinal and ethical theology seem to him to be unbearable retardations which answer questions which neither he nor anybody of his acquaintance had ever thought of asking. Without the lively curiosity of the student there is not much chance of effective and lasting teaching as anyone experienced in the field can testify.

Theological educators will have to come to the painful realization that their primary responsibility is not to teach the well-rounded scope of the traditional Christian faith and thinking. Rather, it is to serve as resource persons who guide the growing interest of the student to the treasures of the past if and when his interest is quickened. Then, he will ask about the relevance of those thought-structures for us now and, afterward, for the significance they must have had for the people who once had stressed them so much.

It is an unreasonable fear to assume that a student who has seriously studied the present-day human predicament will no longer ask any further questions. On the contrary, the scores of laymen, psychiatrists, and social scientists who inquire adamantly as to the genuine meaning of religion testify to the opposite.

Another misconception has to be cleared out of the way of successful theological studies. Most students today are in dire need of financial support whether they are already married or not. Usually this need is met by so-called week-end work in neighboring churches. The idea that a student could wholeheartedly attend to his studies for a full week and then start working all over again over the week end shows respect neither for the limitations of his energies, nor for the demands of studies and church work.

The rationalization for any such illegitimate setup is that this gives the student a welcome introduction to the life and work of a minister. To call this assumption mistaken is a grandiose understatement. If it is any introduction, then it is a miserable one. The minister who hires the untrained student is well aware that the young man works for money without having real qualifications. The remuneration will be correspondingly meager, so much so that it is frequently and with bitter, but appropriate, irony called slave-labor. And that is what it is.

Knowing the student's inadequacies the minister will not entrust him with any decisive or delicate church work. On the contrary, he is apt to relegate to his student-assistant all the little chores which he hates to do himself or is not good at himself. What sort of introduction to the ministry is that? On a casual week-end basis the student is hardly able to establish sound personal relations with anyone in the congregation. If he would like to do so—and who would not who wants ever after to be worthy of his name as minister—then his involvement with his parish duties interferes as to time, energy, and emotional involvement with his studies at school. In turn, he will be professionally ill prepared for his later duties. The vicious circle is closed.

The National Council of Churches would be well advised to make more fruitful use of the fact that more than one hundred million people in this country are affiliated with churches. Could the Council with its authority bring the local churches to save on some stained glass windows and other precious material when constructing their palatial edifices in order to make some scholarship money available for theological students?

The only way in which the practical training of the prospective minister can be made valuable is to put it on the same level with his theoretical studies in terms of time allotment. The time must be divided equally between the classroom and parish work. The duration of his total studies would increase from three to four years, but the gain in professional proficiency would justify fully this prolongation. To expect that in view of the complexities of our living the minister is sufficiently instructed and prepared within three short academic years, full of mere memorizing of predominantly historical subjects, is a detrimental miscalculation.

The nature of the practical training also needs to be changed radically. It should become an integral part of the total educational process and involve the minister-supervisor as much as the student-trainee. No one can teach who does not at the same time learn. First of all, the minister who wants to train future ministers, needs to be in close and sympathetic contact with the school of his trainee, its outlook, purpose, and most of all its faculty. He must know what the school is trying to achieve and agree with it in order to co-operate fully.

But the minister in charge of a prospective colleague must also be willing and able to criticize constructively his own work and parish. To look at one's professional habits with an objective detachment is difficult, though indispensable when one attempts to train. This does not mean that the minister in charge should constantly apologize or belittle his work. Yet he must find it possible to reflect upon that which he is doing to introduce the student to it.

Through such a mutual learning process where theoretical school knowledge and practical experience are exchanged the cleavage between theology and the ministry can be bridged. The student can see why he learns what he learns in school. The minister comes back into the fellowship of further learning. The schools have the opportunity to check constantly whether their curriculum corresponds to the needs of the parish situation.

Such teamwork between schools, ministers, and students demands much readiness on all sides, not the least on the part of the congregation, to invest time, energy, and money into this sort of endeavor. The resulting stimulation for all involved surely will be more than a mere recompense. But the thought that such an undertaking might be the only possible way to make and keep the ministry of today relevant transcends the calculation solely of immediate advantages and returns. The enthusiasm of dealing with the fundamental experiment of whether the Christian faith, the church, and its ministry are still meaningful in our society is bound to provoke the spontaneous co-operation of all involved. Moreover, it might very well attract even those who for a while already have given up any hope and withdrawn from the church.

II

To concentrate now on an actual study program in the area of religion and mental health the following offerings will have to be considered.

The basic need of the incoming student is to understand the sociological characteristics of the church and the society in which it serves today. Usually, the beginning theological student has little awareness of the social implications of church work. He lacks the methodological techniques for investigating the communal pressure of a specific social structure upon the church. Hence he is unaware of the equally important social influence which the church has or could have on its communal surroundings. Often enough, a student will assume that the church consists of a collection of well-meaning, likehearted individuals, exclusively given to the cultivation of their religious sentiments. He sees no defect in such an understanding of the church and believes in fostering such an attitude among his future parishioners.

A course in sociology will focus on a discussion of the different social structures in this country, their origin, characteristics, and interplay with each other. Implied is an investigation of the respective social images and aspirations since they are primarily apt to impress a specific value-orientation upon their adherents. In turn, the religious feelings are transformed in accordance to social motivations. The different classes have their own gods and idols which they worship.

Naturally, the investigation of the social influence on religious orientation demands a sociological scrutiny of the church. How does the church respond to social pressures, how far does it create social consciousness and influence social developments? Ministers and theologians have a distaste for considering their church as a social institution in co-operation and in competition with other communal institutions. Nonetheless, without social sensitivity on the part of the minister, at least, the church is unwittingly overrun by stronger social forces and becomes solely the loudspeaker for the social idiosyncrasies of its most influential and determined members.

A course in sociology, geared especially to the need of the theological student, is the best groundwork for the subsequent consideration of psychological implications. That sociology is chronologically an even younger academic discipline than psychology should not obscure the fact of the primacy which social circumstances have in creating psychological problems, even though the latter come foremost to the attention of the pastor. Psychology, having originally emerged from philosophical, biological, and medical observations of individuals, has moved constantly toward a higher awareness of the bearing of social factors on the individual. A course in psychology for prospective ministers benefits from the instructor's full acquaintance with social psychology and those psychiatric writers who have taken the social facets in psychopathology and psychotherapy seriously, as, for instance, Karen Horney.

The student is usually overeager to learn about psychiatry proper. At Harvard the experiment was made of inviting a practicing psychiatrist to a weekly seminar at the Divinity School. He tried to explain to the students what a practicing psychiatrist does, his attitude, and his way of looking at the personal problems of the patient. The result was unsatisfactory. A psychiatrist feels uncomfortable on the dry dock of theoretical discussions. He cannot demonstrate his work; hence, he gets merely entangled with philosophical issues which do not do justice to psychiatric practice.

The discussion of the psychiatrist with students showed that they were quite ignorant when it came to psychological and psychiatric terms. A clinical psychologist was therefore called in to give a course dealing with the psychology of personality, abnormal psychology, psychopathology and an introduction to psychotherapy. Each session of two hours weekly was divided between a theoretical presentation, a case discussion, and a seminar which allowed the students to verify their impressions, correct misapprehensions through question and answer, and relate new knowledge to old or to actual experience. It is very important that the student have ample opportunity to integrate the theoretical and the practical course offerings into his own understanding. The reading of a textbook alone, without the presence of an experienced clinical psychologist, is certainly inadequate.

With solid preparation in psychology the student is ready to profit from an introduction to psychiatry in action. The administrator of a mental hospital, preferably a teaching hospital, in the vicinity will be glad to provide the opportunity for such a course. Usually an advanced resident and a representative of the theological school set up a program of two half-days a week. One half-day is given to observing the work of the attendants and later on acting as attendants on a ward, followed by the auditing of a staff conference. The other half-day belongs to discussion with the psychiatrist in charge of the group. The student learns about the whole sequence of important events in the patient's hospital stay. An admission conference will bring together the different items of information which the admitting psychiatrist, the social worker, the psychologist, and the chaplain have collected concerning the background and actual problem of the patient. The student becomes aware of the diverse factors contributing to mental illness and the reaction of specific social, religious, and racial groups to the occurrence of mental disturbance and the hospitalized patient.

The psychiatric conferences on the diagnosis and suggested treatment initiate the student into familiarity with the many ways in which psychotherapy is administered according to the specific need. He will be given the opportunity to observe therapeutic processes and their effect on the patient. A friendly contact with some of the patients with the permission of the hospital staff and in accordance with the hospital routine certainly does no harm as long as the student does not seek to have a specific therapeutic or religious impact on the patient. The purpose of the course is an introduction to psychiatry and not to hospital chaplaincy as a specialized ministry, to which pastoral clinical training constitutes a far better preparation later on. Thus, the theological student is not to play chaplain or promote his private brand of Christianity in the hospital. Rather, the student ought to learn, positively or negatively, how the chaplain, the home minister, and the relatives relate to the patient in the hospital and how the patient reacts to their behavior.

Discharge and re-education into an active, independent life within the family, the community, and occupation deserve special attention from the prospective minister. He should know about the difficulties and fears which befall patient and relatives alike when the moment of discharge approaches. He must know of the prejudice of many people toward former mental patients. He must also know how hard it is for a person who has received so much security and attention in the hospital to stand now on his own feet and meet realistically the demands of his environment. To minister to him in this period of readjustment without promoting undue dependence is a delicate and essential task which may very well hamper or promote the ultimate fruition of psychotherapy.

A mature and well-prepared teaching fellow in the field of religion and mental health should be always at hand during the times when the course meets. The psychiatrist is not qualified to deal with students' questions about how psychiatric experiences relate to the Christian faith, how this hospital experience of the student is properly integrated into the rest of his theological studies or pastoral experiences. The chaplain might be able to answer some inquiries which concern pastoral counseling, but he will easily speak exclusively from the viewpoint of a hospital ministry.

A young teaching fellow is chosen to be with the students at the hospital as far as a resource person from the theological school is concerned, not only because an older, full-time professor in the field could not afford enough time and energy for such a job, but he would also be already too remote from the student. It is much better to have a teaching fellow act as liaison. He is still close enough to the student's experience to invite his confidence and to show enough patience and understanding to meet the student where he is. The student needs this freedom to verbalize all his ideas, fears, ignorance, and suspicions without having them exposed to an official member of the faculty who participates in decisions on his academic future.

The aim of such an introduction to psychiatry in action at a hospital is manifold. First of all, it should provide a firsthand account of the nature of psychotherapy and a mental hospital, their potentials, and their limitations. To know them is important when the minister has to encourage any of his parishioners to seek psychiatric help. People are full of misconceptions and suspicion regarding psychiatry and hospitals in general. Precise knowledge concerning psychiatry furthers a better understanding between ministers and psychiatrists and their co-operation. Furthermore, the minister will be called upon to visit parishioners at the hospital. He is expected to evaluate the realistic and unrealistic desires and complaints of the patients, to relate them to the proper official. He will check first with the doctor or the nurse in charge whether his visit with the patient is in order, what the situation is, and how he can be most helpful in mediating where mediation is called for. He is also to act as a spokesman for and to the family of the patient whose relation with the doctor is not what it could or should be.

For the educational purpose of the theological school, however, the feedback from such an introductory course relates to two areas of the curriculum. The hospital experience activates the student's interest in the religious resources which help people to live a meaningful and orderly life, sustain them in moments of crisis, and aid them in regaining their spiritual, emotional, and mental health. Since these questions on the part of the student do not relate properly to any single theological discipline it is important that a member of the faculty, equally well versed in doctrinal, ethical, and pastoral theology, deal full time with the attempt to interrelate these theological disciplines with the stimuli and the challenges which arise from a close contact with the social sciences and psychiatry in the student mind. To ignore them or treat them peripherally with a few side remarks when expounding properly theological subject matters robs the training of the future minister of its very best and central possibility—namely, to make the Christian faith, the church, and the ministry relevant to our time.

Whether the instructor in religion and mental health copes with these questions under the traditional academic headings of psychology of religion, sociology of religion, pastoral theology, pastoral psychology or any other, like pastoral counseling or practical theology, is quite secondary. The main point is that it be done and how it is done. A few remarks may be in order here.

Since the subject of religion and mental health is new to the theological curriculum and its drawing area almost unlimited, it is important that the chief instructor clearly outline and limit his primary goals. The administration and the rest of the faculty must have the assurance that the program on religion and mental health will work responsibly with whatever resources of instruction, students, and outside assistance are available. The prevailing atmosphere in a school, its religious, theological, denominational, geographical, and academic characteristics have to be taken carefully into account. The success of the program depends on how selective the school is determined to be in the admission of students with respect to maturity and open-mindedness.

If promising students come to a theological school, they merit freedom to learn and constant stimulation of their desire to grow through increased understanding of themselves and the subjects. Many a theological student who has learned in his recent college years to study independently and do research likens theological education to his long-since-past high school days rather than recognizing it as a graduate school of higher learning. No field lends itself better to independent and pioneering study and research than that of religion and mental health. The problems are new; they require imagination, objectivity, and intellectual honesty. Yet, the person of the student and his ability to learn from personal experience are even more important than solid, objective investigations.

The promise of a well laid-out study program in religion and mental health is practically unlimited. Teacher and student participate together in the slow but sure evolution in the interaction of the Christian faith and Christian Western culture with science and a highly technical civilization. The old battle lines between biblicism and the natural sciences have given way to a much more central and acute problem, that of the human self-understanding. No one can excuse himself as a disinterested lay-observer. When the nature, place, and function of the human being in this world are decided, everybody's self-respect and future are at stake. To take no stand means to abdicate irrevocably to the mechanization of people in the world of tomorrow.

Certain topics must be thought through and treated by the chief instructor in the field of religion and mental health, who meets and leads secular professionals in their mutual discussions with theological students. The intrinsic temptation for theology to understand the personality on its own terms before any theological bias tends to blur the picture, calls for careful scrutiny.

The tension between the traditional theological concept of the ministry and the contemporary demands on the minister needs to be thoroughly ventilated before the possibilities and limitations in the communal teamwork between minister and other professional agencies can be evaluated. The question will arise whether Erich Lindemann's attempt to subsume the minister, the psychiatrist, and other professionals under the common title of care-taking professions is valid. Does this common denominator do justice to the prophetic aspect of the Christian ministry or not?

Once the position of the minister in the communal interplay is clarified, the delicate topics arise as to how far and in what way the minister will participate in mental health education in the community, how far he will deal with personal and interpersonal problems with strongly emotional undertones before he refers them to the psychiatrist, what his relation will be to a parishioner who is undergoing treatment, and so forth. Pastoral counseling cannot be learned from books alone. But it is certainly appropriate to discuss especially those personal obstacles and detrimental attitudes of the minister which are bound to interfere with his effectiveness as a counselor. To point problems out to a student who has had no experience whatsoever in counseling is a waste of time. However limited such experience still may be, it alone prods the counselor to learn from his mistakes by understanding them and his own part in them better.

The student needs the private and the group opportunity to reveal and criticize his counseling approaches and manners in different situations. The feeling of freedom and mutual respect in group discussions of counseling done by members of the group enable the student to avoid the usual withdrawal of the minister into professional isolation and competitive dishonesty among colleagues. The psychotherapists seek each other's supervision and criticism in order to maintain objectivity, personal mental health and efficiency as therapists. Why is such mutual service and frankness so rare among ministers?

Through carefully guided and controlled group interaction the future minister becomes aware of the emotional potentials and dangers of close group feelings within the parish situation and will learn how far he can utilize and channel them. Today, the average parish is marked by either an almost total absence of any group cohesion, sterile social chumminess or, more recently, the highly explosive manipulation of group reactions on a quite intimate scale without the always needed professional skill on the part of the group leader.

Above all, any instruction and training in the area of religion and mental health must make it crystal clear to the student that it can but send him off into his independent learning process in the actual ministry, be it the parish, teaching, any form of chaplaincy or a still other kind of specialized ministry. The student therefore needs close contact with as many ministers as possible who are willing to share with him their specific experiences, questions, doubts, hopes, and findings.

Besides the internship with one particular minister in action, the campus residence of outstanding representatives of the different ministries with ample occasions for informal interchange between them and the students is highly commendable. The student must know that he is participating already in the total attempt to deepen and constantly renew the relevance of the Christian ministry to his contemporaries. To thus enlist his total involvement and recruit his highest ambitions and capabilities will save the theological student from looking back on his student years as an irrelevant, detached, and one-sided period of mere indoctrination and polishing of professional tricks while he marks time as far as his personal growth and real interests are concerned. The theological student who does not understand his studies as already a mutual ministry of teacher and student for each other and the church universal will hardly understand his later ministry to a congregation much better.

All these programmatic and sketchy remarks on the instruction of religion and mental health in theological schools have grown out of the experience at Harvard and other institutions. It is obvious that none of the suggestions offered can claim absolute tenability, relevance, or long-term usefulness. Actually, it is my hope that soon they will be desperately outmoded since theological schools will have taken up the challenge for further thought and experimentation in this endeavor, for closer co-operation among the schools in the area of religion and mental health. It is the hope that this will lead to a fuller understanding of the vital role of religion in our culture and an understanding of mental health which goes beyond the mere desire to keep people out of hospitals.

Appendix:
The Minister and His Counselee

The counseling activity of the Protestant minister is receiving more and more attention within and outside the churches. Its contribution to the maintenance and restoration of public mental health is generally accepted. Theological schools are seeking to improve their academic and practical offerings in the area of preparing prospective ministers for their counseling with parishioners. Nevertheless, no clear-cut empirical study has yet been undertaken in order to ascertain the place of counseling within the total context of the pastor's work, its relation to the pastor's training, theological outlook, and attitude toward his counselees. To complement this descriptive investigation, covering a random sample on one hundred Protestant ministers in Boston and fifty in San Francisco, the second section of the research report contains the results of a parallel study of the counselees of these ministers.

Admittedly this study is preliminary and designed only to initiate on firm statistical grounds further and broader empirical knowledge in the field of pastoral counseling. The Harvard University Project on Religion and Mental Health is indebted to the General Service Foundation for making this study possible. Mr. Eugene F. Nameche, a graduate student in psychology, has set up the research design with the help of some faculty members of the Department of Social Relations at Harvard University. With the assistance of Mr. Tilden H. Edwards and others he has undertaken and directed the actual interviews and produced the resulting findings.

It goes without saying that this, like any other research study, bears the interest and bias of the investigator. Mr. Nameche, in consultation with the director of the Project, has selected the areas of investigation, To him go the credit and responsibility for the collection and presentation of the actual data. The editor was keenly interested in having the facts speak for themselves and insisted therefore that no interpretative comments should color the picture or anticipate prematurely the conclusions which can be drawn from such an investigation. It is certainly hoped that the findings will arouse enough interest to stimulate subsequent and broader studies in this area. Upon their basis it will be possible to come to precise conclusions as to how seminary training can be improved and how active ministers can increase their usefulness as pastoral counselors.

I

What questions can be answered by empirical investigation that cannot be answered without collecting data? Some of the questions to be answered by this research are these: (1) Just how much counseling is being done in the churches? (2) What types of problems are being encountered? (3) What is the relation of a minister's

221

theological position to his counseling activities? (4) What effect does training in psychology and counseling have on a minister's later work as a counselor? (5) To what extent are ministers active in their communities' mental health endeavors? and (6) What are the most immediate needs in programs for training pastoral counselors? The present study has been focused on these questions, but also offers supplemental information on several related problems in our understanding of the minister as counselor.

The first phase of this study was conducted in Greater Boston during the academic year 1957-1958. To obtain generalizable information a stratified random sample of 100 of Boston's Protestant clergymen was used, and an elaborate interview schedule was developed. The method of this research was that of a descriptive survey.[1] The sample—stratified according to denomination—included a total of twenty-three denominations, although 74 per cent of the sample (hence 74 per cent of the churches in Greater Boston) was composed of five denominational groups, namely, Congregational, Episcopal, Baptist, Methodist, and Unitarian.

By way of background it may be well to describe briefly the situation in which the Protestant churches of Boston find themselves. First of all, Greater Boston's Protestantism probably differs from that of other large Northern cities only in that it is located in a predominantly Roman Catholic area. (Sixty-three per cent of the churches studied were located in areas where Roman Catholics constituted the majority of the population.) In terms of social strata, although there were an equal number of low and high socio-economic (Protestant) churches, the Protestants rank consistently slightly higher in income, education, and occupation than their Catholic neighbors. The median average size [2] of the Greater Boston churches is 420 members, and the churches on the average have about 45 per cent of their members (about 200 persons) active at least to the point of attending Sunday services of worship.

Denominationally, Boston is characterized by a preponderance of churches that tend toward liberal expression, although a vigorous minority of biblically conservative churches is also present. The large Episcopal church body appears to be the only sizable Boston congregation not to tend toward one of the theological extremes. The Protestant population of Boston, then, probably differs slightly from other Northern cities not in social structure so much as in biblico-theological extremism. The ministers of the city appear highly educated—over half of them have done pre-doctoral study after seminary, and 11 per cent have already earned the doctor's degree.

A note at this point is necessary to explain the basic paradigms which were used in this study to observe ministerial counseling. In addition to the replies to the 74 items on the interview schedule, eight variable matrices (groups of items) were developed as conceptual forms which would view, measure, and interrelate the important factors and underlying dimensions of pastoral counseling. They fall into four classes:

1. Situational Variables
   a. Church Size—The average of total church membership and Sunday church attendance
   b. Predominant Social Class—The relative preponderance of the social strata of the congregation
   c. Staff Adequacy—Administrative factors within the church affecting the pastoral counseling function
2. Relation to Mental Health Facilities
   d. Minister—Community Interaction—A scale of the ways and degrees to which ministers are in contact with the mental health resources in their locale
3. Counseling Training
   e. Heteronomy-Autonomy Rating—A measure of the relative authority attached to the biblical account; ranging from plenary biblical literalism (heteronomy) to total freedom from the Scriptures (autonomy)
   f. Training in Psychology—A cumulation of the minister's formal and private training and experience in psychology and related disciplines
4. Counseling Activities
   g. Theological-Psychological Perspective—The point of view from which the minister looks at the counseling function and situation
   h. Counseling Involvement Score—The minister's actual involvement in and identification with the counseling function. A combination of factors that distinguish "active" from "inactive" clergymen with regard to their counseling activities.

These eight variable matrices formed the basic structure and conceptual vantage point for the research interviews. It was not known by the ministers, however, that such was the case. The actual interview schedule was organized in a manner logical to the minister, and the particular questions were asked in an order that would appear reasonable and inoffensive.

Constant reference will be made to the relationships between these variable matrices as we attempt now to answer the six research questions of this study.

1. *How much counseling is being done in Protestant churches?*

Before reporting the information received concerning ministers' present pastoral counseling activities, it is necessary to repeat the all-important definition of counseling which has been used throughout this study. "Counseling" was defined as "those problem-centered interviews, which are, in the main, initiated by the counselee." The purpose of this definition was to exclude the more routine pastoral calling of the ministers from our data, but to allow for that pastoral call which turns into a real counseling session.

The average amount of time spent in counseling each week by the parish ministers studied was 3.76 hours. The average counseling session was 55 minutes in length. One fourth of the ministers did virtually no counseling at all, while another fourth spent less than three hours per week in this role. Although these figures might appear surprisingly small at first sight, when multiplied by the total number of Protestant clergymen in Greater Boston it is found that over 2600 hours of counseling are spent and the same number of persons are seen per week through pastoral counseling in this city. This figure does not include those persons seen at the pastoral counseling clinic at Boston University or any of the counseling done by ministries to university students or other nonparish organizations.

To find out how the pastoral counseling role of ministers compared to their other duties in terms of the amount of time spent, the ministers were asked to rank the following five activities: Administrative duties, Sermon preparation and preaching, Teaching, Pastoral calling and social activities, and Counseling activities. Counseling was found to rank fourth in terms of the relative time spent—only teaching required less of the minister's time. When asked to rank the same activities again in terms of their importance for carrying out one's ministry, the clerics generally ranked counseling third; sermon preparation and preaching, and teaching ranked first and second respectively. Although administrative duties often took most of the minister's time, they were usually felt to be the least important of the pastoral responsibilities.

The ministers who were doing more than the average amount of counseling were asked how many additional hours per week they could use for counseling, and they reported that their churches could use at least six more hours each week for counseling purposes. In spite of this need for more time, however, the ministers reported that they very seldom, if ever, turned down a request for counseling—that instead they would sacrifice other time and obligations to do the counseling needed. Three-fourths of the ministers would increase the amount of their counseling if they had the freedom and time; one-fourth would keep it about the same; and only one per cent would decrease it. This desire to increase the amount of pastoral counseling is partially explained by the fact that a similar three-fourths of the ministers reported that minister-parishioner relations were closer or improved after a counseling session; about one-fourth said they remained about the same; and only 2 per cent of the men reported that counseling caused the minister-parishioner relationship to become more difficult or strained.

Ministers of churches in the lower socio-economic strata do relatively more counseling than their colleagues in churches of higher income, educational and occupational groups. The size of the church, the adequacy of its staff, the location of the church, and other such factors were not related to the amount of counseling being done by the ministers.

Of the three age groups found in churches—youth, young adult, and adult—the young adult group (ages 18-35) was the one which received the most counseling from their ministers. This occurs in spite of the fact that the adult (over 35) proportion of a congregation is usually larger than the other groups. Of all counselees seen approximately 10 per cent were in no way connected with the churches of the ministers who counseled them.

2. *What types of problems are being encountered?*

Only about 10 per cent of the problems brought to ministers in counseling initially pertain to religious questions. Marriage and family problems are the most frequent of the problems encountered; psychological distress problems are second in frequency; youth-behavior problems, third; alcoholism, fourth; and problems of aging, fifth. (All these occur more frequently than religious questions.) Ministers felt themselves most capable of working with marriage and family problems, and least capable when working with persons with psychological distress or difficult emotional problems.

When the types of problems encountered were classified into groups entitled least difficult and most shallow, moderately difficult, and most difficult or "deepest," it was found that the types of problems encountered were related to the ministers' denominational position in an interesting and unsuspected way. Ministers of conservative denominations were found to work most with the shallow or least difficult problems; the most liberal denominations counseled on the moderately difficult problems; and the denominations of "middle Protestant orthodoxy" counseled primarily on problems classed as "deepest" or most difficult. On no other matters concerning pastoral counseling are the "middle orthodoxy" and liberal denominations found to differ. It is suspected that they differ on "types of problems encountered" primarily because the parishioners of those denominations have variant ideas about the roles and responsibilities of their clergymen. The socio-economic difference (the liberal groups are higher on the socio-economic ladder) may also be relevant.

3. *What is the relation of a minister's theological position to his counseling activities?*

The most important finding of this study toward answering Question 3 is that there is no simple answer. We have already noticed a tendency for theologically conservative ministers to be slightly less involved in counseling than less conservative ministers. We can add that the conservatives also have less contact with their community's mental health resources. They tend to view counseling situations from an almost entirely theological, not psychological, perspective, and they frequently have a more judgmental attitude toward mental illness than do more liberal ministers. However, all these findings do not necessarily point to the conclusion that ministers who lean toward biblically conservative positions in theological thinking are doing a less adequate job in their pastoral counseling. In fact, other findings of this study suggest that in Greater Boston the churches of these ministers simply have fewer "potential counselees." This occurs for Boston's more biblicistic

Protestant churches because these churches are almost universally made up of cultural subgroups (usually of Scotch, Nova Scotian or Scandinavian extraction). It is admitted that this subgroup typology is probably uncommon for biblicistic churches generally, but in this study it is clear that it has caused considerable reluctance on the part of these parishioners to take their problems to the church or any other social institutions, and has thereby seriously affected the possibilities for pastoral counseling in these churches. Since this research has shown that biblically oriented ministers are neither less trained nor less interested in pastoral counseling than other ministers, interpretations that point to these conclusions should be avoided.

4. *What effect does training in psychology and counseling have on a minister's later work as a counselor?*

Among the measures of training in psychology and counseling was the number of courses taken in each at the undergraduate, seminary, and graduate levels of study. The average minister has had about three undergraduate courses and two seminary courses in psychology. About 30 per cent of the ministers have done some graduate study of psychology as well. In terms of course work in counseling, however, the situation is considerably worse. Half of the ministers have never had any formal counseling instruction at all; another fourth of them have had but one seminary course in pastoral counseling. Almost all the men who had received any formal counseling instruction at all, had done so at the seminary level.

Another index of the ministers' preparation for counseling was the number of counseling (psychological or pastoral) books they could recall and the number which they owned. The average minister could recall the titles and authors of about seven books and owned five. Books by Carl Rogers, John S. Bonnell, Seward Hiltner, Leslie Weatherhead, Rollo May, and Richard Dicks were those most used, and were considered the most valuable among the ministers. Fifty-six per cent of the ministers had made reference within the last six months to some form of counseling literature. Similarly, one-fourth of the ministers were currently subscribing to journals (pastoral, psychiatric, or psychological) on counseling. Another one-fourth of the group had subscribed to pastoral counseling journals in the past, but had discontinued their subscriptions.

When asked to evaluate the literature currently being published on pastoral counseling, 38 per cent of the ministers evaluated it very positively, 50 per cent had both positive and negative comments about it, and 12 per cent offered wholly negative evaluations. The negative comments of the last two groups were mainly of two sorts: (1) That pastoral counseling literature invariably emphasized either the theological or psychological approach at the expense of the other, or (2) That the counseling literature is so elementary that it is of no use after any experience in the counseling function.

In evaluating their academic study of psychology (not pastoral), 71 per cent reported it was highly valuable, 19 per cent felt that it was moderately valuable, and 10 per cent felt that it was of no value. It can be noted from the figures above on pastoral counseling literature, that the evaluation of psychology course work received nearly twice as strong a positive vote. In an appraisal of their seminary training in pastoral counseling 66 per cent of the ministers stated that it was highly inadequate, 8 per cent that it was moderately adequate, and 26 per cent that it was adequate preparation for their work as a counselor. Of course, older ministers constituted most of the former group, but satisfaction with current training in pastoral psychology was far from universal. This became apparent when 67 per cent of the ministers answered affirmatively the question, "If training in pastoral counseling were made available in this area now—say involving one afternoon a week for two or three months—would you be interested in such training?" The large majority who said they would not be interested in such training explained that time would not allow it. Less than 10 per cent of the ministers felt that they did not need more training.

On being probed as to what type of training in specific would be most valuable to them, the ministers emphasized the need for practical training, and felt that a case method study with ministers and professional therapists present would be most helpful. Marriage and family, and psychological distress problems were the problem areas in which the ministers felt they needed the most training.

When queried on the present trend toward large-scale incorporation of psychological studies in seminary education, only 3 per cent of the ministers said that this trend would be harmful to religion in the long run, 16 per cent said that it would be only partially helpful, while 81 per cent felt that it would have no harmful effect on religion.

When asked about extracurricular training in mental hospitals, four-fifths of the ministers reported that they had never worked in a mental hospital, one-tenth had had a six-week clinical pastoral training program there, and one-tenth had done more than three months of work as an attendant or staff member. About three-fourths of all the ministers who had had this experience working in mental hospitals valued it very highly and recommended it for seminary students training for the parish ministry. The remaining quarter of this group felt that counseling experience in a parish situation would be of more value for ministerial students than hospital work.

Turning for a moment to the question of graduate study for clergymen, it was found that ministers who have never done graduate work beyond seminary do considerably less counseling than ministers who have done some pre-doctoral work or who have received their doctor's degrees.

In summary, it was found that the ministers who had the most psychological training were the most involved in their counseling activities, and had more interaction with their community's mental health agencies and therapists than other ministers. There was no difference on these matters between ministers with little psychological training and those with none at all. The ministers who had had training in counseling but who did not have much training in straight academic psychology, did not feel so well equipped for their counseling functions as did those with a "straight" psychology background but no counseling study.

5. To what extent are ministers active in community mental health endeavors?

Although Greater Boston is comparatively fortunate in the number and quality of its mental health resources, the needs of the inner and middle sections of the city are far beyond the area's facilities. The ministers' interaction with the city's mental health resources is considerably less than it might be because of sheer lack of knowledge. The average minister is acquainted with about four mental health agencies and one private therapist, psychiatrist, psychologist or other counselor. He uses mental health agencies about three times in two years, and makes referrals to a private therapist only once in five years. Over one-fourth of the ministers studied had never made use of mental health agencies, and twice as many had never referred any parishioners to a private therapist. Although these figures are rather small, when multiplied by the total number of Protestant (parish) ministers in the city, it is found that last year some 1050 referrals to mental health agencies and 140 referrals to private therapists were made.

The major problems which have given rise to the use of mental health agencies were youth-behavior problems, marital problems, and alcoholism (in that order). These three types of problems constituted over two-thirds of the reasons for referral to mental health agencies. The problems referred to agencies tended to be more social in nature than those referred to private therapists: the latter were mainly problems of personal adjustment or psychological distress. There were three major deterrents of referral to private therapist (and occasionally to mental health agencies as well), namely: (1) perpetual overcrowdedness and shortage of professional therapists' time, (2) reluctance and hesitancy on the part of counselees to receive help on "mental" problems, and (3) minimal use of the channels of communication between ministers and private therapists.

Considering minister-community mental health interaction from the other direction, it was found that 55 per cent of the ministers had never been approached by any mental health agencies, while 36 per cent had been called upon only once. The remaining 9 per cent of the cases usually involved ministers who were serving on community mental health committees, thereby having frequent contact from the agencies. There was considerable dismay on the part of many ministers concerning the one-way communication between the clergy and mental health agencies. (Four out of five of the ministers felt that minister-community mental health interaction should be improved.) It was hoped that mental health groups would begin to initiate relationships with the clergy, at least in the form of providing information about the facilities and programs available. With the aforementioned qualifications, 85 per cent of the ministers stated that the co-operation they had received from mental health agencies and therapists was more than satisfactory.

A final finding on minister-community interaction showed that 84 of the 100 churches observed were without group volunteer service to mental health agencies or institutions; 13 churches had one group volunteering service; 3 churches had more than one group in this type of social work. Many ministers reported that individual members of the congregations were volunteering help to mental health institutions, and others said that some of their church groups were serving at medical, but not mental, hospitals.

Approximately one-fourth of the ministers reported that none of their parishioners had ever been admitted to a mental hospital; one-fourth reported that some members of the church had been admitted, but none during the past year; another fourth said that one member of the congregation had been admitted during the past year; 15 per cent had two parishioners admitted last year; and 10 per cent said more than two were admitted last year. For parishioners returned from mental hospitals (60 in number) 41 per cent of the ministers said these ex-patients' relationship to the church was better and more active than it was before admittance to the mental hospital; 49 per cent said it was about the same as before; and 10 per cent said that the church relationship was less active or worse than before admittance to the hospital. Slightly less than half of the ministers volunteered the information that special efforts were being made to provide a receptive atmosphere in the church for the returned mental patient.

6. *What are the most immediate needs in programs for the training of pastoral counselors?*

Since there was a consistent and marked tendency for ministers in the field to evaluate their training in "straight" academic psychology higher than their training in pastoral psychology, it seems fair to suggest that seminaries should move in this direction. Likewise, since many ministers agreed that skill in pastoral counseling comes only with considerable experience in the actual parish situation, the proper time for the bulk of training in counseling should be held for postseminary days. Again, it is felt that ministers generally have more of the necessary apparatus for translating the theoretical training (to be acquired in seminary) into practical application (in their churches) than they have interest or time once out of seminary to ground themselves in a firm understanding of human behavior.

Similarly, if the function of the seminaries in training ministers for pastoral counseling were mainly to acquaint them with the corpus of the academic literature of psychology and psychiatry, it is suggested that summer clinical training while in seminary or postseminary conferences in applied pastoral counseling, or the ministers' private study of the pastoral counseling literature would give the necessary clinical tools for his counseling function. The situation frequently reported today by clergymen concerning their training for pastoral counseling is that they have a considerable store of techniques but no firm foundation of psychological knowledge for dealing with the problems encountered in pastoral counseling.

It is encouraging to note the healthy attitude regarding persons returned from mental hospitals which most of the clergymen are attempting to instill in their congregations. Along with efforts to provide a restorative atmosphere in the church's social life for the mentally disturbed, ministers are also seeking to educate their congregations on problems of mental health—especially in the breaking down of judgmental and chiding attitudes toward persons who are mentally sick.

Although the San Francisco study provided us with much valuable new information, its primary goal was to serve as a parallel and reflecting glass for our earlier investigations.

San Francisco was chosen as a locus for this study because it had two important features in common with Boston. It is approximately the same size as Boston, and has a very heavy Roman Catholic population. Also of great importance for comparative purposes were the differences between the two cities. Whereas Boston is an old and relatively stable urban center, San Francisco is a much younger and more mobile city. The more secure, patterned culture of the East is mirrored in Boston; the newer frontier culture of the West is reflected in San Francisco. While Greater Boston is very low on the scale of population growth and geographical expansion, the Bay area of San Francisco is near the top.

Whereas Boston is probably distinctive in the nation for the diversity and comprehensiveness of Protestant religious traditions, San Francisco is very largely a center of conservative Protestantism. In the Bay Area, fundamentalism is larger than the moderate and liberal bodies combined. In Greater Boston, fundamentalism is slightly smaller than either the moderate or liberal groups. A second important difference between the two cities is that Boston's Protestant churches are almost twice as large as those in San Francisco. The average church size in Greater Boston is 420 members; in the Bay Area it is 230 members. Both of these socio-religious differences between the two cities relate directly to pastoral counseling.

We shall concentrate on the important differences which appeared in the data of the two cities. Our hope can be only to paint a general portrait of our subject rather than to describe its anatomy.

A method of stratified random sampling was used to obtain interviews with 50 Protestant ministers. Twenty-one denominations were represented: Thirteen of the denominations were theologically conservative (fundamentalist). Four bodies, Baptist, Lutheran, Methodist, and Presbyterian, constituted half of the total population—hence half of the sample. There was some difficulty getting all the ministers in the original sample because of vacation schedules, thus slight adjustments were necessary in some cases. In only two cases did ministers refuse to be interviewed.

In San Francisco the people in the upper levels of the social structure represent a "secular minority" with little or no church involvement. In Boston, by contrast, these persons are found either in the large liberal groups or in the sizable Episcopal group. The average church member in San Francisco is far more involved in his church than is Boston's average layman—another correlate of conservatism.

The clergy of the two cities differ most markedly on educational background: the San Francisco group is far less educated. Only five per cent have even engaged in doctoral study; while far less than that have completed it.

These observations about the type of Protestantism that is found and its social setting enable us to construct a number of hypotheses about pastoral counseling in the Bay Area. The hypotheses, and a word of rationale where appropriate, follow:

1. Less pastoral counseling is being done in San Francisco than in Boston. (We suspect that the strength of conservatism in the Bay Area will outweigh other factors.)
2. Fewer "deep" psychological problems are handled by San Francisco pastoral counselors than by less conservative groups of ministers.
3. There is less interaction of the clergy with community mental health services in San Francisco than there is in Boston.
4. San Francisco's clergy is comparatively poorly trained for counseling.
5. Ministers in the Bay Area are more theologically than psychologically oriented in their counseling.
6. More role-conflict will be observed in the San Francisco clergy than in the Boston group. (The rigid moralisms of the fundamentalists are at odds with the "acceptance orientation" of secular counseling.)

Each of these hypotheses has been examined. Whereas in the Boston research only seven correlations were significant, in the San Francisco study sixteen significant relationships were found between the variable matrices. All the important relationships found in the Boston study were confirmed in the Bay Area, and nine new—but obvious—relationships emerged. This difference occurred primarily because the San Francisco clergy are a more homogeneous group in their theological orientations, and their congregations are likewise more homogeneous in the socio-economic positions. In Boston there was too much diversity of religious position and social class for clear-cut correlations. Almost all the "new" correlations were in the direction expected. For example, conservatives were found to be low in community interaction and low on psychological training; ministers low in psychological training had a theological perspective in counseling and were not involved in community mental health efforts; pastors doing little counseling were not involved in community mental health activity, and so on. These new findings will not be reported in detail here because they are only confirmations of trends that were reported in the Boston data.

1. *Less pastoral counseling is being done in San Francisco than in Boston.*

This hypothesis must be rejected. The contrary was found. The average amount of time spent each week in pastoral counseling by Boston ministers was three hours. The average San Francisco pastor counsels 3.5 hours per week.

In spite of the conservative dominance in the Bay Area, other factors pyramided to overbalance our expectations. The lower social class index of San Francisco's churches was of most importance. The members of most of these churches cannot afford psychiatric counseling or cannot risk the embarrassment of being a "mental case," as the jargon has it. Hence the only kind of counseling open to them is pastoral.

Another reason that the Bay Area clergymen counsel more than would be expected is that their churches are small enough that they have considerable personal contact with their parishioners. When size of church is held constant, ministers of small churches do the most counseling. An example will illustrate this seeming contradiction: "Prospect Church" has 800 members, and its minister counsels eight hours per week; "North Church" has 150 members, and its minister counsels five hours per week. Although the ministers of large churches counsel more than the ministers of small churches, they do not counsel proportionately more.

Whereas half of Boston's clergy is negligibly involved in counseling (less than three hours per week), only one-third of San Francisco's clergy can be said to be negligibly involved. Similarly, San Francisco has more ministers extremely involved in counseling than does Boston. Both groups rate counseling about the same in importance when compared to their other duties. Counseling generally ranked third: less important than preaching and teaching, and more important than pastoral visiting and administrative duties.

Even more than in Boston, ministerial counseling almost always made the minister-parishioner relationship closer and more personal than before. Ninety-six per cent of the Bay Area clergy—this is much more than Boston—would increase the amount of their pastoral counseling if they had the time and opportunity. Lastly, the young-adult age group receives more pastoral counseling in the Bay Area than in Greater Boston.

2. *Fewer "deep" psychological problems are handled by San Francisco pastoral counselors than by less conservative groups of ministers.*

This hypothesis has been confirmed, though some reservations are in order. The reservations are necessary when we look at the types of problems encountered. The two groups of clergy deal with an equal number of psychiatrically light problems—religious questions and vocational guidance: The West Coast group handles a few (but not many) more "moderate" problems—problems of youth behavior and of aging; and the East Coast group handles slightly more of the "deeper" type problems—marital and family, and psychological distress problems. These differences, in themselves, are not great enough, however, to reach a categorical conclusion that the Bay Area counseling is more superficial. The distinctions—shallow, moderate, and deep—are generally true when related to types of problem, but they need not be. A youth-behavior problem, for example, can range from a slight disciplinary discussion to a full-blown personality disorder.

Another slight reservation is in order when we note that three times as many Bay Area pastors reported that alcoholism was one of their major counseling problems. We suspect that such a frequent mention of it by these clergy is helped along by their moralistic world-view. There was some indication of this also among Boston's conservative clergy.

More reliable data for this hypothesis is available if we look ahead to the counselee data from the Bay Area. In San Francisco it was found that only 9 per cent of the parish counselees interviewed had problems that belonged more appropriately in psychiatrists' hands. In Boston the figure was 36 per cent. Similarly, 75 per cent of the San Francisco parishioners had problems that were of moderate seriousness—appropriate for a pastoral counselor: the Boston figure was 52 per cent. Clearly, on these, our most reliable judgments, the Bay Area pastors do far less counseling on "deep" psychological problems.

3. *There is less interaction of the clergy with community mental health services in San Francisco than there is in Boston.*

This hypothesis is supported in every facet of the relevant data. Over half of the Bay Area pastors have never used a community mental health service. Half of them don't know a single private therapist (psychiatrist, psychologist, or other counselor). Two-thirds of them have never referred a counselee to anyone else.

Although we have not been able to compile complete and detailed information on the subject, our suspicion is that there are almost as many mental health services in the Bay Area as there are in Greater Boston. The reason for less contact is not that the facilities don't exist. It is instead related to the tendency of the conservative clergy to remain an island to themselves. Some "religious" mental health agencies are coming into existence now, so it is somewhat unlikely that co-operation with "secular" mental health forces will grow as much as would be expected in Boston.

We do not imply that the clergy of the Bay Area are not interested in problems of mental health. There is a growing concern with these problems. Especially the young clergy are becoming active. However, the seminaries on the West Coast have been slower than their Eastern counterparts to become involved in this area, and it is unlikely that the clergy will show the awareness or depth of concern about mental health evidenced by the Boston clergy for some time to come. Ministers as a whole bemoan the overcrowded conditions of mental health facilities, but are very complimentary of the efforts that are being made in the mental health professions. The pastors are willing to refer their parishioners to agencies, especially if they have had some personal contact with the personnel of the agencies. Like their Boston counterparts, the Bay Area clergy are greatly distressed by the lack of co-ordination of knowledge about the mental health facilities available.

4. *San Francisco's clergy is comparatively poorly trained for counseling.*

Without even comparing it to the highly trained ministry of Boston, there is a marked lack of counseling training in the San Francisco clergy. Almost two-thirds of the ministers were trained at conservative seminaries which until very recently had no pastoral counseling training. Three-fourths of the clergy had done very little or no reading in the pastoral psychology literature. Half of them have had nothing but introductory psychology course training.

There is some evidence of attempts to compensate for this lack of training, however. More of the West Coast pastors subscribe to pastoral counseling journals and more are seeking experience working in mental hospitals than in the Boston group. The ministers evaluate their training in academic psychology very highly, but are even more critical of their little pastoral counseling training than Boston's ministers.

Ninety per cent of the pastors would enroll for pastoral counselor training if good opportunities for it were available: They do not feel the seminaries are doing an adequate job. In spite of their conservative leanings, the ministers encourage the trend of more psychological study in seminary even more vigorously than do the Eastern ministers.

The lack of training among these pastors accounts in part for their feeble knowledge of mental health facilities and the infrequency of serious psychiatric problems in the counseling they do. It contributes also to their inability to view the counseling relationship in psychological terms. This is our next topic.

5. *Ministers in the Bay Area are more theologically than psychologically oriented in their counseling.*

Again, with little ambiguity, our hypothesis is heavily supported. The predominance of conservatism and the general lack of psychological orientation in San Francisco's clergy account for the thoroughness of a theological approach to counseling. On these matters twice as many of the Bay Area pastors were totally theological in their perspective on the counseling relationship as were Boston pastors. This orientation would become particularly obvious when such problems as guilt, anxiety, moral questions, and alcoholism were under scrutiny.

Parallel to their conservative theological orientation, the San Francisco pastors showed over twice as much directiveness in counseling as did the Boston ministers.

It was clear that minister and parishioner alike saw pastoral counseling as an opportunity for guidance. Advice giving occurred in almost half of the Bay Area cases, while it was found in only one-seventh of the Boston counseling.

6. *More role-conflict will be observed in the San Francisco clergy than in the Boston group.*

The Bay Area pastors are not completely unaware of the inconsistencies involved in their theological views and the basic requirements of effective counseling —acceptance, a nonjudgmental attitude, an egalitarian relationship, and so on. Although not many can verbalize their conflicts, item-analysis shows that there is considerable unexpressed evidence to support the role-conflict hypothesis. The pastor as a symbol of moral excellence and the nonjudgmental counseling role do not fit easily into one person without some evidence of conflict.

In Boston where there was relatively little of the moralistic element in pastoral relationships, this role-conflict only infrequently emerged. The Boston ministry saw counseling as an integral part of their over-all pastoral endeavor. They distinguished the counseling role from other pastoral roles, but did not find it at odds with their other efforts. In San Francisco, there was a less clear-cut picture of pastoral counseling. Considerable prodding was required to keep the ministers from equating pastoral calling and pastoral counseling. The counseling role was not particularly well circumscribed for them, and thus their role-conflict was unconscious rather than ready to awareness.

II

Research on "the minister as counselor" was mainly concerned with the extent of pastoral counseling and the minister's own understanding of the counseling role. The primary goal of this study is also the gathering of descriptive information, but this time we shall look at the counseling situation from the counselee's point of view. The discrepancies between how the minister sees counseling and how the parishioner sees it were often astonishing, and these discrepancies will be the focus of our attention. The differences between the minister and the counseled parishioner in the perception of what happens in counseling will be discussed first. Then we shall report what a parallel sample of uncounseled parishioners think about pastoral counseling. All this will be done in the light of the following seven major research questions:

1. Who comes for counseling, and to which ministers do they go?
2. How does past and present religious involvement relate to counseling?
3. What do parishioners expect from pastoral counseling?
4. Of what does counseling consist?
5. What does pastoral counseling change?

6. How do parishioners compare pastoral counseling with other kinds of counseling?

7. How informed are parishioners of the mental health movement? Of the pastoral counseling movement?

On almost all these questions information is available from both parish counselees and noncounselees. (Some questions could be answered only by counselees.)

During the academic year 1958-1959, a sample of 50 counselees and a control group of 25 noncounselees were obtained through ministers who had co-operated on the former year's research by this Project. Though the ministers of the former study were a random sample of Boston's Protestant clergymen, the sample of parishioners was anything but random. In the first place, only those ministers were selected to help on the counselee study who belonged to one of the five categories in a typology of counselors developed from last year's research. This eliminated half of the ministers from consideration. Second, only 29 of the 50 ministers remaining were willing and/or able to co-operate in procuring for us counseled and uncounseled subjects. A comment on this selective process is in order.

A large number of ministers (about 30 per cent) said that they could not ask any of their counselees to be interviewed because this would involve a breach of the trust that was integral to the counseling relationship. When we explained that they were simply to ask their counselees if they were willing to be interviewed, thereby giving to us only the names of persons who had already agreed to be interviewed, roughly a quarter of the ministers persisted on the "breach of trust" theme. This group consisted mainly of Unitarians and fundamentalists. For the others, when it was learned that we wanted to speak only to persons who wanted to be interviewed, and when we assured total anonymity and no interest in the personal aspects of the counseling problem, the procuring of subjects was further impeded only by problems of scheduling.

Summarily, our sample was made nonrandom by (1) the typology of counselors, (2) the lack of co-operation of certain ministers, and (3) the problem of scheduling interviews. This last factor, for example, gave us a disproportionately large group of women in the sample since their schedules were more amenable for interview time.

In addition, selectivity was particularly obvious for our group of noncounseled parishioners. It became apparent early that when we requested one noncounseled parishioner from each minister, the minister would in most cases call upon someone in his church whom he knew particularly well. The result was that the uncounseled sample became skewed toward higher education and occupation, and was composed of the older and most active members of the church, who in general were more "liberal" than other members of the congregation.

The members of the counselee sample were not stratified according to denomination because of the selectivity problems already mentioned, but were members of nine of Boston's ten largest denominations. The groups were Baptist, Congregational, Episcopal, Evangelical Covenant, Evangelical United Brethren, Methodist, Nazarene, Presbyterian, and Unitarian.

Interviewees for this study were from all possible gradations of education, occupation, marital status, age, and church activity.

With the assistance of the large quantity of data collected in the study of ministers in Boston last year, we were able to develop a typology of counselors along the two dimensions that affect a minister's counseling most—namely, his religious position and his previous training and experience in counseling.

Along the dimension (continuum) of religious position were defined three groups according to their interpretation and use of the biblical account. A scale of seven items was used to determine each minister's position. The first group were those ministers who interpreted the Bible literally and understood it as God's absolute and sovereign law, wholly outside of man and not affected by him. This group is popularly known as "fundamentalists." We shall use the word "conservative" to describe these ministers remembering that it has been defined by our scale of religious position and not arbitrarily. The parishioners of the "conservatives" in this study were made available to us from the lowest 10 per cent of the scores on the religious position scale. This scale was called the heteronomy-autonomy scale in last year's study.

The second type of minister on this continuum is called "moderate" as a popular name with our technical meaning when talking about these ministers. The "moderates" take the biblical account with ultimate seriousness, but are neither literalists nor liberals. The denomination most positioned as moderate was the Episcopal. Nonfundamentalist Presbyterians and nonliberal Congregationalists also usually fall into this category. The ten middle ministers on our religious position scale were asked to co-operate in the counselee study and made up the "moderate" group. Those who were most liberal: that is, free from attachment to the biblical account, made up the third type of minister on this continuum. These men treated the Bible as a valuable piece of religious literature but attributed no finality (normativeness) to its message. This group was almost invariably Unitarian and consisted of the ten most liberal ministers in last year's sample.

Our other dimension for the typology of counselors was developed to distinguish between clergymen "active" in pastoral counseling and those "inactive." For this scale items were used representing a cumulation of the minister's past counseling training and experience, and his past and current involvement as a pastoral counselor. To get our subjects from the "active" and "inactive" counselors the top 10 percent and the lowest 10 per cent were used. Thus the "inactives" were as minimally trained and involved in counseling as any group could possibly be, while the "actives" were highly trained (usually to at least the Master's Degree in Psychology level) and highly involved (from 12 to 25 hours per week of actual counseling). Each minister was requested to provide three parishioners, two counseled and one uncounseled. Although there was some variation, no minister was represented by more than this number.

This research design provides for the multiple comparison of different types of parishioners from different types of counselors. The major limitation, of course, is the small numbers that are involved. Therefore, it is important that not too much confidence be placed in the exact percentages reported. We have far too small a percentage of the total number of parishioners to describe more than trends and suggested relationships. Comparisons with other research findings, however, lead us to suspect that contradictions to the trends and relationships here described exist.

The interview schedule for the counselees consisted of 87 items, about half of which were "open end." The noncounselee schedule had 63 items, roughly one-third "open end" and two-thirds categorical. The questions were carefully designed to be inoffensive to the respondents, and no "prying" whatsoever was done into the more personal aspects of counseling. It was interesting to note, however, that well over half of the respondents offered considerable detail concerning their counseling problem even though such information was not at all solicited.

1. Who comes for counseling, and to which ministers do they go?

An attempt was made to discover the major sociological factors that were connected with a person's going to his minister for counsel. First of all, it is clear that women go to their minister considerably more often than do men. This occurred even after adjusting for the fact that there are more women in the congregations and that they were more likely to be in our sample. It is not infrequent that women come to ministers for their husbands, and that only after considerable persuasion does the male concede to enter a counseling relationship.

Although the adult group in the congregation supplies more counselees for a minister than the youth and young adults, it is only the young adults (18-35 years) that receive a disproportionately large amount of counseling. White-collar workers receive the most counseling; blue-collar people the second most; and professionals the least. Proportional to their representation in the congregation, blue-collar workers receive more counseling than would be expected, professionals the same as would be expected, and white-collar people less. Counselees are slightly more educated than the rest of the congregation, however, despite the slight occupational lag. This apparent discrepancy can be resolved by noting that generally the upper educational levels of each occupational group were the levels most likely to appear for counseling. Ministers "active" as counselors got the bulk of the highly educated and most gainfully employed counselees. Conservatives and "inactive" ministers tended to get the blue-collar and uneducated counselees. Roughly half of all counselees are married; 30 per cent are single; and 20 per cent divorced or widowed. This last group is considerably larger than its occurrence in the congregation.

Turning to the question of which ministers tend to be singled out for counseling, it is well to recall the main findings of last year's research. There it was learned that the most active counselors were most likely to be ministers of the lower-class churches; "moderates," theologically well trained in psychology and counseling, in the middle-aged group of their profession; those who saw counseling both theologically and psychologically; and those who preached personally relevant sermons. In addition to this description, we suggested that the minister's personality (his traits, personal stability, sensitivity) played a large part in determining whether or not he would be sought out as a counselor. This hypothesis was certainly born out in the counselee study, but was shown to be heavily counteracted by the parishioners' role-expectations for their minister. Rather than saying that they went to their minister because of his personal qualities, counselees most often reported that they went because it was part of the minister's job. Similarly, when asked how they would choose a pastoral counselor if another counseling problem arose, the subjects said simply that they would go to their own minister or one they knew—making no mention of personality attributes necessary or even stipulating that their counselor should have had training in the counseling function. Only for counselors who were theologically moderate was there any crossing of denominational lines by the parishioners. Both the conservative and liberal clergymen counseled almost entirely among their own parishioners and at least within their own denomination. The inactive counselors also were called upon only by their own parishioners. Three-fourths of all counselees had been members of their counselor's church for at least three years. Only the active and theologically moderate counselors were likely to be involved with parishioners who were new to their churches; the liberals tended largely to counsel old members.

A rather crude summarization of our data would suggest that parishioners in distress generally are not too cautious about whom they choose for help. They go to the nearest concerned person who might have had some previous knowledge or experience with the type of problem they face. Only about one counselee in five expects any sort of professional help from his minister. The rest simply "need someone to talk to."

Before moving away from our topic let us consider the other side of our question: namely, "Why do many people not go to ministers for counseling?" The major reservations that were offered by the noncounseled group of respondents were, "Ministers are too moralistic and I couldn't talk to them," "Ministers don't know anything about counseling people," and "I just wouldn't want anyone to find out I had those kinds of problems." The moralism reason was the one most dominant for uncounseled and counseled parishioners alike, though the latter consistently reported that early in counseling this fear was wholly dispelled. Social reserve played the strongest role for persons who had no knowledge of pastoral counseling whatsoever. Parishioners from the liberal denominations were by far the most reserved about counseling in general; the conservatives had the least hesitation. About half of the noncounselees would not want to be counseled by a conservative minister because they felt there would be a lack of objectivity, freedom, and understanding, and too much "God-talk." One-fifth did prefer a conservative counselor because he would provide "better standards and more spiritual security." Thirty per cent said it would make no difference to them if the counselor were conservative, moderate, or liberal.

2. How does past and present religious involvement relate to counseling?

In checking the religious background of our group of counselees, a most interesting finding emerged. We learned that counselees were themselves likely to have been highly involved in the church during their youth, but that their families had seldom been active in church affairs. It appears, then, that the church as a "refuge" has played a strong part in the lives of these parishioners. The research indicated strongly that this use of the church as a "refuge" was in some cases superficial and occasional, but in others a matter of total personal commitment. Since all counselees mentioned the danger of "running to their minister with every little detail," it is valid to assume that whether the church was being used opportunistically or committedly, considerable thought went into the decisions of whether or not to go to a minister.

Although our uncounseled group knew their ministers far better than average laymen, the counselees knew their ministers (past and present) about the same as the rest of the congregation—certainly not better. The counselees also were no more active in current church affairs than the rest of the congregation. In terms of "daily religious activity" it was indicated that counselees are considerably less active than the average noncounseled parishioner.

The intergroup differences found on these matters were as follows: (1) the counselees of the active counselors knew their minister better before counseling than did those of the inactive group; (2) parishioners of the theological moderates and conservatives were much more involved in daily religious activity than those who go to the other types of ministers; and (3) the persons who went to conservative and inactive counselors tended to be the least active in the current affairs of the church.

An attempt was made to measure the degree of "functionality" in our respondents' religious behavior. The meaning of "functionality" for our purposes is roughly "the extent to which a person uses his religion (daily religious activity, church membership, and religious symbol-system) for purposes which are not defined as ultimate by his church body." The counselees were about the same as the rest of the congregation in terms of having a primarily functional or nonfunctional religion. Parishioners who were counseled by liberal and inactive ministers possessed a highly functional religion; those of active counselors had middle-functionality; and those of the conservatives and moderates were the least functional.

Lastly, the respondents were asked, "What is the main satisfaction you get from your participation at the church?" The answer fell into the categories of service (helping others), fellowship, worship, and intellectual stimulation. Sixty-five per cent of the uncounseled group mentioned service and fellowship as their main satisfactions, and seventy-five per cent of the counselees mentioned worship and intellectual stimulation. This is a huge difference statistically and should have many ramifications for understanding counselee behavior. For interpretation purposes this finding can be explained by suggesting that persons under distress are very active cognitively, and that many parishioners bring these cognitive needs to the church. At the same time, persons under somewhat less distress (noncounselees) use the church mainly to satisfy social needs.

3. *What do parishioners expect from pastoral counseling?*

To answer the question above by replying that counselees don't expect much would be accurate in one sense but misleading in another. It is true that parishioners do not expect much (if any) professional help from their minister; but they do expect concern, sympathy, and understanding. Their early response to counseling is very favorable over 90 per cent of the time. And after the first session 8 out of 10 counselees come to expect more help from their minister than they had anticipated originally.

Two-thirds of the noncounselees expected that if they went to a minister for counseling, there would be no change (positive or negative) in their personal relationship to him. The facts of the matter are that 9 out of 10 persons who receive counseling do change their relationship to the minister—almost all (95 per cent) end with a "better," closer relationship.

Last year it was learned that less than 10 per cent of all problems brought to ministers pertain to explicitly religious problems. When we asked the uncounseled parishioners what per cent of a minister's counseling pertains to these problems, 80 per cent of them greatly overestimated the number. Parishioners generally think that the majority of pastoral counseling is done on "solely religious matters." These two areas—namely, one's relationship to the counselor and the types of problems brought to counseling—are the most misconceived of all parishioner knowledge and preconceptions about counseling. These areas of misinformation seriously affect who comes to counseling and what problems are considered appropriate for ministerial attention. On this last matter, only 16 per cent of the noncounselees thought that any problem was appropriate to be taken to a minister, and psychological distress problems were only infrequently mentioned as appropriate. This, too, occurs in spite of the fact that psychological distress (or personal adjustment) problems are the type of problems that are most often brought to ministers.

4. *Of what does counseling consist?*

Pastoral counseling, first of all, consists of taking a personal problem to a minister. Roughly 60 per cent of the counselees had decided on their own to go to a minister; 35 per cent were encouraged by someone else to go; and in 5 per cent of the cases counseling had begun during a pastoral call or visit by the minister. Pastoral calling, therefore, appears almost negligible as a time for serious counseling, though it can provide the framework for the indispensable precounseling communication that might be necessary for some parishioners. This function of pastoral calling, however, remains to be empirically demonstrated. Of those counselees who were encouraged by someone else to see a minister, two-fifths were sent by their family, two-fifths by friends, and one-fifth by professional counselors or therapists.

The major types of problems occurring in our sample were these: psychological distress problems (40 per cent), marriage and family problems (24 per cent), youth-behavior problems (12 per cent), and illness, alcoholism, religious problems, and vocational problems (6 per cent each). This is roughly the breakdown of problems that ministers reported in last year's study, though they emphasized the frequency of marriage and family problems more. We cannot say which of the two sets of figures is the more accurate, but it seems fair (and the most accurate estimate available) to suggest that the average of the two sets of figures would best approximate the total population.

Twenty per cent of the counselees had spent one or two sessions (about 50 minutes each) with their minister; 25 per cent had had three to five sessions; 20 per cent had had six to nine sessions; and 35 per cent had seen the counselor ten or more times. Active counselors were seeing their parishioners over the longest period of time, but a counseling relationship with an inactive counselor would seldom go beyond two meetings.

Regarding the depth or seriousness of the counseling problems, 12 per cent were analyzed by our interviewers to be "no problem at all," 52 per cent were considered "counseling-moderate," and 36 per cent were "psychiatric-serious." A rather clear "hierarchy" emerged finding the shallow or no-problem cases being handled mostly by the inactive and conservative counselors; the liberal ministers handled problems of moderate depth; and the active and theologically moderate counselors handled the deepest, "psychiatric-serious" problems.

A third of the problems brought to the clergymen were of recent origin; half of them had been matters of concern for at least six months; and a sixth were perennial. Only one counselee in four had any hope of an immediate solution (these were the less serious problems); one in five clearly knew that there was no solution at all.

An evaluation was made of who "directed" the counseling sessions—the minister, the parishioner, or both. In two out of three cases the minister and the parishioner both shared the directing of the case; a fifth of the time the minister was totally nondirective; and in one case in seven he was totally directive. This analysis also was carefully done, though, of course, it rests on the counselee's interpretation of what transpired. The trend observed is that ministers are slightly more nondirective than directive in counseling. The "actives" and the "theological moderates" were the least directive of the five types of counselors. Eighty-five per cent of the counselees approved of the method (mode of directiveness) used, and 15 per cent were ambivalent or negative about it.

When questioned on the amount of insight their counselor had demonstrated, 10 per cent reported low insight, 40 per cent moderate, and 50 per cent a high degree of insight and sensitivity. The active counselors were universally reported to be high in insight, but both the liberal and the inactive ministers tended to be regarded as deficient on counseling acumen. Three out of four parishioners looked forward to new sessions with their pastoral counselor: conservative counselees were the only group not to anticipate favorably a new session.

In exactly half of the counseling cases studied, there had arisen some explicitly religious material. This material usually took the form of prayer or "God-talk," and confession was on occasion effectively used. In the other half of the cases no explicitly religious material occurred. Conservative counselors used explicit religious material the most; active counselors, second most; and inactive counselors used it the least.

5. What does pastoral counseling change?

In thinking about the kinds of changes that occur in pastoral counseling, we were interested in two major areas—psychological change, and changes in religious activity. Our measures of psychological change were admittedly quite superficial and limited: It is impossible in survey research to study something as complex as behavorial change. The measures on changes in religious activity, on the other hand, are in most cases multiple and carefully scaled.

At the most general level of change—over-all change in the counseling problem —65 per cent of our respondents reported general over-all improvement; 30 per cent, no change; and 5 per cent, a relapse to a condition worse than when counseling was begun. The least improvement shown was in the group that was counseled by the inactive ministers. It should be noted that the active counselors' clients did not show significantly more improvement than those of the other types of ministers. This is explained by the fact that the "actives" deal with the far more serious and difficult problems. When "success" is reported of a long-term counseling case by these ministers, it might safely be assumed tthat a major psychotherapeutic change has been effected. Most of the long-term counseling done by the "actives" is done with cases equally as complex as those being handled by competent, professional therapists. Our group of ten active counselors were working on two problems of homosexuality, two of alcoholism, one ambulatory schizophrenic, and four "neuroses." In over half of these cases, the pastoral counselors had tried to turn over the cases to psychiatrists but were told that they (the ministers) could handle them as well as a professional therapist.

In spite of not being able to report a great over-all improvement, the counselees of active ministers report a far greater amount of change in self-knowledge and self-acceptance than do other counselees. The inactive ministers are the lowest in providing their counselees with increased self-knowledge and self-acceptance, and the conservative counselors are exceptionally low in communicating self-acceptance to their counseled parishioners.

Exactly half of the counselees interviewed reported no change in the amount or significance of their religious activity. For the 50 per cent that reported change in this area, virtually all of it was positive—toward a more active religious life. The areas in question were one's relation to the church, attitudes toward ministers, the extent of one's devotional life, and the evaluation of the importance of pastoral counseling in ministers' functions. The greatest changes took place in the counselees' relation with ministers: 85 per cent of the respondents reported that they now saw ministers as "more human" and "less pious." The least change occurred with regard to counselees' relation to the church. Only one counselee in three had become more active in church affairs since undertaking pastoral counseling.

The changes reported in counseled parishioners' devotional life (half of the counselees were more active in personal devotions) most often were not conscious to respondents. When asked if any change had taken place on this count, they frequently replied, "Well, yes, now that you mention it. I have been much more active devotionally since counseling, though I don't think there has been any talked-about connection between this and my counseling." On all these areas of religious change, the counselees of active and theologically moderate counselors showed the greatest increase, and those of the inactive and liberal clergymen showed the least change.

6. How does pastoral counseling compare with other counseling?

The most unexpected finding concerning the relation of pastoral to other counseling was that exactly one-half of all parish counselees had had some previous counseling experience. Only 15 per cent of this former counseling had been pastoral, but 85 per cent had been psychiatric. Thus, because of this high frequency of counselees who had had both pastoral and psychiatric counseling, we shall use statements from these respondents to understand these parishioners' perceptions and evaluations of their two types of counseling experience.

One very important clue for understanding the parish counselee was observed. It was learned that although the persons who had been counseled by both ministers and professional therapists expected that the latter would have more training, the counselees would nevertheless use the same criteria for evaluating both their counselors. For example, the factors mentioned for causing dissatisfaction with psychiatric counseling were (1) institutional unconcern, (2) personal unconcern (on the part of the therapist), (3) money, and (4) not liking the interpretation suggested. When the respondents were asked what it was that interfered most with pastoral counseling, they again came up with all the previously mentioned factors except, of course, money. Most apparent in all the replies was that all the counselees wanted was someone who was very seriously concerned about them; if they had to choose between getting a well-trained counselor and one who had great concern about them and their dilemma, they would almost always choose the latter.

The group of counselees who had received help from both the clergy and the psychiatrists, were asked to evaluate which counseling seemed the more effective and more rewarding. The possible responses were as follows: the pastoral counseling was worse; both were about the same; and the pastoral counseling was better. No one reported the pastoral counseling as worse; 50 per cent said the pastoral counseling was better. At least two reservations must be used in interpreting this finding. First, our data are only "self-reports" and someone with more refined and professional criteria might judge differently. Second, since our research was by its very nature more identified with pastoral than with psychiatric counseling, there must have been some tendency for the respondents to give us the answers they thought we wanted to hear. Even taking these factors seriously into account, such a favorable response to pastoral counseling is striking. The main reasons for dissatisfaction with nonpastoral counseling have already been mentioned—the high cost and the personal unconcern on the part of the therapist stood out. Of all the persons who had received pastoral counseling, over 90 per cent would go again if the situation warranted. Of all those in our sample who had received psychiatric help, 45 per cent would go again.

The noncounseled parishioners were asked to rate how important counseling was to a minister's duties. About a third said it should be his primary function, 60 per cent said it was important but not his most important role, and 7 per cent said it wouldn't matter if a minister counseled or not. This rather high regard for counseling once its importance has been brought to their attention indicates that the education of parishioners about ministerial counseling should not be met with much disfavor.

Presently, two out of three parishioners said they would go to their minister for counseling if the situation warranted it. Of the one in three who would not go, most of them had a "social reserve" about going, namely that they would not want the minister (or anyone else) to find out that they have any problems.

7. *How informed are parishioners of the mental health movement? Of the pastoral counseling movement?*

Perhaps the major reason that so many people go to their minister for counseling is that they have no one else to turn to. Mental health facilities and personnel are seriously behind the needs of large cities. Last year's research indicated that most agencies have impossibly long waiting lists, the hospitals can handle only the most critical cases, and therapists' time for taking on new cases is almost negligible. Not only is the over-crowdedness of the mental health resources an important problem, but the layman's knowledge of what facilities are available and how one gets in touch with them is another serious problem to be met. This parishioner research suggests that about two persons in five are aware of their community's mental health facilities, and that only one in five would know how to go about getting service from them. (Clergymen are often sought for help on these matters.)

Counselees are generally more informed than the rest of the congregation about their community's mental health facilities and the private therapists available, and are usually more knowledgeable about the problems of mentally disturbed persons. Concurrent with having more contact with the mental health field, the counselees were found to be more critical and more aware of the shortcomings of that field than are uncounseled parishioners. The counselee group, along with their greater involvement in the problems related to mental health, evidenced considerably more realism about the actual predicaments in the field of mental health.

With regard to the pastoral counseling movement, about 60 per cent of our respondents were aware that considerable attention is being given to pastoral counseling in the churches. Since our respondents were either counselees or very active church members it is likely that less than half of the members of an average congregation are aware of the seriousness of attention being given pastoral counseling by their denominational administrators and educators. Most of the parishioners who do know something about pastoral counseling have learned it through their ministers, but the use of other media for educating laymen seems to be on the increase in this area. Ministers who are theologically moderate stand far ahead of the other groups on informing their parishioners about pastoral counseling. The parishioners of liberal and inactive counselors are the least informed.

About half of the persons interviewed had read something that pertained to religion and mental health, but in three out of four cases the material was very untechnical and nonauthoritative. Only one parishioner in twelve had read anything that is normally considered part of the pastoral counseling literature. Regarding the literature in the field of mental health, about half of the parishioners were totally uninformed (except that they had seen one or two articles in the newspapers about it). The other half of the parishioners had either learned something about mental health in college or made a point of reading magazine articles about it. Only one parishioner in ten in an average congregation ever talked to his minister about what is happening in the field of mental health.

In San Francisco the sample was about one-half as large as it was in Boston. Twenty-five counselees and 15 noncounselees were interviewed. All but one of them were members of churches pastored by ministers whom we had interviewed earlier concerning counseling.

As in the former "counselee" research, respondents were chosen from five types of ministers. Two typologies were used: one was theological position—conservative, moderate, and liberal; the other was counseling training and involvement—active and inactive counselors. For each of the five categories above, five counselees and three noncounselees were chosen, thus giving a total of 40 in the sample. The selection of respondents was the same as in the Eastern study. After a minister had been interviewed and it was certain that he belonged in one of the five categories, he was asked to procure one of his counselees and one other person from his church (a noncounselee) for interviews. This was done until five counselees and three noncounselees were acquired for each of the appropriate categories. Many of the same problems arose in the Bay Area as had arisen in Boston in getting enough respondents. The liberal group was again the most reluctant to co-operate in the research, while the conservatives were again the most suspicious, though co-operative. Like Boston, however, once the parishioner interviews got under way, rapport and mutual confidence was readily established, and far more material than was even asked for from the respondents came our way.

Although the Protestant churches of the Bay Area are as a whole of lower socio-economic stature than those of Boston, it did not follow that the parishioners interviewed were of lower social class position. The reason for this is that while Boston clergymen counsel at all social levels about equally, the San Francisco pastors tend to counsel the better-educated and higher-income and occupational groups more than would be expected. The net effect of this is that both groups of clergy are counseling people of the same status—though the Boston clergy generally ministers at higher status levels.

On the conservative-moderate-liberal theological dimension the West Coast parishioners were found to parallel their pastors: they are more conservative than the Eastern group.

As with the "minister as counselor" data, we have generated some hypotheses about expected differences between our East Coast and West Coast studies. The hypotheses are listed below. No attempt has been made to offer many statistical distinctions between the two cities because of the smallness of the Bay Area sample. Only trends and large differences are reported. The hypotheses follow:

1. The average parishioner is more amenable to pastoral counseling in San Francisco than he is in Boston.
2. Problems brought to Bay Area pastors are less serious than those brought to the Boston group.
3. Bay Area ministers are more directive in counseling than are Boston ministers.
4. San Francisco parishioners undergo less change in counseling than do Boston counselees.
5. There is more specifically "religious" content in the West Coast ministers' counseling.
6. Pastoral counseling will compare less favorably with "secular" counseling than it does in Boston.
7. West Coast parishioners are less informed about the field of mental health and the pastoral counseling movement than are Boston's parishioners.

All of the foregoing hypotheses have been confirmed by a comparison of the San Francisco and Boston data. They have been confirmed clearly and decisively—as decisively as small-scale research can do. Having reported this, our task remains to show why and to what extent these hypothetical statements have held true. After completing this elaboration we shall conjecture about the extent to which our Boston data can be generalized to the country as a whole.

1. *The average parishioner is more amenable to pastoral counseling in San Francisco than he is in Boston.*

Bay Area laymen appear to have an almost totally uncritical attitude toward religion. They participate much more actively in their own church work than do Boston laymen, and consequently their church group forms a subculture through which they interpret the rest of the world. Ministers are seen as quite competent guides to every facet of daily behavior; the minister has a superior and authoritative position in the layman's eye which favorably inclines him toward seeking pastoral counsel. Boston parishioners, in contrast, are far more critical of their clergy and appear quicker to search out their pastor's limitations. The result is that Boston laymen are far more dubious about their pastor's capabilities in counseling than were the San Francisco respondents.

2. *Problems brought to the Bay Area pastors are less serious than those brought to the Boston group.*

Confirmation for this hypothesis was both direct and indirect. Whereas 36 per cent of the Boston clergy's counseling was concerned with problems that were clearly psychiatric in seriousness, only 9 per cent of San Francisco's cases were so involved. Most Bay Area counseling is done at a level which is appropriate for a counselor—neither totally superficial nor demanding psychiatric attention. The Boston pastors, on the other hand, were involved in much more serious and complex work. About 10 per cent of the Greater Boston clergy were involved in full-fledged psychiatric therapy, but only 2 or 3 per cent of the West Coast ministers were so involved.

Further support for this hypothesis was found when it was noted that very few of the problems worked with in San Francisco were described as psychological distress problems. Instead of these ambiguous and involved problems the Bay Area pastors worked with more religious questions and the other more superficial types of problems. Similarly, the duration of counseling needed to work with parishioner problems on the West Coast was much shorter than it was in Boston.

Parallel to the more superficial nature of Bay Area counseling was the finding that there was more and quicker improvement regarding the counseling problem than was reported in the East. This finding on the surface might indicate better counseling on the part of West Coast ministers, but our other data in fact point to the opposite conclusion. The problems of parishioners on the West Coast are more readily solved simply because they are not so deep or complex as they are in Boston.

3. *Bay Area ministers are more directive in counseling than are Boston ministers.*

The authoritarian aspects of conservative religiosity were expected to be manifested in the San Francisco pastors' counseling. Indeed, they were. Not only were advice giving and directive counseling much more frequent among the Western group, but it was learned that the counselees of West Coast ministers do far less talking during the counseling sessions than do their Boston counterparts. Data on four items showed that the San Francisco clergy not only tended to dominate most counseling interviews, but that this was exactly what their parishioners expected and wanted. In terms of growth and development, this sort of counseling is minimally effective, but in the more superficial cases with which these pastors generally deal it is unlikely that much harm was done. Whereas in Boston it was found that pastoral counseling is no more directive than most psychiatric counseling, in the Bay Area pastoral and psychiatric counseling are clearly of two different breeds. The relative newness of the pastoral counseling movement on the West Coast is obviously related to their less progressive methods. Conservative ministers tend to and are expected to serve a type of policeman function, even in their counseling work. The moderate and active groups of counselors were the least directive of the five types of ministers.

4. *San Francisco parishioners undergo less change in counseling than do Boston counselees.*

In the Boston study we distinguished two kinds of change that related to pastoral counseling—change in religious activity and psychological change. In both these areas West Coast counselees changed less than the Eastern group. With regard to changes in religious activity, San Francisco counselees became slightly more active than they had been earlier, but the change was not nearly so great as it was for the Boston group. The reason is simple. The Bay Area respondents were far more active in church affairs to begin with, so the possibility of positive change was not so great. Although they were no more active in church affairs than non-counselees, these parishioners were almost twice as active as the Boston respondents. This greater religious activity is related to the smaller size of the West Coast churches as well as the well-known greater enthusiasm of fundamentalist bodies.

Regarding psychological change in counseling our measurements were difficult to make because the counseling of the West Coast clergy was neither long enough nor intensive enough to produce psychological change. It can be reported, however, that the change that did occur was almost entirely positive. Although self-report data are extremely tenuous on such matters as psychological change, they do show in all our counselees research that there is very little pastoral counseling that is seen to be harmful.

5. *There is more "specifically religious" content in the West Coast ministers' counseling.*

In the Boston study we learned that roughly half of the Protestant clergy used some form of "explicitly religious" material in their counseling. In San Francisco this material arose 80 per cent of the time. Usually it took the form of talking about God or prayer, and was used instead of any other type of counseling. Worth noting was the observation that Boston parishioners tended not to want any explicitly religious content in their counseling, but the San Francisco group both expected it and was disappointed if it did not appear. This and related observations force us to conclude that two radically different approaches to counseling are being demonstrated by our pastors. The major line of difference seems to be along the directive-nondirective dimension. Almost all the conservative wing of the church (ministers and parishioners alike) tends to function under a directive relationship between pastor and parishioner, whereas the nonconservative ministers are more willing to take the risks of not being directive. The moderate pastors have, in both cities, been found to be the least directive of the three theological types.

6. *Pastoral counseling will compare less favorably with "secular" counseling than it does in Boston.*

Our data support this hypothesis generally, but not with the strength that has affirmed the former statements. In both Boston and San Francisco pastoral counseling is rated higher than "secular" counseling by the persons who had had both. Also in both cities the pattern prevailed that pastoral counseling tended to come after "secular" counseling or therapy.

Even less referral of counselees between psychiatric workers and the clergy was found in the Bay Area than in Boston. There were no referrals minister-to-minister among the West Coast pastors, whereas in Boston there is twice as much referral of cases to other clergymen as there is to professional therapists. This problem is partly being ameliorated by the establishment of some psychiatric facilities by the Bay Area churches, but to date these efforts aid only an infinitesimal number of all the church people who could use professional help.

As in Boston, half of the parish counselees had experienced some form of previous counseling. One important difference arose in reference to the Boston finding that these counseling experiences were very much alike. In San Francisco the experiences were not very much alike. Where professional help had been employed there was usually a psychiatric, accepting, nondirective orientation to the counseling. When the counselee came to his pastor this atmosphere was usually radically changed into a moralistic, advice-giving, directive approach. Thus the Bay Area counselees saw the church and the psychiatric clinic as two radically different sources of help for the same problem: In Boston the two institutions were seen to be more complementary than competitive. The net effect of all this was that although pastoral help is preferred to psychiatric help in San Francisco among the parishioners we studied, it is not so strongly favored as it is in Boston. In Boston positive psychological change was reported in 65 per cent of the pastoral counseling cases. In San Francisco only 30 per cent reported this improvement.

7. *West Coast parishioners are less informed about the field of mental health and the pastoral counseling movement than are Boston's parishioners.*

In the Bay Area there was almost no knowledge of the mental health facilities available, no knowledge of private therapists, no contact with agencies or counselors, and no awareness of any of the new pastoral counseling clinics. A small part of this lack of information is accountable by the fact that there are slightly fewer mental health facilities in the Bay Area than in Boston. But most of the reason for it must be attributed to the relatively more isolated way in which the conservative churches function in society.

Regarding the parishioners' reading in the field of mental health, they were no less read than Boston laymen. Also it was found that Bay Area ministers play a larger role in informing their parishioners about happenings and new material on mental health than do the Boston pastors. Apparently the West Coast laymen are directed more to general knowledge about mental health and pastoral counseling, than to immediate contact with professional workers in the field.

REFERENCES

1. Herbert Hyman, *Survey Design and Analysis* (Glencoe, Ill., The Free Press, 1955). "*Descriptive* surveys are especially valuable for the accurate conceptualizations of a heretofore unstudied field, and *explanatory* surveys (i.e., controlled experimental studies of large groups) are most fruitfully employed in a later stage of knowledge— when experimentation with an already defined phenomenon is valuable."
2. The median is a measure of central tendency and the point in a distribution which has 50 per cent of the cases above it and 50 per cent below it. It is a valuable descriptive statistic when there are skewed distributions or when there are extreme cases at either end of a distribution which would distort the mean or average values. In this report "median" and "average" have been used synonymously.